THE DEVIL'S

ABOUT THE AUTHOR

David O'Donoghue is a native of Cork city. He has worked with RTÉ news and for the French international news agency Agence France-Presse in Paris. Dr O'Donoghue has taught journalism at university level in the UK. He helped to launch Ireland's first independent national radio station, Century Radio, in 1989, and currently works as a parliamentary reporter in Oireachtas Éireann.

David O'Donoghue holds a PhD from Dublin City University and is the author of two previous books: *Hitler's Irish Voices: The Story of German Radio's Wartime Irish Service* (Belfast, 1998); and *The Irish Army in the Congo 1960–1964: The Far Battalions* (Dublin, 2005).

THE DEVIL'S DEAL

The IRA, Nazi Germany
and the Double Life of Jim O'Donovan

David O'Donoghue

NEW
ISLAND

THE DEVIL'S DEAL
First published 2010
by New Island
2 Brookside
Dundrum Road
Dublin 14

www.newisland.ie

Copyright © David O'Donoghue, 2010

The author has asserted his moral rights.

ISBN 978-1-84840-080-1

All rights reserved. The material in this publication is protected by copyright law. Except as may be permitted by law, no part of the material may be reproduced (including by storage in a retrieval system) or transmitted in any form or by any means; adapted; rented or lent without the written permission of the copyright owner.

British Library Cataloguing Data. A CIP catalogue record for this book is available from the British Library.

Cover design: Inka Hagen

Front cover images: Jim O'Donovan at Dublin's Bridewell Garda Station, 1941 © Irish Military Archives; Seán Russell Statue, Fairview Park, Dublin © www.shanetobin.com; Hermann Görtz funeral, Dean's Grange Cemetery, Dublin, 1947 © *The Irish Times*
Back cover image: Aftermath of Coventry bombing, 1939 © The National Archives, UK

Printed and bound in Great Britain by
CPI Antony Rowe, Chippenham, Wiltshire

10 9 8 7 6 5 4 3 2 1

*In memory of Lt. Jim O'Donoghue,
Bandon, County Cork (1902–1920)*

CONTENTS

Foreword by Diarmaid Ferriter ix
Acknowledgements xii

1. Origins of a Revolutionary..............1
2. The Unfinished Portrait................11
3. Active Service.........................19
4. The Road to Civil War..................38
5. Picking up the Pieces..................60
6. A Call to Arms........................83
7. The German Connection.................112
8. 'Our Friends' in Berlin...............133
9. Carnage in Coventry...................153
10. The Road to Internment...............167
11. A Guest of the Nation................178
12. A Time for Reflection................211
13. Belated Thanks from the Third Reich...228

Postscript...............................246
Appendix 1: The S-Plan...................250
Notes....................................278
Select Bibliography......................321
Index....................................325

FOREWORD

Jim O'Donovan lived a long, eventful and in many ways difficult life. David O'Donoghue's vivid exploration of that life has resulted in an absorbing and well-researched account of O'Donovan's preoccupations and prejudices, his dreams and delusions, and the Ireland that produced him.

From being a young chemistry student in the UCD labs, he became the IRA's leading explosives expert during the war of independence and was a member of the General HQ staff of the pre-treaty IRA. As David O'Donoghue has observed, he was 'not someone to stand still for very long'. After enduring periods of imprisonment in the civil war, during which he boasted of outdoing Christ by fasting for forty-one days, he unsuccessfully attempted to establish a paint manufacturing business, eventually began working for the ESB, published the innovative and radical *Ireland To-Day* magazine, retained his belief in violent Irish republicanism, and, under the influence of Seán Russell, drew up the notorious and disastrous 'S' (Sabotage) Plan, the basis of a bombing campaign in Britain, which originated in ideas he had formulated during his civil war imprisonment.

Never one to shirk confrontation with those in power, he rebutted Episcopal pronouncements, remained preoccupied with the civil war period and those he regarded as treacherous, and eventually became the IRA's chief liaison officer with the Nazis, making four visits to meet German agents on the continent. O'Donovan exaggerated the strength of the IRA and indulged in fanciful projections, suggesting that a German victory in World War II would result in Ireland becoming 'a virile entity, freely functioning in a noble European federation, instead of the miserable, misshapen land of decay and hopelessness'.

He was to endure further confinement as an internee in the Curragh where he spent twenty-three months during World War II, suggesting to Gerry Boland, the minster for justice, 'Your government should with greater justice occupy my position'. As the author notes, in one of the many wry observations he makes on O'Donovan's stance, 'O'Donovan's lack of subtlety proved to be his undoing'.

This was true of much of his life; as one of his fellow internees commented, 'he just carried on in his own old way'. One of the values of this book is that it underlines the human consequences of O'Donovan's refusal to compromise; the toll it took on his wife and children, and the dilemma of being unable to repair ruptured family relationships. In untangling the webs of his career with insight and clarity, David O'Donoghue has revealed the difficulties of an individual who 'nailed his colours to the mast early on and remained steadfast', despite the formidable odds against success. When newspaper articles began to appear in the 1960s exposing his links to German military intelligence, he was unrepentant: 'linking in any way with Germany might now seem remote, foolish and in some vague way treacherous … but in essence it was not a crazy scheme'.

FOREWORD

It would be easy, from an early twenty-first-century perspective, to dismiss him as dangerous and delusional. He could have taken an easier and eminently more respectable post-civil war route, like his brother Dan, who became secretary of the Department of Social Welfare, or his brother Colman, who became a diplomat. What he became instead was a man whose whole life and loyalties were shaped by the Irish war of independence and civil war and the difficulties of dealing with the legacies of those conflicts. In documenting his experiences, in chronicling his voice and thoughts and those of his contemporaries, David O'Donoghue has illuminated, with verve, many aspects of the difficult and often tortuous experiences of an important generation of Irish republicans.

Diarmaid Ferriter,
University College Dublin
March 2010

ACKNOWLEDGEMENTS

This book could not have been written in such detail without the help of Jim O'Donovan's children: Mrs Aedine Sànta, Mr Gerry O'Donovan, Mrs Sheila Hanna and Mr Donal O'Donovan (sadly, the latter two members of the family are now deceased). All four of them agreed to be interviewed by the author as well as providing family papers and photographs for inclusion in this biography. The author is grateful to them for their insights into their father's long and complex life.

Additional material relating to Jim O'Donovan's life and times are to be found in the following institutions: the National Library, Dublin; the Oireachtas Library, Dublin; the National Archives, Dublin; University College Dublin's archives; the Manuscripts Department of Trinity College Library, Dublin; and the UK National Archives, Kew. The author is indebted to the directors and staff of the foregoing bodies for their help. In particular, the help of

ACKNOWLEDGEMENTS

Mrs Maedhbh McNamara and Mrs Eileen O'Donoghue of the Oireachtas Library, and Mr Séamus Helferty of UCD's archives, is much appreciated. The author is grateful to Commandant Victor Laing and his team at the Military Archives in Dublin for their courtesy and assistance in providing access to various files on Jim O'Donovan over a number of years. Dr Patrick Wallace, director of the National Museum, has been most supportive of this project, not least in kindly granting permission to reproduce Leo Whelan's group portrait of the IRA's general headquarters staff in 1921 (of which Jim O'Donovan was a member).

The author wishes to acknowledge the generosity of Mrs Drue Heinz for the award of a fellowship at the Hawthornden International Retreat for Writers. It was at this remote Scottish castle that the first eight chapters of *The Devil's Deal* were written in draft form. Without this sanctuary to work in, the book could not have been kick-started and may not have got off the ground. The work was subsequently completed at various other locations, including the Irish Writers' Centre, Dublin and the Tyrone Guthrie Centre at Annaghmakerrig, County Monaghan (whose director, Dr Pat Donlon, was a great source of encouragement).

Many individuals helped the author to tread the biographer's perilous and unsteady path. Most of them are named in the relevant chapter notes. But the author wishes to thank in particular the late Mr Derry Kelleher of Greystones, County Wicklow, who provided a comprehensive list of ex-internees who had attended an anniversary dinner in the 1990s. Their names and addresses were written on the back of a hotel menu. This led the author to undertake a series of interviews with IRA veterans in Belfast, Tipperary, Cork and elsewhere who had been in the Curragh camp with Jim O'Donovan in the early 1940s.

The author also wishes to thank Mr Seán O'Mahony, Mr Tim Pat Coogan and the late Mr Michael MacEvilly for sharing their encyclopaedic knowledge of twentieth-century republican history. In addition, the personal recollections of the late Lieutenant-

Colonel Seán Clancy – who lived to the ripe old age of 105 – proved to be invaluable in reconstructing the daily travails of a young IRA volunteer in Dublin during the war of independence.

The author acknowledges the help of Mr Seán Ó Briain in translating Irish-language texts, and the following for translating German-language texts: Ms Anna Brüning White, Ms Stefanie Unland and Mr Dominic Gilmore. In addition, Mr Thomas Turpin was particularly helpful in uncovering recent historical aspects of Trinity College, Dublin, as they relate to this biography. The assistance of the following in unravelling the myriad mysteries of computer technology is much appreciated: Ms Onora Brassill, Mr Colm Breen and Mr John Chambers.

My former RTÉ colleagues Mike Burns and Seán Duignan generously recounted the details of their 1969 meeting with the Coventry bomber, Joby O'Sullivan from Cork. Mr Brendan Ó Cathaoir, formerly of *The Irish Times*, and Major Mark Hull of the US Army both acted as advisors over a long period.

The author is grateful to the biographer and historian Mary Kenny who kindly acted as a sounding board during the gestation period of this work. In particular, she was the first to spot the close parallels between Jim O'Donovan's own life and the life of the new state he had played such a key role in creating. In addition, Mr Michael Halpenny was most helpful in tracing the S-plan, Jim O'Donovan's blueprint for the 1939–1940 IRA bombing campaign in England; and Mr John McCabe, alumni director of St Aloysius' College, Glasgow, provided vital details of Jim O'Donovan's school days in Scotland.

The following members of the Oireachtas assisted the author in verifying and detailing various aspects of Jim O'Donovan's life: Martin Ferris TD, Senator Terry Leyden, Finian McGrath TD, Arthur Morgan TD, Senator Denis O'Donovan, Dr Rory O'Hanlon TD and Ned O'Keeffe TD.

The author is particularly grateful to the current Sinn Féin President, Mr Gerry Adams MP, MLA, and the former Sinn Féin

ACKNOWLEDGEMENTS

President, Mr Ruairí Ó Brádaigh, for their help in dealing with a number of detailed written queries.

The author recognises the assistance of his literary agent Mr Jonathan Williams and his editor Ms Deirdre O'Neill for their advice and hawk-eyed editing skills. Finally, the author acknowledges the support and encouragement of his publisher, Mr Edwin Higel, the founder of New Island Books.

David O'Donoghue, Ph.D.
Wicklow, July 2010.

1.
ORIGINS OF A REVOLUTIONARY

There are beginnings and beginnings, some more auspicious than others. The origins of this biography's subject, James Laurence O'Donovan, are relatively inauspicious, but few if any could have predicted what lay ahead for him. As a member of the 13-strong headquarters staff of the pre-treaty IRA, O'Donovan would be assured of a footnote in the history books. But from the apparent triumph of the mid-1921 truce (bringing an end to the bloody Anglo-Irish war), the treaty talks in London and independence from Britain in January 1922, came the chaos of civil war and lasting political divisions. Later still came O'Donovan's role in the IRA's infamous S-plan bombing campaign in England (1939–40). There was also the ignominy of internment (1941–43) at the hands of his ex-IRA comrades who were then occupying the seat of government in Dublin. Harder to fathom were O'Donovan's links with the Third Reich, including clandestine pre-war visits to Hamburg, Brussels and Berlin. In addition, he seemed all too eager to shelter the German spy Hermann Görtz – offering the Nazi emissary every facility at a time, in 1940, when Ireland's fragile neutrality was teetering on the brink.

But all these adventures – some might say misadventures – lay far in the future for Jim O'Donovan, who was born at Castleview, Roscommon town, on 3 November 1896, the fifth of seven children born to a middle-class Cork couple, Daniel O'Donovan and Margaret Brennan. Mrs Margaret O'Donovan's family lived at Kilbrogan House, Bandon, and owned a hotel and shop in the west Cork town. Daniel O'Donovan hailed from a farming family in the parish of Desertserges, outside Bandon. His job as a gauger with the UK customs and excise service meant that he could be reassigned anywhere within the United Kingdom at any time. In fact, just six weeks before Jim was born, his father had been transferred to Roscommon from Wakefield, Yorkshire.[1] And so it was that eight years later, in 1904, the family found themselves on the move again, leaving the north-west boglands of Ireland for the smokier climes of Glasgow. From one Celtic corner of the kingdom to a very different one. Jim O'Donovan attended the Scottish city's Jesuit-run St Aloysius' College from 29 August 1904 to 27 June 1913. (In fact, the school records are incorrect, since Jim stayed behind to complete his final year studies after the family had left for Ireland, eventually following them home in 1914.) His two older brothers, Peter and Colman, also attended the college, as did Jim's younger brother Daniel (whose record states that he left the college for Ireland on 20 May 1914, but it seems the school authorities mixed up Jim and Dan, hence the incorrect dates). The family lived at 8 Lyndhurst Gardens in the affluent Kelvinside district of Glasgow. St Aloysius' current alumni director, John McCabe, notes that:

> James completed the course but there is no record of his national leaving certificate exams. His class records throughout his time at this school indicate that he was of reasonable academic standard and that in his earlier years he was always in the top five in a class of

thirty-five. The fact that he stayed on to the sixth form shows that he was of above average academic ability as his year group at that stage had shrunk to twelve pupils. His strong subjects in the final year were English and the mathematical disciplines; an interesting point is that he did not study Latin or Greek, which were the most popular subjects and those for which St Aloysius' was noted.

A school picture, taken in 1909, shows the 12-year-old Jim O'Donovan sitting cross-legged in the front row of his class, at the knee of a stern-looking Jesuit priest. The prefect of studies at St Aloysius' at the time was Fr Eric Hanson SJ, who ran the college from 1901 to 1926. Fr Hanson is still recognised today as having been 'the most influential and successful headmaster' in the school's 150-year history.[2] Jim O'Donovan's son Gerry recalls that in 1914:

> World War I had just started and he applied to go to the [Royal] Navy. He had a physical and got a 'thank you' signed, with a printed signature, by Winston Churchill, as First Sea Lord, thanking him for his application, but his eyesight wasn't good enough.[3]

The O'Donovan family returned to Ireland in 1913, leaving Jim behind to complete his final year studies. They took up residence in Drumcondra on the northside of Dublin. His daughter Aedine thinks her father's isolation in Glasgow at that time, aged only sixteen, had a marked effect on him:

> A lot of his behaviour may have come from the fact that he stayed alone in Scotland after the family came back [to Dublin], to finish his schooling. I don't know how much that affected him, but a lot of the poems he wrote were written at that time … some of them are quite moving, showing the person that nobody really knew, but that was there – the person with real feelings and romantic ideas and things that you never saw.[4]

With good final exam results (in a 1947 curriculum vitae, O'Donovan claimed to have obtained the Scottish leaving certificate, although there is no record of this at St Aloysius' College), Jim enrolled at UCD's department of chemistry, then situated at Earlsfort Terrace near St Stephen's Green, in autumn 1914. His early course subjects were French, Irish, maths, mathematical physics, political economy, chemistry and experimental physics. According to the university records, O'Donovan failed his first-year science exams in the summer of 1915. It appears, however, that he re-sat and passed those exams in the same year, because he took his BSc degree 'within the usual three-year time-frame'.[5]

As 1916 drew to a close, O'Donovan received a letter from one of his former teachers at St Aloysius' College in Glasgow. It is clear from the letter, dated 30 December 1916, that Fr Geoffrey Bliss is disagreeing with O'Donovan's anti-conscription stance on World War I – the conflict was then at its height and would last for a further two years. The Jesuit priest wrote:

> As to the war, I know enough of Irish history – ancient and recent – not to have any harsh feelings towards Irishmen who are not willing to stand side by side with us in this quarrel. But the same knowledge gives me a very warm feeling of admiration for the many Irishmen who have judged Belgium's case to be as bitter as their own land's, and her spirit akin to hers, and have drawn the sword not from love to England but for reverence to their own land and its history … you will say that I do not sympathise with your position. I do not fully simply because I do not fully understand it. But I will ask you to believe me when I say that I have known you personally and therefore know that no 'ugly names' are possible here, or can explain why you do not fight.[6]

ORIGINS OF A REVOLUTIONARY

It is worth noting that by late 1916, the young chemistry student no longer considered the war a worthy cause, as he had done when applying to join the Royal Navy two years before. He was clearly opposed to conscription and was already turning his attentions to domestic issues that had been reawakened by the Easter Rising earlier that year. While unwilling to criticise his former student for not fighting in the Great War, Fr Bliss could not have foreseen that twelve months later O'Donovan would join the IRA and begin a very different fight, this time for his own country's freedom.

The young student took to his new college life in UCD with relish and settled in without delay. He had found his niche and was setting out on a course that would see him become, within a few short years, the IRA's top explosives expert during the war of independence. The university chemical society's handbook for the 1916/17 session lists J. L. O'Donovan as a committee member of the society, scheduled to deliver a paper, on 28 March 1917, entitled 'The Isomerism of the Cinnamic Acids'. A year later he had taken over the post of honorary secretary of the chemical society and already held a B.Sc. honours degree with which he had been conferred in autumn 1917.

The honorary president of UCD's chemical society was Professor Hugh Ryan (1873–1931), while the president was Assistant Professor Thomas Dillon.[7] O'Donovan's daughter Sheila recalls that at UCD her father 'came into contact with republican sympathisers such as Dillon, Michael Tierney and Turlough MacNeill. They used to go camping together ... that is where he got involved in IRA activity'.[8] Professor Dillon was active in the republican movement and would soon recruit his young student as an IRA volunteer, with a specific brief to develop new explosive materiel for the armed independence struggle. At this stage of his college career, O'Donovan was also doing research work for the Nobel's explosives company. On 6 March 1918, he delivered an address on atomic weights. Despite the backdrop of World War I

– Ireland was still within the UK, but conscription did not apply – there was a leisurely atmosphere within the privileged circle of the university chemical society. Professors and students partook of tea at 4.30 p.m. each Wednesday during term, with papers being read at 5 p.m., followed by a discussion 'in which all present are invited to take part'.

Contemporaneous notes written by O'Donovan on the back of his UCD chemical society 1917–18 handbook, disclose that he was already shifting towards a radical republican standpoint in his dealings with the student representative council, the chemical society itself and the university's governing council. His scrawly handwriting records that 'as secretary, chemical society, UCD, I led protest against honorary degrees being given to American soldiers on score of war service'. He also protested against 'English soldiers' (presumably he meant Irishmen in British army uniform) attending lectures at UCD.[9] O'Donovan's notes record his intention 'to urge all graduates to join and record their votes at the triennial election of members of the [university] senate'. He wanted what he termed 'royal members' of UCD's senate 'to register as national [members]'. In addition, O'Donovan acted 'to impress upon all graduates the importance of using their votes as graduates for [electing] members of the governing body'. In the formal, pedantic style he would employ in official IRA communiqués in later years, the 21-year-old chemistry graduate formalised his anti-British, pro-nationalist resolutions as follows: 'The chemical society of University College, Dublin, in meeting assembled, desires to convey to the students' representative council of UCD the following statements and demands, and to insist upon the extreme urgency and importance attending the fulfilment of the actions suggested....' Obviously, the long years of formal, classical schooling at St Aloysius' College had not gone astray for the Jesuits' *enfant terrible*.

As O'Donovan progressed in his studies at UCD's department of chemistry, working towards obtaining a master's degree in science, he would match his words with deeds that would bring him inexorably along the path of armed struggle. His role would not be that of a front-line fighter, however, but a key back-room strategist, developing new types of explosive devices for use in the looming war of independence which ran from January 1919 to July 1921. Circumstances combined in a way that favoured the young graduate, placing him in a pivotal position to assist the IRA's strategy. The failed 1916 Rising had backfired on the British when public opinion abhorred the executions of the republican leaders. (According to his son Donal, Jim O'Donovan 'disapproved of the 1916 Rising'. His decision to join the republican movement came some time later, in December 1917.) But those who were spared the firing-squad or the hangman's noose lived to fight another day. Many, including Michael Collins, returned from Frongoch internment camp in Wales, or prisons elsewhere in Britain, to regroup and retrain for the coming fight. Slowly but surely, O'Donovan was gaining expertise as a chemist, specialising in the manufacture of explosives – and helped in no small measure by his mentors, Professors Ryan and Dillon.

But the young student's progress was not without mishaps. One incident in particular remains memorable for all the wrong reasons. Having attended his lectures and completed his duties as honorary secretary of the chemical society, O'Donovan had taken to working late in the university laboratory at Earlsfort Terrace in central Dublin. In later years he recalled making

> ... poison-gas, tear-gas and things like that. I took it that we were going to use these gases, and I did not think very much of the possibilities, but I learned from Dick Mulcahy ... that what we were really working on was to take safeguards against poison-gas, the use of which, during the imminent imposition of conscription, was expected. It was presumed that gas was going to be used at some stage of the war here and that it would be of benefit to be forearmed. I was

> working with Dr W. D. O'Kelly also on the making of helmets and goggles and masks which would absorb the poison-gas, active charcoal being one of the filter ingredients of the mask. I had to make the poison-gases myself, and carried out all experiments connected therewith by myself. During one of these experiments it blew up and I got all the liquid gas on my face. I thought I was blinded but, fortunately, after about 15 or 20 minutes, I found I could open my eyes. My face was a mass of water blisters and I had to be off work for about a week. The liquid form of the gas was, of course, much more virulent and damaging than the gas itself, which is what would be normally used in [an] attack. I could thus lay claim to be the first poison-gas casualty in Ireland, if not the only one ever recorded.... Professor Hugh Ryan knew from the signs of my equipment and materials (left about after I was disabled) that I was working on these gases, but he had to pretend he knew nothing about my work.

This last observation confirms that Professor Ryan was willing to look the other way when IRA work was going on in his chemistry department. The young student knew he was in danger of being caught, adding:

> There was always an element of suspicion about my work, but this chance had to be often taken. For instance, at the time of the tear-gas incident, there was only one person in the building when the liquid blew up during my preparation of the poison-gases. He was a laboratory superintendent and when he found me wandering about in instinctive search of water after being blinded, he was free to think what he liked. I could not say whether he was friendly or

otherwise, but even if he was not he would probably keep his mouth shut. Perry was his name and he was the only person who actually saw me out of action. After the explosion, and when I had recovered my sight, he wanted me to go to Vincent's Hospital, but I could not go there as I would have been subjected to awkward questioning.[10]

In less favourable circumstances, the exploding gas incident could have led to O'Donovan's arrest and expulsion from UCD. But it seemed as if staff in positions of authority were prepared to be helpful to him, if only by saying nothing and turning a blind eye to his experiments. Thus, the next day's intake of students – and, more importantly, the college authorities – were none the wiser about the events of the night before and the existence of a bomb-maker in their midst.

The sinister and deadly nature of O'Donovan's work in this period is contained in his revelation that the Volunteers' leadership was thinking of using chemical/disease warfare against British forces in 1918:

Consideration was also being given to the possibility of infecting the horses in the various cavalry barracks with glanders or some similar infectious disease. Another aspect of bacteriological warfare was the possibility under consideration of spreading disease, e.g. botulism, on which I wrote a couple of articles about 1918. The whole thing arose out of the conscription scare because in the highest circles, even in the Castle, it was definitely expected that conscription would be applied here. It was the nearest miss that this country ever experienced. As regards this infection, botulism, I don't know what the full application of it would have been. It was for human use, but what the proposed application of it was I cannot say. Its effects were only passing, resulting in dizziness, sickness and affecting the sight, etc. The above illustrates a couple of unusual possibilities that were considered from the military angle. After the conscription time, about March 1918, would have been the critical period.[11]

Despite the apparent 'lone ranger' aspect of O'Donovan's IRA activities at UCD in the 1917–19 period, he was not, in fact, doing a solo run with the backing of a few professors. Other students were also active in the armed struggle to end British rule. They included Seán MacBride (1904–88) who recalled in his memoirs that he was able to fire on British troops near Westland Row railway station (since 1966, renamed after Pádraig Pearse, the 1916 commander in chief), and then race back to attend lectures at Earlsfort Terrace, thus escaping arrest and providing a valuable alibi. In addition, Richard Mulcahy, who would become chief of staff of the Volunteers during the war of independence, was briefly at UCD at the same time as O'Donovan.[12]

The nearest Jim O'Donovan got to embracing the constitutional path was a brief flirtation – albeit in an anonymous background role – with a radical republican party, Córas na Poblachta, in early 1940. The new party, which never succeeded at the polls, was formed by IRA volunteers in protest at what they saw as de Valera's wartime 'collaboration' with Britain.[13] But O'Donovan's decision to dabble fleetingly in fringe politics lay two decades ahead. In the intervening years he would have to soldier through the crucible of the war of independence and the civil war, followed by bankruptcy, economic renaissance and the call to fight an ancient enemy again, but this time on English soil.

2.

THE UNFINISHED PORTRAIT

It all started with a leak in the roof of artist Leo Whelan's Eccles Street home in Dublin. It was November 1945 and the world was still reeling from six years of conflict which had only just ended. But in Ireland – most of which had escaped the war – things moved to a different rhythm and there was time to deal with more mundane matters. The leak prompted Whelan, a noted portrait painter and member of the Royal Hibernian Academy, to clear out the attic of his home and move all the materials to his studio in Lower Baggot Street. But as he set about the task of saving paintings from the rain, Whelan was in for a shock. Lying in a corner was a large (9' x 6') rolled-up canvas that had lain untouched and unseen for almost a quarter of a century. It was a long-lost and almost forgotten piece of work, still unfinished all those decades later. Whelan unfurled the painting and gazed in disbelief. Thirteen sober men in grey suits stared back at him. They could have been the board of directors of a bank. But the well-cut suits with starched collars and ties in which Whelan had chosen to portray them, belied the fact that the group comprised the general headquarters staff of the pre-treaty IRA in December 1921. Five months earlier, in July 1921, the truce had marked an end to the war of independence with Britain which had run its bloody course from the start of 1919. The British prime minister, David Lloyd George, was now willing to begin peace treaty talks in London on a measure of Irish independence. The thirteen men in the portrait had effectively taken on the might of an empire and forced the British to the negotiating table.

Frozen in time, the IRA leaders looked out from the group portrait with resolute, fixed expressions. Their average age was only thirty. And they could hardly have guessed what awaited them after the moment of apparent triumph in late 1921. Independence from Britain, in January 1922, heralded acrimonious splits (principally over the terms of the Anglo-Irish treaty which kept the six counties within the UK) and a brutal civil war (1922–23) scarring the Irish body politic for generations to come.

By 1945, the Irish question had been all but forgotten abroad in the wake of World War II, which had left tens of millions dead on battlefields around the globe. In an Irish context, however, Leo Whelan's unfinished painting was a poignant reminder of a lost unity of purpose. The resolute determination of the IRA leadership and its tough military tactics – in which Jim O'Donovan, as director of chemicals,[1] had played a part – had brought about a truce and peace talks. But the treaty, signed in London on 6 December 1921, resulted in partition and, although ratified by a 64–57 vote in Dáil Éireann on 7 January 1922, quickly led to bitter divisions both within the republican leadership and in the country at large.

The sorry tale of internecine conflict must have passed through Leo Whelan's mind as he surveyed his historic painting, which would be publicly displayed by the Royal Hibernian Academy for the first time in 1946. Shortly after rediscovering the long-lost work, the artist told a newspaper reporter that he

… was at the old Gresham Hotel on the historic night of December 6, 1921, when news of the signing of the Treaty in London had electrified the atmosphere. He was introduced to General Mulcahy and later someone in the party suggested that he should paint the GHQ staff.[2] He agreed, and on the following day Gen. Mulcahy gave him the list of the members and arranged sittings. Mr Whelan made individual portraits at his studio at 64 Dawson St, and later transferred them to the larger canvas. It was exciting work and often the men had to rush from the studio after sittings of a few minutes. At other times despatch riders raced to the studio to arrange or cancel sittings. Michael Collins was, according to Mr Whelan, the worst sitter of all. The big, burly Corkman could not manage a moment's quiet. He was forever twisting and turning in the chair and was liable to dash from the studio without warning to attend to urgent business.[3] The individual studies of Collins, Rory O'Connor and Liam Mellows have been disposed of by Mr Whelan. The painting of Collins is in England, that of Rory O'Connor is in the National Gallery, while Mr de Valera is the owner of the study of Liam Mellows.[4]

But the group portrait was destined never to be fully finished:

Sittings were infrequent and hurried in the tense days that followed and progress was slow. The death of Mr Whelan's father in March of the following year further delayed the work. When the civil war broke out a few months later, the artist resignedly rolled up the nine feet by six canvas, which was more than three-quarters finished, and placed it in the attic of his home.[5]

Almost 25 years on, some in the portrait were dead (victims of assassination or state executions), while others had taken the political path but remained enemies because of the lasting civil war divisions. Some chose to become career soldiers in the new Free State army, while others dropped off the radar screen and faded from public view. By 1945 only one, Jim O'Donovan, had remained committed to what he saw as the legitimate principle of an armed struggle to free the Six Counties from British rule.[6] He would outlive them all, dying in June 1979 at the age of 82.

It is instructive to consider the unfinished IRA group portrait at this remove, almost 90 years after it was begun – it is currently on display at the National Museum in Collins barracks, Dublin, having previously been displayed at the National Gallery and later in the Officers' Mess in McKee barracks – and see what happened to the thirteen men portrayed on the canvas:

J. J. 'GINGER' O'CONNELL (1887–1944), was assistant chief of staff during the war of independence. He supported the 1921 Anglo-Irish treaty which granted independence to twenty-six of the thirty-two counties of Ireland, leaving Northern Ireland within the United Kingdom. He became deputy chief of staff of the new Free State army in 1922 and remained in the army for the rest of his career, occupying a number of senior posts.

EMMET DALTON (1898–1978), director of training. Pro-treaty. He accompanied Michael Collins to London during the treaty negotiations in 1921. He was with Collins when the latter was shot dead at Béal na mBláth, County Cork, on 22 August 1922. After the civil war, Dalton worked as a film producer in Hollywood and London. In 1958, he co-founded Ardmore film studios in Bray, County Wicklow.

LIAM MELLOWS (1892–1922), director of purchases. Anti-treaty. As a prisoner of the new provisional government during the civil war, Mellows was executed (along with three other prisoners) on 8 December 1922 in reprisal for the shooting of two government

TDs the previous day (one of whom, Seán Hales, died of his wounds).

PIARAS BÉASLAÍ (1883–1965), director of publicity. Pro-treaty. TD from 1918 to 1923. Major-general in new national army. Resigned from the army in 1924 to write and also work with the Irish language movement. His best-known work is *Michael Collins and the Making of a New Ireland* (London, 1926).

MICHAEL COLLINS (1890–1922), director of intelligence. Pro-treaty. Held a number of ministerial posts in the First Dáil (1919–21). A member of the delegation that negotiated the Anglo-Irish treaty of 6 December 1921, Collins became chairman of the provisional government formed to implement the accord. When civil war broke out in June 1922, he became commander in chief of the government forces. Died in an ambush by anti-treaty forces at Béal na mBláth, County Cork, on 22 August 1922.

RICHARD MULCAHY (1886–1971), chief of staff. Pro-treaty. TD 1919–61, holding various ministerial posts. After leading the Volunteers during the war of independence, Mulcahy became chief of staff of new Free State army during the civil war, following Michael Collins's death. Mulcahy played a leading role in the Blueshirt movement in the 1930s. He was a founder member of Fine Gael and led that party from 1944 to 1959. He retired from politics in 1961.

GEARÓID O'SULLIVAN (1891–1948), adjutant-general. Pro-treaty. High-ranking IRB man (with Collins, Mulcahy and Mellows). He retained the same post in the new Free State army from 1922 to 1924. Later in the 1920s, he became the army's judge-advocate general. O'Sullivan was a TD for Carlow-Kilkenny 1921–23, and for County Dublin 1927–37 (following the assassination of Kevin O'Higgins). He was prominent in the Blueshirt movement for a time.

EAMONN 'BOB' PRICE (1892–1951), director of organisation. Pro-treaty. Member of Michael Collins's 'squad'. Joined Free State forces during civil war and reached rank of Major-General. At request of General Richard Mulcahy, Price wrote a report on the Ballyseedy massacre in County Kerry, in which anti-treaty forces were killed by a land-mine. He withdrew from military and political activity after 1923. Eamonn Price's sister, Leslie de Barra (née Price), was married to General Tom Barry, who led the flying columns in west Cork during the war of independence.

RORY O'CONNOR (1883–1922), director of engineering and O/C Britain. Anti-treaty. Captured following government attack on Four Courts garrison, Dublin, on 28 June 1922. Along with Liam Mellows and two other prisoners (Joe McKelvey and Dick Barrett), O'Connor was shot by firing squad on 8 December 1922 in retaliation for the shooting of two government TDs.

EOIN O'DUFFY (1892–1944), deputy chief of staff. Pro-treaty. IRB supreme council 1917. TD 1921–22. He became commissioner of the Garda Síochána in 1922 and was appointed head of the army during the Curragh mutiny of 1924. Éamon de Valera sacked O'Duffy as Garda chief in 1933. He became leader of the Blueshirts the same year and subsequently president of Fine Gael. He later left that party and, in 1936, organised an Irish brigade to fight for Franco in the Spanish civil war.

SEÁN RUSSELL (1893–1940), director of munitions. Anti-treaty. Following the civil war, Russell rejected the democratic path, believing that only a military campaign could achieve a united Ireland. Appointed IRA chief of staff in 1938, he called on his old war of independence colleague Jim O'Donovan to design a major bombing campaign in England (the 1939–40 S-plan). Russell raised funds for the campaign in America. By May 1940, he was in Berlin, seeking weapons and other help from the Nazi regime. In August 1940 he died of a perforated ulcer aboard a German

U-boat en route for Ireland. Frank Ryan (a senior IRA figure who had fought with the International Brigade in Spain) was also aboard the vessel but returned to Germany where he died in 1944.

SEÁN MACMAHON (1894–1955), quartermaster-general. Pro-treaty. An IRB member, he became chief of staff of the defence forces from September 1922 to 1924. Forced to resign over the army mutiny of 1924, he later withdrew from all military and political activity.

JAMES O'DONOVAN (1896–1979), director of chemicals. Anti-treaty. O'Donovan was imprisoned during the civil war and later started his own chemical business in Dublin, which later went bankrupt. He joined the Electricity Supply Board (ESB) in 1930 as a manager. In 1938, he returned to active service with the IRA, drawing up the S-plan to bomb England. The bombing campaign ran from January 1939 to March 1940. As the IRA's chief liaison officer with Nazi Germany, O'Donovan covertly visited the continent on four occasions in 1939 (once to Brussels, twice to Hamburg and finally to Berlin) to establish links with German military intelligence. He was interned in the Curragh camp from 1941 to 1943. He took no further part in militant republicanism after his release and retired from the ESB in 1962. When he died in 1979, he was the last surviving member of the IRA's pre-treaty headquarters staff.[7]

Between the truce of July 1921 and the disputed treaty of December that year, all thirteen members of the GHQ staff were fitted for generals' uniforms at Callaghan's outfitters on Dame Street, Dublin. But the uniforms were destined to be worn only by the nine GHQ men who opted for the pro-treaty side following the Dáil's ratification of the treaty in January 1922.[8]

A key question remains: how did the apparent initial unity of the IRA GHQ staff lead to discord and civil war? And was it simply a matter of disagreements over the terms of the Anglo-Irish treaty?

THE DEVIL'S DEAL

As we shall see in the next chapter, Jim O'Donovan would find himself taking sides not only against the treaty but also in a bitter internal dispute between those who, like himself, favoured military control of the state through the IRA's army council, and the pro-democracy elements led by Collins and Mulcahy, who were determined that power would be vested in Dáil Éireann and not in the military. O'Donovan's stance on these crucial issues would bring him into conflict with his former commanding officer, the new Free State's minister for defence, General Richard Mulcahy.

3.

ACTIVE SERVICE

Jim O'Donovan was awarded a Bachelor of Science degree in 1917 and immediately began studying for a master's degree, which he obtained in 1919. His graduation was to prove a baptism of fire for the young chemist, who was still working on new types of explosives for use by IRA volunteers against British troops. But his first contacts with the republican movement date from Christmas 1917 when 'through personal friendships with the Ryan family I became acquainted with Dick Mulcahy [then a UCD medical student, who married Mary 'Min' Ryan in June 1919] and many other personalities associated with the Volunteer organisation'. He dates his active IRA service from 1 January 1918 when, for three months, he was an attaché to the Irish Volunteers. As a chemistry student he attended Sinn Féin lectures by Gavan Duffy and Eoin MacNeill. His academic work went far beyond the theoretical into practical methods of bomb, land-mine, grenade and incendiary manufacture. O'Donovan described his breakthroughs as follows: 'The principal explosive used at this time of our own make was the one from nitrated resin … which I christened "War Flour" from its resemblance to Indian meal or coarse flour. I was working all the time towards a simpler explosive … for which my model was cheddite [a high explosive notable for its stability] and was christened by me "Irish Cheddar". It was not perfected for some time.' Irish Cheddar eventually supplanted War Flour, which was 'not very stable and, as a result, a bit dangerous'.[1]

In later life, O'Donovan boasted of his work in designing explosives, especially grenades, for the Volunteers. In his statement to the Bureau of Military History, written in 1957, O'Donovan explained the shortcomings of his early bomb designs, confirming that the timing fuses and detonators 'were never 100%'. But he made progress and

> … was able to get very quick results. I remember at one time getting a beautiful grenade turned out in a week – a vast improvement on anything that had been done before in the way of moulding the wall with its sectional grooves. I always maintained that our final grenade was really superior to the Mills.[2] The fragmentation, which measures the final hurting power, was a matter for frequent testing. A grenade that would split in two and ignore the grooving would obviously be virtually useless. In a lean-to corrugated iron shed at the 'Bottle Tower', Churchtown, I carried out tests with Seán Russell by counting the fragments actually left behind plus those which had escaped, making holes in the roof.

Describing his various grenade designs, O'Donovan continued:

> In the explosive grenade, the object was to have a thick cast-iron wall serrated in such a way in the mould as to reduce by fragmentation to a theoretical 48 fragments upon explosion, each of which would be similar in effect in action to shrapnel; whereas in the

case of incendiary work, a soft and easily consumed wall was what was required, preferably itself made of inflammable material, which would be destroyed in the process, and the contents such as to produce intensely high temperatures in the least time.[3]

However, the reality for young IRA Volunteers on the ground could sometimes be at variance with O'Donovan's somewhat exaggerated opinion of his technical prowess. Seán Clancy, who fought the Black and Tans on Dublin's northside – as a member of B company, 2nd battalion, Dublin brigade IRA – recalls that the grenades did not always explode. According to Clancy, street ambushes were 'very prevalent':

> The Black and Tans appeared on the scene and they were our main target here in Dublin at that time. Our job was – in small groups, in turn – to attack them in their movements in the streets. They used to travel in Crossley tenders. At first they were open and were very good targets for hand grenades. We used hand grenades mostly; any rifles in Dublin after 1916 were sent to different parts of the country where they were needed more. But small arms were used and hand grenades in particular.

The street encounters, usually carried out in broad daylight, were fraught with danger:

> It was a question of having a go and disappearing. We were very badly armed and we weren't prepared to stand up and fight for a period. The procedure – in Dublin anyhow, as distinct from the country – was to let fly at Crossley tenders that were carrying British troops, and then disappear. We had an advantage that way; we knew the streets and knew the area pretty well. They were strangers and I suppose were more nervous than we were.

Clancy recalls that British troops always opened fire on the IRA,

> ... but they often missed. We'd have disappeared after getting rid of our weapons. Each of us might have one hand grenade. After letting fly at a passing lorry, we might miss it often or sometimes the old grenades might not explode at all. Once we got rid of the hand grenades we were gone around the corner ... sometimes we had revolvers, but even revolvers were scarce. In a small group of four, five or six there might be one or two revolvers but each of us would have at least one hand grenade anyhow. [After an engagement] somebody would be held responsible for collecting the weapons. There might be a couple who would take responsibility for them and would take them back into the dump again. Each company had a dump [which] was usually situated in some back garden or a stable. At that time, you often had stables with horses where we used to keep our dumps. From time to time, we used to lend the contents of the dumps to other groups.[4]

In his own words, O'Donovan was the 'earliest investigator into replacement of purloined commercial explosives by those of home manufacture'. In addition, he was 'engaged on anti-gas defence preparations in anticipation of the possibility of conscription'. But conscription was never introduced in Ireland during World War I and, in fact, it was not used in Northern Ireland during World War II either. O'Donovan reveals that he was personally 'invalided by gassing for a few days at this period [early 1918]'.

Details of O'Donovan's experiences in the 1918–23 period – which includes the war of independence and subsequent civil war – are relatively sketchy. They comprise hand-written notes, letters and IRA communiqués, as well as material in his army pension applications in 1933 and 1935. In addition, O'Donovan provided

ACTIVE SERVICE

a 13-page account of his 'Work for and in the munitions and chemicals dept, GHQ, for Irish Volunteers and IRA 1917–1920' to the Bureau of Military History (BMH) in the 1950s. This material did not become publicly available until half a century later. Since material sought by the BMH covers only the 1913–21 period – that is from the formation of the Volunteers to the July 1921 truce – it does not include any civil war data. When signing off on this BMH material on 13 September 1957, O'Donovan added the following note: 'If time permits, I intend to add a further instalment to bring this evidence down to 1921.' But he never got round to doing so. Instead, he began penning a series of unpublished memoirs after his retirement in 1962, but these were never completed either.

An overview of what had occurred in the 1918–23 period emerges from O'Donovan's two applications for army pensions: in 1933, i.e. an invalidity pension concerning the May 1922 injury to his right hand; and in 1935, concerning his active service during the war of independence.[5] In order to obtain these pensions, O'Donovan used two laws introduced by the new government of Éamon de Valera, who on 9 March 1932 had taken over as head of government from W. T. Cosgrave's Cumann na nGaedheal administration, which had run the country for the ten years since independence. The legal provisions were the Army Pensions Act 1932 and the Military Service Pensions Act 1934 – essentially introduced by de Valera to provide a stipend for ex-IRA men who had fallen on hard times in the preceding decade. Many who had opposed the treaty (signed in London on 6 December 1921) were looked on unfavourably by the 1922–32 administration and found it hard to get employment. Emigration, principally to America, was often the only way for them to survive. This was not so in O'Donovan's case, however, because – since 19 November 1930 – he had been on the Electricity Supply Board's payroll.

He first applied for an army invalidity pension on 25 February 1933, and on 12 May that year 'was awarded an annual pension in respect of wounds to the value of £75 per annum'. O'Donovan had told the pensions board that 'from June 1921 until March 1922' his 'remuneration as whole-time director of chemicals was received out of Dáil Éireann funds to the extent of £25 per month'.[6]

Under the terms of the subsequent 1934 Act, O'Donovan sought a military service pension in 1935 and to this end was interviewed by J. M. Somes, an accountant with the Munster & Leinster Bank's O'Connell Street branch in Dublin. When asked to provide referees 'who could testify as to your statements', O'Donovan named Richard Mulcahy and Thomas Dillon, then professor of chemistry at University College Galway. The choice of referees was instructive: as the key player who had recruited him to the Volunteers, Dillon would presumably not have hesitated to vouch for his former student; but the same could not be said for Mulcahy. The retired general and minister for defence, who in the mid-1930s was an opposition TD, had not met or spoken to O'Donovan since the acrimonious treaty split in January 1921 when both men had quarrelled over the transfer of executive powers from the IRA's army council to Dáil Éireann.[7] In any case, there is no record of either Mulcahy or Dillon being asked to provide a reference for O'Donovan in 1935.

O'Donovan claimed that his initial active service ran continuously from 1 April 1918 to 31 March 1919 when, as a UCD postgraduate student, he worked as an attaché to the Volunteers: 'Investigations continued. Procuring war-like materials and carrying out tests, often with considerable dangers.' To vouch for his IRA activities in this 12-month period, O'Donovan cited Dillon and Mulcahy, in addition to Michael Lynch, O/C Fingal battalion and later O/C Dublin brigade IRA.

In the period from 1 April 1919 to 31 March 1920, O'Donovan continued to describe his role as that of an IRA attaché: 'Increasing activity. Extensive filling of Mills grenades at 10a, Aungier Street and other "shops". Testing bombs and various new explosives with O/C Dublin brigade, etc. Series of articles on the manufacture and care of explosives in *An t-Óglach* [an IRA journal] 1st and 15th March 1920.'

O'Donovan was speaking from personal experience when he said that testing bombs involved 'considerable dangers', as he had sustained a serious injury (while stockpiling grenades in the run-up to the civil war) leaving his right hand permanently disfigured. He first gave details of the incident when applying for an invalidity pension. On 25 February 1933, O'Donovan wrote to the pensions board from his home at 12 Tivoli Terrace South, Dún Laoghaire, describing himself as a 'permanent civil servant' (he had joined the state electricity board two years earlier). The pension board comprised Mr John McCoy, Dr E. O'Hogáin, and Major D. J. Doyle. O'Donovan told the board that his right hand had been injured by an explosive in May 1922, as a result of which two fingers were completely amputated and one partly amputated. According to O'Donovan's evidence to the pensions board, for which he cited Seán Russell as a corroborator, the accident had happened on 10 May 1922 (i.e. a month after the anti-treaty IRA had formed its own GHQ staff, and six weeks before the start of the civil war) at Monasterevin, County Kildare. The incident fractured all the bones in his right hand, causing the 'loss of portion of hand and also two and a half fingers'. O'Donovan had been 'demonstrating [the] composition of grenades and [their] use in action' when the explosion occurred. He was rushed to Kildare county infirmary where he was treated until 29 June 1922.[8]

O'Donovan's son, Donal, recalls that 'the doctors wanted to amputate his hand but he refused. He was lucky that they were persuaded not to amputate, as they had wanted to, because he could write with that hand all his life. He had bits of grenade shrapnel coming through the skin.'[9]

Jim O'Donovan also revealed to the pension board that a 'part contribution' towards expenses of hospital treatment in Kildare was made by Austin Stack in his capacity as minister for finance (i.e. of the shadow, anti-treaty administration). On his discharge from hospital, O'Donovan was detained at Naas military barracks from 29 June to 8 July 1922. From there he was taken to the Curragh military hospital on 8 July where he remained for treatment until 15 September. Thus, O'Donovan followed all the opening salvoes of the civil war (including the bombardment of the Four Courts on 28 June and the assassination of Michael Collins on 22 August 1922) as a detainee. O'Donovan had been present in the Four Courts following its initial occupation by the anti-treaty GHQ staff on 9 April 1922, but he subsequently left to work with Seán Russell on stockpiling weapons and explosives in the run-up to the civil war.

On 12 May 1933, the army pensions board recommended that a full pension (i.e. 50 per cent of his final army salary) be awarded to O'Donovan. For the rest of his life, he would wear a leather glove to conceal his maimed hand. Apart from feeling self-conscious about the injury, and although he was able to write despite it, he knew the authorities had his medical records and could more easily identify him from then on.

There were several versions of the incident in which O'Donovan's right hand was maimed. One account puts the blame on an inexperienced IRA recruit. Over half a century later, O'Donovan told James Toner that 'he lost his fingers during an IRA training session. A young IRA recruit was being shown how to throw a grenade. He pulled the pin and froze. Jim said that he had to prise the younger man's hand open to retrieve the grenade and it exploded just after it left Jim's hand as he threw it.'[10] James Toner's father, Edward, was at Clongowes Wood College in County Kildare in the early 1920s when Jim O'Donovan was teaching there and they became lifelong friends. Another version was that 'there was a bit of bravado, and he didn't pay much attention to the time that had elapsed since pulling the grenade's pin'.[11] Both these incorrect versions of the same event were doing the rounds amongst ESB staff in the 1950s. In later life, O'Donovan told his son Donal yet another version of the story:

He told me that he brought the nobs out to Whitehall Lodge, to the Bottle Tower church. The fuse was too short or something and it went off and damaged his hand, while his peers were looking on at the great experiment. It's funny that there are different versions, isn't it?[12]

In his pension application papers, O'Donovan claims to have worked unofficially for the IRA general headquarters staff from 1 April to December 1920, with Richard Mulcahy as chief of staff. He adds: 'Then officially taken on to GHQ staff in December 1920 as director of chemicals.[13] Previous to this, no rank or status, except as attaché.' In his pension claim, O'Donovan fails to mention that both he and Seán Russell, among others, were appointed to an expanded GHQ staff following the deaths of Dick McKee and Peadar Clancy in Dublin Castle on 21 November 1920. (The two leaders were arrested, tortured and executed in the wake of the killing of fourteen British agents by Michael Collins's 'squad'. On the same day, known as Bloody Sunday, British troops killed twelve people and wounded sixty at Croke Park.) O'Donovan continues: 'Explosives shop started in Peter Street dispensary immediately following GHQ appointment. Staff engaged and department functioning about January 1921. Perfection of incendiary grenade. Manufacturing, testing and distribution of explosives, etc.' Richard Mulcahy is cited as the sole referee for this period. In his statements to the Bureau of Military History, O'Donovan recalled that from the 'principal workshop' in the dispensary 'we could see through the windows the frequent comings and goings of troops and Tan lorries issuing from Ship Street barracks'.

The testing of his incendiary grenades made for some hair-raising episodes, as O'Donovan recalled:

I remember the first official try-out of this product, which took place in the basement of 44 Parnell Square in the presence of [Peadar] Clancy, Seán Russell, Mick

Lynch, probably Seán Mooney (then brigade adjutant) and others. This was a memorable occasion, as units were drilling upstairs while we occupied the dark basement. In view of the job being undertaken, the drilling was an important adjunct as it tended to conceal the activity in the basement. A manually ignited fuse was used on this occasion, not one operated by a hammer and cap mechanism, as the purpose was simply to try out the actual incendiary materials in association with primers and the container. It was, as far as I remember, a cigar-lighter fuse, and its progress was visible in the dark, so that the excitement and tension grew as the flame visibly progressed. During the silence of waiting, the marching and drilling upstairs filled the expectant basement. It was a complete success in every way and McKee was highly excited and congratulated me, shaking both my hands. When we had finished, the upstairs building began to fill with smoke but by then we, the experimenters, were gone.[14]

O'Donovan goes on to explain, albeit obliquely, his elevation to the IRA's command structure: 'The deaths of Dick McKee and Peadar Clancy removed the two men with whom I was most intimately connected at this period. It was on the death of Peadar Clancy that a fully organised munitions department – functioning under a director of munitions and, equally, a director of chemicals – was decided upon.'

For his activities during the period from 1 April to 11 July 1921, O'Donovan offers the following brief outline: 'Ireland generally, Liverpool and London. O/C Richard Mulcahy. Director of department of chemicals, GHQ staff. Organisation of the department. Purchase of raw materials. Establishment of workshops. Manufacture, testing, distribution of explosives.'

In a memo dated 16 December 1970, O'Donovan revealed that in 1921 he had received a German-language explosives manual from a friend, Dr Paddy Brown. To avoid suspicion, he had the book rebound in a new cover entitled 'Study of Wild Flowers'. The book's real title was *Spreng- und Zündstoffe* (Explosive and Incendiary Materials). It was written by a German professor, Dr Hermann Kast, and published in Braunschweig in 1921.[15]

O'Donovan's deposition under the terms of the Military Service Pensions Act 1934 places him as a member of the IRA GHQ staff from 12 July 1921 (the day after the truce) to 30 June 1922 (i.e. the surrender of the Four Courts by the anti-treaty garrison) 'with the rank of commandant-general'.[16] 'District or districts in which active service was rendered: Ireland generally and London. O/C R. Mulcahy to 12 January 1922 [i.e. the day after he had written to Mulcahy demanding an IRA convention with a view to vesting supreme power in the army]. Several explosives shops established. Staff considerably increased. Organisation of large-scale purchases. Explosives shop established in Greenwich, London.' Thirty years later, in his deposition to the Bureau of Military History, O'Donovan explained the significance of the Greenwich facility:

> In the latter stages, pre-truce, I got a lot of chemical raw materials through Francis FitzGerald who owned a chemical factory in Greenwich. He was a brother of Desmond FitzGerald. He was an extremely useful introduction. It took time to develop this source of supply because the quantities involved were very much bigger. We got the stuff consigned in new bags as bicarbonate of soda or any commercial material such as baking soda, cream of tartar, etc., all of which resembled our raw material which was potassium chlorate. We could get over the basic raw material which I had adopted as being the most practical for our use.[17]

Under the heading 'Absence from duty and cause', O'Donovan notes: 'Hospital from about 23 May 1922 to 29 June 1922 as a result of a bomb explosion in Monasterevin. Under arrest as from

29 June. Referees for this period: 1. Richard Mulcahy; 2. John Joyce O/C F[ree] S[tate] army in Naas barracks on 29 June 1922; 3. Seán Lemass (as barrack adjutant, Four Courts).' In fact, O'Donovan's recollection of his hospitalisation is about two weeks out. He was admitted to hospital on 10 May.

By way of explaining his absence from front-line duty, O'Donovan added the following explanation to his pension application:

> Prior to the complete re-organisation of the GHQ staff by the creation of new technical and other departments in December 1920, I was specifically enjoined by Richard Mulcahy on no account to join any infantry unit as my services were stated to be of much greater value if I remained completely unattached. Even before this became a definite injunction, it was also the implicit attitude early in the period on several occasions when I endeavoured to join the ranks as a 'volunteer'. Owing to my unattached status, not being associated with a definite unit in the early period, I have not been able to seek or obtain the corroboration that would otherwise have been available.

In other words, the back-room nature of his earlier work was making it difficult for O'Donovan to plead his case for a full senior officer's pension in 1935, some fifteen years after joining the IRA general headquarters staff.

On 29 November 1935, O'Donovan wrote indignantly to the secretary of the military service pensions board to ask why he still had not received a service certificate. In the same letter, he seeks to distance himself from any suggestion that he wants recognition for his wartime role, stating that his sole reason for applying for a pension is 'my accumulated indebtedness in respect of the enterprise I undertook in order to give employment to the ex-members of my former IRA department – amounting to over £2,000.' The enterprise was the City Chemical and Colour Company, which went bankrupt. Apart from that ill-fated venture, O'Donovan had been relatively penniless since his release from prison in July 1924 until he was hired by the ESB in November 1930. But, understandably, he wished to put a gloss on his pension application and thus played the old-soldier card, even though he had only just turned thirty-nine.

Two and a half months later, on 14 February 1936, O'Donovan made the following sworn statement before an advisory committee of the military service pensions board:

> The only explosive that was available to us was gelignite, which was not entirely suitable. It was more desirable to have our own supplies. I graduated in 1917. When I joined the Volunteers I was a research graduate. All my spare time was spent working for the Volunteers. Once I was appointed, I had no other interests in life. I might say, with truth, all my spare time. The beginning of 1918 was the first official contact. Mulcahy was in the university at that time. My brothers were in ambushes and that kind of thing.[18] I wanted to join them but would not be permitted because at that time I was not known to the authorities ... I went full-time in June. I had a contract from Clongowes from which they would not release me.[19] They would not agree to it. June 1921, I was whole[-time]. December 1920 I was eventually made director of chemicals. It was Dermot O'Hegarty [who] proposed to put it through. Before December 1920 I was not whole-time but whole spare-time. I have [*sic*] come up in the night time. I had a motorbike.

O'Donovan continued to press his case for an army pension and, as a result, was questioned by members of the military service pensions board at army headquarters in Parkgate Street, Dublin, in February 1936. The question and answer session provides some interesting information:

> Q. You were full-time during the Truce [i.e. July to December 1921]. Seán Russell was working side by side with you?
> A. It was from May 1920. Chiefly before that I had been with Dick McKee and Mick Lynch.
> Q. Seán Russell was casting grenade cases?
> A. Prior to that it was more of battalion kind.
> Q. Seán is not touching the pensions at all? It's a pity anyway for some fellows who were part-time.
> A. I was in touch with his staff, October 1922 and March 1923.

O'Donovan then tells the inquiry that he was arrested on 15 March 1923 and released on 17 July 1924, adding: 'It was the second last day [before the final release of internees]. Seán Russell was about the only one that was left over until the following day'. The question and answer sessions continued as follows:

> Q. On 11 July 1921, you were wounded during your service?[20]
> A. Yes.
> Q. Was that accident in the factory?
> A. We were just opening a new munitions factory in Monasterevin and we were both there, Seán Russell and myself. We both did the manufacturing in a hurry and I had the testing of it. The others were spectators. There was nothing wrong with anything, except that we rushed the thing so much that the whole thing was too hot. The detonator was sensitive. It was the vibration of the hammer that set it off instead of travelling through the fuse length.

ACTIVE SERVICE

Despite O'Donovan's detailed submissions to the inquiry, it seems that the army pensions board was in no hurry to grant him a service pension, although it had approved an invalidity pension in May 1933. The military machinations moved slowly at times. Some eight months later, on 24 October 1936, the advisory committee took sworn evidence from Ernie O'Malley (O/C of the IRA's 2nd southern division during the war of independence, who went anti-treaty in 1922 – he was assistant chief of staff during the civil war) on behalf of James Laurence O'Donovan:

> Q. He joined the Volunteers in January 1918. He was investigating the replacement of purloined commercial explosives. He took explosives on which he was working as a research graduate for Nobel's, brought them home and tried to see if they could be made by some home process.
> A. I suppose he was working with Hugh Ryan.
> Q. Yes. He got gassed during the course of his experiments.
> A. So he would. I did, too.
> Q. He was working from the very start on this thing. He had definitely left Nobel's; Hugh Ryan was working at Nobel's at the time.
> A. I expect he used the laboratory in the college [UCD]. They could get supplies through Tom Daly[21] who started importing stuff so that they could get the raw material.
> Q. Had they that place in Galway?
> A. The importing place was in Mary Street, Dublin.
> Q. He did the work in Galway?
> A. I think he was in Dublin, probably, at the time. I do not know when he went to Galway.

On 30 October 1936, the army wrote to O'Donovan informing him of its decision to award him one-third of a full rank C pension based on his years of active service. On 2 November, O'Donovan wrote back to protest that he was entitled by seniority to a rank B pension:

> The findings are not acceptable to me. After the deaths of Dick McKee and Peadar Clancy, I was immediately summoned by Diarmuid O'Hegarty and informed that I was to consider taking over and developing the department relating to every aspect of explosives, etc., and discuss the matter later with D. Mulcahy. This I did and accepted immediately the subsequent re-organisation of the entire staff – completed in December 1920 – ratifying and regularising that appointment. I was present at all full GHQ staff meetings and when, a short time later, it was decided to minimise the risks attendant upon frequent meetings of the entire staff, by the formation of groups, I was never absent from the meetings of the QMG [quarter-master general's] group, which comprised: S. MacMahon, Liam Mellows, Seán Russell and myself, as often as not with the chief of staff [Mulcahy] (*ex officio* head of each group) also present. The department of chemicals was entirely separate and completely on a par with the department of engineering and the department of munitions. Recognition was given to my office and rank when, during the Truce, Cathal Brugha [minister for defence, replaced by Richard Mulcahy on 9 January 1922] issued commissions, mine being that of a commandant on the GHQ staff, i.e. commandant-general, exactly as in the cases of the directors of purchases [Liam Mellows], engineering [Rory O'Connor] and munitions [Seán Russell]. At the historic meeting of the cabinet with the GHQ staff (25 November 1921), I was present along with the

other 12 members of the staff and the entire cabinet. When subsequently the then minister for defence (D. Mulcahy) commissioned Leo Whelan RHA to paint the GHQ staff as represented by its wartime (i.e. pre-Truce)[22] personnel, I received the summons to be painted on 11 or 12 January 1922, at the same time and in the same manner as all the other fully recognised members of the GHQ staff.[23]

O'Donovan's protest letter is interesting from a few angles. Firstly, he attaches great importance to his inclusion, at the behest of Richard Mulcahy, in Leo Whelan's group portrait of the 1921 IRA leadership. The clandestine underground nature of the GHQ staff organisation in the war of independence period[24] meant that formal documentation was sparse and, thus, the portrait became more significant with the passage of time. Secondly, O'Donovan also sets much store by the meeting of the GHQ staff with Cabinet members, which he attended, on 25 November 1921. It is clear that, just five weeks before Britain handed power to a new Irish government, O'Donovan considered the delicate relationship between both groups – IRA GHQ and Cabinet (although there was a partial overlap since some GHQ members were also TDs) – to be critical with regard to the future governance of the nascent state. In fact, as we shall see in the next chapter, he strongly disagreed with the decision to transfer any powers from the IRA leadership to an elected parliament, thus giving Dáil Éireann control over the new Free State army from January 1922.[25]

But to return briefly to his quest for a pension, there was bad news in store. On 30 June 1938, the department of defence informed O'Donovan that it 'was unable to revise his award'. He appealed against the decision that same year but, according to the file, was unable to pursue the appeal 'due to ill health'. (The ill health plea may have been a ruse, since O'Donovan was then about to resume IRA active service at the behest of a new chief of staff, his old friend Seán Russell.) The eventful war years went by, and on

8 February 1945 O'Donovan sought a reopening of his pension case 'based on a document which only recently came to light'. The document was a letter, dated 3 December 1920, to the chief of staff [Mulcahy] from Diarmuid O'Hegarty, director of organisation, regarding the successor to Peadar Clancy as director of chemicals, referring to Jim O'Donovan's anonymous articles in *An t-Óglach* on 1 and 15 March 1920. Enclosing O'Hegarty's 1920 letter, O'Donovan wrote to the office of the minister for defence, Oscar Traynor: 'Incidentally, I was surprised recently to learn that neither of these gentlemen [Richard Mulcahy or Diarmuid O'Hegarty] had been called as witnesses in connection with my award. Only such high officers of long association could adequately support and fully interpret my then status.'

This time the Department took O'Donovan's point and, on 20 April 1945, Diarmuid O'Hegarty – the IRA GHQ's director of organisation until December 1920 and, in 1945, a commissioner of the Office of Public Works – was summoned to give evidence at the department of defence at Mobhi Road, Glasnevin. O'Hegarty stated:

> I remember document of 3 December 1920 but not the enclosures. [Peadar] Clancy looked after manufacture of munitions and was also quartermaster of the Dublin brigade. HQ staff before then [comprised] chief of staff, quartermaster general, director of training, and director of intelligence. The great difficulty was [in procuring] arms, ammunition, mines, etc. We had come to the conclusion to put the supply of arms under the quartermaster general. Mr O'Donovan's article probably suggested the manufacture of chemicals separately from munitions under separate directorships. The problem of getting explosives for mines and grenades was difficult – we had used explosives from quarries, etc.

O'Hegarty concluded:

> I don't see any justification for differentiating between the directors of munitions and chemicals, and purchases and engineering. The function of the director of chemicals [i.e. Jim O'Donovan] was the research into new sources of supply and the making of chemicals. The departments of chemicals and munitions were very closely associated. If I were the referee, I would feel compelled to give him upgrading for special services.

Eventually, the army heeded the Old IRA man's advice, although it is interesting that at no time was Richard Mulcahy asked to give evidence on O'Donovan's behalf. Given the animosity between the two men, the army bosses probably felt it was better not to reopen old wounds. In any event, on 20 October 1945, the army granted O'Donovan a rank B pension under rule 4 of the first schedule of the Military Service Pensions Act 1934. It had taken the army ten years to accede to this request, although the smaller invalidity pension had been granted almost on request in 1933.

4.

THE ROAD TO CIVIL WAR

Jim O'Donovan was uneasy at the pace of events which appeared to have been accelerating since the truce in July 1921 and which went into overdrive following the contentious signing of the Anglo-Irish treaty on 6 December 1921. By the mid-1930s, when seeking an Old IRA pension for his war of independence service, he was still referring back to his attendance 'at the historic meeting of the Cabinet with the GHQ staff' on 25 November 1921, emphasising that 'I was present along with the other 12 members of the [IRA GHQ] staff, and the entire Cabinet.' This comment, together with a reference to his commission (from defence minister Cathal Brugha) as a commandant-general on the GHQ staff, indicates that O'Donovan was unhappy not only with the terms of the treaty but also with what transpired after the Dáil ratified the treaty on 7 January 1922.

For the rest of his life O'Donovan maintained that the majority of GHQ staff, including himself, had not been kept in the loop when it came to discussing the draft treaty, i.e. before it was signed in London. In a detailed reply to a questionnaire from Florence O'Donoghue[1] in 1952, O'Donovan outlined how he was outmanoeuvred by the pro-treaty faction at the joint meeting of Cabinet ministers and GHQ staff, which had been summoned for the Mansion House in Dublin by Gearóid O'Sullivan, the adjutant-general. According to O'Donovan, the GHQ staff were all in attendance punctually at 5 p.m. but 'we waited until about 9.15 p.m. before being called in'. In other words, the Cabinet kept the GHQ staff waiting outside for over four hours. According to O'Donovan's notes, those present at the joint meeting were: 'Pres[ident] de Valera, [W. T.] Cosgrave, [Robert] Barton, [Michael] Collins, Dick Mulcahy, Owen O'Duffy, Ginger O'Connell, Gearóid O'Sullivan, Seán MacMahon, Bob [Eamonn] Price, [Emmet] Dalton, Seán Russell, Joe Vize (not really entitled to be present), Rory O'Connor, Liam Mellows and myself. Absent: [Arthur] Griffith and Gavan Duffy.' O'Donovan suspected that

> ... almost certainly the draft Treaty and the very latest developments had been the subject of Cabinet discussion while we waited in the room next door, there was no presentation of a draft Treaty nor indeed any primarily political subject to the GHQ Staff. I fancy the position was that – through Collins – Mulcahy, O'Sullivan and Diarmuid O'Hegarty (who might be regarded as the Big Four, with Collins, O'Sullivan and O'Hegarty as the Big Three) were made aware of all the political developments, but the bulk of the rest of the GHQ Staff were not informed.

O'Donovan recalls that 'many rows' took place at the joint GHQ/Cabinet meeting:

> De V[alera] seemed all thro' the conference to be deeply affected by a sense of impending disaster and disunity. When vigorously insistent that the army would have to be under his control and responsible to

the Cabinet nominated by him, he spoke very autocratically and was accused of this by Gearóid O'Sullivan and others who resigned partly on this account. Gearóid O'Sullivan, Ginger O'Connell and Owen O'Duffy (the latter two or three times) tendered their resignations and withdrew them again. O'Duffy was squabbling about his status, insisting that he should be Deputy Chief of Staff and Ginger Assistant Chief of Staff, labouring the distinction. This was conceded.... Pres[ident] de Valera ordered the re-issuing of the oath [of allegiance to the Republic] to be renewed (if previously taken) by every member of the staff. This was agreed to be done immediately. Some general mumblings about postponement so as not to interrupt meeting were raised by Mick, Dick, etc. and then it was agreed that Dick M[ulcahy] should take it that night and he then administer the oath to us within the following day or so. THIS WAS NEVER DONE. [O'Donovan's emphasis].²

Looking back 30 years later, O'Donovan reflected that while 'to de Valera and Brugha, the coming rift in the Army was clearly inevitable and it had become a struggle to retain control over the actual organisation … this was not apparent to me at the time'. O'Donovan summed up his aim, in the critical November/December 1921 period, as being 'to prevent the Army as a whole from being seduced from its original aims and control and become merely the nucleus of the new Army which would be the servant of the Provisional Government. This same question of control was to loom later as the important issue at the [IRA] Conventions [26 March and 9 April 1922] – namely, if the Army is to become the tool of the majority of Dáil Éireann who had agreed to vote for the Treaty, then the Army should logically withdraw its allegiance to the Dáil of 1919 and resume its independent status as a Volunteer Army'. O'Donovan conceded to Florence O'Donoghue that 'the proposal to revert to Volunteer Army status, free of Dáil control' was another way of describing 'the establishment of a military dictatorship'.³

Clearly, O'Donovan could not accept that, with Mulcahy and Collins in charge, power was inexorably slipping from the IRA's supreme command structure to the elected members of the Dáil – specifically the cabinet ministers who were intent on quashing all resistance to the treaty and quickly establishing their right to govern the new country as a functioning parliamentary democracy. Although it took him 30 years to admit it openly, this model of governance was not what O'Donovan had in mind at all.

Historian Tom Garvin notes that:

> The IRA had become increasingly restive after the 7 January vote [by Dáil Éireann to accept the treaty]. On 13 January, Mulcahy already felt obliged to warn Jim O'Donovan, GHQ director of chemicals, that the Dáil was still the elected government of the republic and that supreme control of the army was vested in that civilian assembly and not in the IRA leadership. The Republic, he assured O'Donovan, was to stay in being until disestablished by the voters and replaced by the Free State.⁴

Professor Risteárd Mulcahy adds: 'Dad did say after the treaty ratification and after he was appointed minister for defence, that the army would remain the army of the Republic. It is recorded in the Dáil Reports. I expect he said it to mollify the anti-treaty volunteers. I cannot recall that he ever said it to O'Donovan'.⁵

Historical writer Tim Pat Coogan notes that:

> ... the split in the Dáil was clearly mirrored in the country as a whole. The big battalions – the Church, business, the bigger farmers, the press and most of the senior Army officers – were on the side of the Treaty. However, the power of the antis was not negligible.

Sections of the IRA, particularly in Cork, were solidly anti-Treaty, and prominent IRA men like the commanders of the Southern Divisions, Liam Lynch and Ernie O'Malley, were opposed. In GHQ, figures like Rory O'Connor, Liam Mellows, Seán Russell and Jim O'Donovan were anti-Treaty. However, it is one of the great 'ifs' of Irish history as to whether anything more than a relatively minor faction fight would have developed had de Valera not thrown his enormous prestige on to their side. His intervention brought incalculable political credibility to the militarists.[6]

Even before the Dáil vote accepting the treaty, however, O'Donovan was hankering after some form of military control of the state in which, presumably, he considered he would play a leading role. When asked by the author if he thought Jim O'Donovan could have made the transition to politics, the retired Fianna Fáil TD Ruairí Brugha (who was an IRA internee in the Curragh in the early 1940s, but not at the same time as O'Donovan), commented:

> I don't think he would have been able to. I am talking about mind-sets, you know. I mean, the fact that Fianna Fáil had to lock up a lot of our fellows didn't affect me in the least. I mean, if you're in government, you're in government and you've got to govern. Whereas you may assume yourself the right to carry a revolver, it doesn't mean that you have it, in so far as the electorate is concerned. You know what I mean? The way I talk now, it would be impossible for an IRA man; he wouldn't understand it. But there is a logic and there is common sense. And you cannot have free elements carrying guns. In the long run, that's not patriotism, it's anarchy – particularly if you haven't got complete control over it. And how do you

achieve that? It's bad enough to see the Free Staters executing 77, as they did – taking them out of jail and executing them.[7]

The seeds of the forthcoming civil war – subsequently called *Cogadh na gCarad* or Friends' War – were being sown by protagonists who only a short time earlier had been unified by another sort of conflict. No sooner had Michael Collins witnessed the lowering of the Union Jack over Dublin Castle in January 1922, followed by the raising of the tricolour, than matters started to go haywire, with the pro- and anti-treaty factions opting to choose separate paths. Of the 13-member IRA headquarters staff in 1921, nine supported the treaty with Britain (effectively partitioning Ireland) while only four opposed it. They were Jim O'Donovan, Rory O'Connor, Seán Russell and Liam Mellows. Outnumbered by more than two to one, the anti-treaty GHQ faction were seemingly doomed in their efforts to take on the new government and somehow achieve a 32-county republic. Nonetheless, O'Donovan did not let his minority position hamper him from trying another throw of the dice as 1922 dawned. This came in the shape of an acrimonious exchange of letters with his former commander in chief, Richard Mulcahy. It seems that O'Donovan was the first to suggest the formation of a separate anti-treaty army headquarters. On 11 January 1922, he was one of eleven signatories to a demand for an army convention – the IRA's supreme rule-making body.[8]

Addressed to Richard Mulcahy TD – deliberately ignoring Mulcahy's position as defence minister in the new Free State government (Eoin O'Duffy had succeeded Mulcahy as chief of staff on 10 January 1922) – the missive from the disgruntled anti-treaty faction read as follows:

> A Chara, we, the undersigned members of the general headquarters staff, divisional commandants, etc., of the Irish Republican Army hereby request that a

convention of the army be called, not later than Sunday the 5th February 1922 for the purpose of considering the resolution attached herewith. We also require: 1. That the machinery for calling and carrying out the work of the convention be made up of an equal number of persons appointed by you on one hand, and by a committee representing the undersigned on the other hand; 2. That a chairman of the convention be appointed by mutual agreement between you and this committee; 3. The basis of representation at the convention shall be: (a) All divisional commandants shall be *ex officio* delegates. (b) Other delegates shall be selected as follows: 1 delegate selected at a company parade where 30 or less attend. 2 delegates where number is over 30 and under 70. 3 delegates where number is over 70.

These delegates shall attend the brigade convention, shall select for the general convention 5% of the total number of delegates to the brigade convention. In the event of 5% amounting to a whole number and a fraction, the number of delegates shall be brought up to the next whole number.

All officers and men are equally eligible for appointment as delegates at company and brigade conventions, with the exception of divisional commandants who are *ex officio* delegates to the general convention.

We will await a reply up to 2 p.m. on the 13th instant to this office.

Signed: Rory O'Connor, director of engineering GHQ; Liam Mellows GHQ; James O'Donovan, director of chemicals GHQ; Seán Russell, director of munitions GHQ; Oscar Traynor, O/C Dublin brigade; A. McDonnell, O/C south Dublin brigade; Liam

Lynch, O/C 1st southern division; M. McCormack, O/C 3rd southern division; Thomas Maguire, O/C 2nd western division; William Pilkington, O/C 3rd western division; M. MacGiollarmaid, O/C 4th western division.

In addition to the above, the O/C 2nd southern division [Ernie O'Malley] is in agreement with the policy outlined herein, but his signature will not be available for some hours. It is understood that other divisional commandants are also in agreement.[9]

Attached to the letter was the following resolution:

> That the army reaffirms its allegiance to the Irish Republic. That it shall be maintained as the army of the Irish Republic, under an executive appointed by the convention. That the army shall be under the supreme control of such executive, which shall draft a constitution for submission to a subsequent convention.

Not so deftly hidden within O'Donovan's tortuous, almost Jesuitical, wording was a blatant attempt to wrest power from an elected government, answerable to Dáil Éireann, and transfer it to an army under 'the supreme control of' an executive. O'Donovan's plan was that such an executive – of which he would presumably be a leading member – was to be 'appointed' by the IRA army convention he now sought. Essentially this move was a showdown between the anti-treaty militarists and their former comrades who, under Collins and Mulcahy, had opted to accept the treaty and pursue the democratic path.

With the benefit of hindsight, it is easy to see that O'Donovan and his three anti-treaty GHQ colleagues (O'Connor, Mellows and Russell) were in a fairly weak negotiating position. While they had mustered the support of two brigade commanders and a further five divisional commanders, the admission that they had not yet secured the signatures of others made their position look less impressive than it might otherwise have been. In addition, it is unclear why Liam Mellows's GHQ title of director of purchases does not appear on the letter. In any case, O'Donovan must have known that 'mutual agreement' on a chairman of the convention would be impossible to achieve, since such an individual could hold the vital casting vote to decide the convention's outcome. He might also have guessed that Mulcahy would see through the complex mathematical formulae in the letter, which were presumably designed to provide the anti-treaty faction with a good chance of carrying the convention and, thus, establishing something akin to a military dictatorship. Perhaps only a qualified chemist could have constructed such a labyrinthine scheme.

Whatever the anti-treatyites' game-plan, Mulcahy was having none of it. In as blunt a rebuff as he was able to muster, he met his opponents' deadline, delivering his reply two days later on 13 January 1922. Under the letterhead of army headquarters, Mulcahy wrote to J. O'Donovan, director of chemicals GHQ, as follows:

> Attached is a copy of a communication received by me on 12th inst., bearing your name typed as a signatory. In reply I have to say: 1. That the Dáil as a whole is the elected government of the Irish Republic and that the supreme control of the army is vested in it; and 2. That the proposal contained in the resolution to change the supreme control of the army is entirely outside the constitutional powers vested in the Dáil executive by the Dáil.
>
> Will you please arrange to meet me at my office at 9.30 a.m. sharp tomorrow, Saturday morning, to discuss this matter.[10]

The letter is signed by Richard Mulcahy, using the Irish version of his name, Risteárd Ó Maolchatha, and the title minister for defence. Mulcahy sent the same reply to all eleven signatories of the 11 January letter, inviting them to his office in order to face them down. The fraught meeting took place as planned and, one of those present, Ernie O'Malley, noted that:

> Jim O'Donovan turned to Collins. 'You are a traitor', he said, 'and you should have been court-martialled long since for treason'. Collins jumped to his feet. There were loud shouts of 'Withdraw', 'Apologise'. Some of our number seemingly did not approve of the word 'traitor'. Mulcahy brought the meeting to order with a few quiet words. Whatever he felt, his face did not show either feeling or emotion. Collins sat with hands propped up, supporting his chin, a fighting expression on his face. 'I will not withdraw the word', said O'Donovan, 'It is true'.[11]

In the event, Mulcahy and his government colleagues were determined to take a tough line against the anti-treaty people. In waging this war of words, which predated the outbreak of the civil war by five months, Mulcahy may have been playing for time. Professor Risteárd Mulcahy notes that in the immediate post-treaty period, his father discouraged Arthur Griffith, who

> ... was very anxious to face up to the army. As early as March 1922, or even before it, he was very anxious to face up to it, but Dad wouldn't accept that from Griffith. He said: 'There is no way we are going to beat these guys now. We have to build up our army.' With O'Duffy as chief of staff and himself as minister for defence they did a huge job in getting the Irish Free State army to the point where at the end of June they felt they could take on the irregulars [i.e. the anti-treaty forces].... That was what really beat the irregulars in the long run – that the army itself was seen to be subject to political control all the time.... Whatever success or failures my father had, one thing he was determined to do always: he had a complete

and utter commitment to democracy, and he modelled the army all the time on being the servants of parliament and the people.[12]

Since neither side was prepared to give way or reach a compromise, the inevitable split occurred with an alternative anti-treaty army headquarters being established. With two groups – each claiming to be the legitimate government – at each other's throats, the country was now facing into a year-long civil war. It was a conflict O'Donovan would survive, but only as a prisoner of the new government, incarcerated along with many others who had backed the anti-treaty side and lost. Before the end of the civil war there would be many escapades as O'Donovan played a cat and mouse game with his former comrades in the decisive conflict that would shape Ireland as an independent 26-county state.

The anti-treaty group went ahead with the banned IRA convention on 26 March 1922, and on 9 April a new IRA GHQ – i.e. an anti-treaty one – was established. On 13 April, the anti-treaty forces occupied the Four Courts and set up their headquarters there. Among those occupying the historical building were Jim O'Donovan, Rory O'Connor, Peadar O'Donnell and Robert Briscoe (who became a founder member of Fianna Fáil in 1926). The government's decision to shell the Four Courts on 28 June 1922 marked the opening shots in the internecine conflict. By that time, however, O'Donovan had left Dublin and was involved with Seán Russell in the manufacture of hand grenades in Monasterevin in preparation for the civil war.[13]

On 8 June, the Second Dáil was dissolved and on 16 June, a general election effectively gave the pro-treaty side a governing majority (the Third Dáil did not meet until 9 September). The Four Courts garrison surrendered on 30 June. At this stage, O'Donovan was a prisoner in County Kildare, still undergoing medical treatment for his badly injured right hand. On 10 July, the anti-treaty director of organisation, Ernie O'Malley, noted in his diary 'Badly want D/Chemicals in Cork, if he has been released.'[14]

THE ROAD TO CIVIL WAR

Two days earlier, on 8 July, O'Donovan had been transferred from Naas military barracks to the Curragh military hospital where he remained until mid-September. On 15 September, he was moved to Newbridge jail from where he was 'mainly responsible' for organising an escape, on 14 October, with Tom Harris (later a Fianna Fáil TD for Kildare 1931–57). O'Donovan told the army pensions inquiry in 1935 that the Newbridge jail escape 'left me free to re-organise department [of chemicals] immediately. In addition, from this date, until date of recapture 15 March 1923, I was given by chief of staff [Liam Lynch] also the post of acting director of munitions.'[15]

O'Donovan's arrest was reported in *The Irish Times* under the heading 'Fight and Arrests', as follows: 'The following official reports were issued by the National Army Headquarters last night – An Irregular named James Donovan [*sic*], described as "Director of Chemicals", was arrested at the North City quay last night by troops from Collins's barracks. Donovan had been engaged for some time past in smuggling explosive material from England.'[16]

On 31 July 1922, Ernie O'Malley – who by then had risen to the rank of assistant chief of staff to Liam Lynch – noted: 'We cannot carry out operations any way successfully owing to lack of grenades, lack of small arms. Owing to a succession of unfortunate incidents the munitions factory has not yet been started. I do not know what happened to the D/Chemicals but I think he has been arrested. The arrest of staff means loss of time, as we have to build up from the beginning'.[17] As O'Malley rightly guessed, the anti-treaty IRA's top explosives expert was at that moment under lock and key in Newbridge jail. It is unclear from O'Malley's papers who replaced O'Donovan as interim director of chemicals on the anti-treaty side. By 6 August, however, O'Malley noted that 'a substitute D/Chemicals has returned from England, where he made some purchases – expect to have some result at end of week'.[18]

Despite O'Donovan's incarceration, covert lines of communication remained open for the anti-treaty IRA leaders, as is clear from a letter Liam Mellows wrote, on 14 August 1922, to O'Malley:

> Séamus O'Donovan, D of C, at present a prisoner at the Curragh, informs us that he has a large supply of raw material on hand in dumps (in city I presume), and that if a good chemist or engineer were available, a lot of stuff could be turned out. Can you supply such a man for this purpose? Ryan, O/C Engineers, 3rd, has been mentioned, but it is not certain whether he is free or not. A better man would be John J. Tallon, who worked for D/C at F[our] C[ourts] up to the attack. As he lived out he was not captured.... Further information re the foregoing is to be obtained from Miss Minnie O'Donovan (Séamus' sister), 13, Grace Park Gardens, D'[rum]condra. She is in touch with the Curragh.[19]

Two days later, on 16 August 1922, O'Malley confirmed to the anti-treaty IRA chief of staff, Liam Lynch, that O'Donovan had been arrested, adding: 'As far as I can see there has been practically no output from this Department. I am looking for another chemist and will see to this Dept … myself in future.'[20]

The anti-treaty side suffered a double-whammy in October 1922. On 15 October, the government brought in emergency powers, effectively establishing martial law. Five days earlier, the Catholic hierarchy had issued a pastoral letter, to be read out at all masses, condemning the anti-treaty IRA. As a result of the pastoral, the anti-treatyites were 'denied the sacraments by many priests and prison chaplains'. In addition, priests were forbidden 'under pain of suspension … to advocate or encourage this revolt, publicly or privately'.[21]

The Irish bishops' stand against the irregulars, effectively backing W. T. Cosgrave's government, prompted Jim O'Donovan to write to Éamon de Valera – as 'President of the Irish Republic' – about organising a republican appeal to the Pope to protest against the Irish bishops' move. In a five-page hand-written memo, dated 6 November 1922, O'Donovan complained that the attitude of the Catholic hierarchy 'is of course that a government set up – no matter whether by fraud, corruption or force – is the lawful government if it shows what appears to them to be adequate indications of stability.' In the same note, O'Donovan all but conceded to de Valera that the appeal to the Pope would fail: 'Father Peter Finlay's private view on the matter of appeal is that Rome cannot but endorse the Irish Hierarchy's views as they are the "on the spot" ecclesiastical opinion. Of course, if the appeal secured the adoption of a policy of non-intervention even, that would be morally tantamount to an endorsement of our views'.[22]

On 19 March 1923, when the civil war was in its final stages, a papal envoy arrived in Ireland, following extensive lobbying of the Vatican by anti-treaty representatives. But Monsignor Luzio was shunned both by the Irish hierarchy and the Cosgrave government, which eventually asked Rome to recall him. Luzio stayed in the Shelbourne Hotel until May 1923 but achieved little apart from having a number of meetings with de Valera, who felt the envoy was not 'pro-republican' and had come at 'a bad time for us'.[23]

The hierarchy's stance against the anti-treaty IRA faction continued to be a cause of rancour with O'Donovan for the rest of his life. Although technically subject to excommunication, the anti-treatyites slowly drifted back to the church after the civil war. For his part, O'Donovan remained a regular attender at Sunday mass but, according to his son Donal, 'would not let a priest into the house'. He kept a copy of *The Imitation of Christ* (first published in 1418) by the German monk Thomas à Kempis, on his bedside locker. O'Donovan's lifelong friend Todd Andrews, on the other hand, never attended mass for the rest of his life in protest at the bishops' stand in 1922. His son David Andrews (a former Fianna Fáil minister for foreign affairs) recalls: 'I would not say he was anti-religious but he never went to mass.' On his deathbed in 1985, aged 86, Todd Andrews met an old priest and was reconciled with the church. 'He recanted and went straight up, I suppose,' says David Andrews, gesturing towards the heavens.[24]

In his unpublished memoirs O'Donovan wrote that during the civil war his area of operation was 'principally Dublin', with Ernie O'Malley as his commanding officer. Professor Tom Garvin notes that in September 1923 Jim's brother, Dan O'Donovan (who became secretary of the department of social welfare in 1946), was incarcerated in Newbridge jail, teaching

> ... courses in constitutional law, local government and Irish history ... he and other lecturers suggested that the military victory of the Free State could be reversed by peaceful means. Non-violent penetration of the local government apparatus would, in the long term, deliver the new policy into the hands of its enemies.[25]

But this was hardly what his brother Jim, a lifelong believer in the armed struggle, had in mind. Garvin notes that 'The genesis of what was to become Fianna Fáil occurred in the Free State's prison camps, much as the IRA had been born in the British camps of 1916–17.' Of course, Jim O'Donovan never joined Fianna Fáil, although his brother Dan and his son Donal did so (in the 1970s, Donal was the party's director of elections for the Wicklow constituency).

An early and major casualty of the civil war was Michael Collins, killed in an ambush by anti-treaty forces at Béal na mBláth, County Cork, on 22 August 1922. The removal of Collins, who was commander in chief of the Free State army, left a gap in the pro-treaty leadership. But his death also left his comrades all the more determined to pursue the democratic path based on the Anglo-Irish treaty they had negotiated and ratified. O'Donovan can hardly have mourned Collins's passing, since he had called for his court-martial as a traitor just seven months before. In the event, Richard Mulcahy succeeded Collins as army commander in chief.

O'Donovan's contemporaneous hand-written notes for the period 26 November 1922 to 21 February 1923 survive in the archives of the Bray Heritage Centre, County Wicklow. (The author is grateful to Mr Gerry O'Donovan for providing photocopies of same, and to Mr Henry Cairns for showing him the originals.) The papers describe a chaotic period during which O'Donovan's home was frequently raided by Free State troops and the 'CID' (i.e. Garda special branch). The notes are not without humour, even given the tense situation. On 6 December 1922, for example, O'Donovan writes:

> Raid at 10.30 p.m. at No. 5 ... seen to be F.S. [Free State troops] ... was just going out back door when I heard them in hall talking. I hurried over wall into next garden and down it over end wall, this out onto field (there was bright moonlight); put on hat and coat and climbed over railings out on to road. Found I had lost the glove that mattered [i.e. the glove he wore to hide his maimed right hand]. Nothing incriminating (worth talking about) had been found, I learned next morning. And the dog who had been barking at me when I had left, had evidently picked up the glove immediately, as it was found in the kennel in the morning. They searched the garden in another minute or so and would have found this tell-tale clue had the dog not helped.[26]

In late 1922 and early 1923, O'Donovan was being put under constant pressure, with raids on his home both late at night and early in the morning. In addition, he was often questioned by soldiers when walking in the street. He was also producing many 'important department circulars' with the aid of a typist in an office, but even then he was not immune to raids. On 15 January 1923, he wrote:

> Was about to start work, had typewriter etc., out, but typist said she was afraid and there had been patrols

about. I said the patrols don't affect us here and she went down to get papers out of dump. She just barely had time to get them back into dump when the military were admitted – mostly officers. She dashed up to let me know but I was just leaving the room (with bowler hat, glove and coat on) when two of them bounded up by me on the stairs. I never felt more hopeless but I summoned a feeble smile and said 'Good morning', and passed down as leisurely as I could, but not to meet them. I was in the hall, I ran as hard as I could down the back garden, having asked the maid to open the back premises first. I got away and was fully resigned to learn of the arrest of both typist and maid. Nothing happened, however – the typewriter had left them cold.

At this time, O'Donovan and others were churning out anti-government propaganda on behalf of Liam Lynch. According to some examples of this propaganda, the Free State had been 'founded on the blood of boys used by the very men who climbed into office over the bleeding sacrifices of those boys'; this was in reply to a government claim that the anti-treaty soldiers were 'children, common thieves and criminals'. Furthermore, the Free State government was accused of having 'borrowed guns from the British by which to shoot down Irish soldiers'. Meanwhile, it was claimed that the 'enemy [i.e. the Dublin government] has used the worst form of terror – far worse than forced themselves to sign the treaty'.

But behind the war of words lay a far deadlier pattern of tit-for-tat killings, with the first official state executions of prisoners beginning in mid-November 1922, a month after the introduction of martial law. On 7 December the anti-treaty IRA shot two government TDs – one of them, Seán Hales, later died from his wounds. The following day, in retaliation, four IRA prisoners were executed, including Jim O'Donovan's GHQ colleagues Rory

O'Connor and Liam Mellows. (The other two were Joseph McKelvey and Richard Barrett.)[27]

On 29 January 1923, Jim O'Donovan received a letter from Liam Deasy, a leading anti-treaty figure, who had been arrested on 18 January and was under sentence of death. Deasy wrote: 'I have undertaken for the future of Ireland to accept and aid in an immediate and unconditional surrender of all arms and men ... as required by General Mulcahy.' Deasy went on to plead for an end to the civil war – which he described as 'a war between families rather than armies' – and called on O'Donovan (and fifteen other anti-treaty IRA leaders, including Éamon de Valera, Frank Aiken and Liam Lynch) to surrender immediately and unconditionally 'together with their arms and equipment'. Deasy warned O'Donovan that the conflict could arrive 'at a point where the war will be waged by both sides against the people ... family against family will be forced to fight in defence until the losses on both sides will be so great, some other power, probably England, will be called on to intervene, and possibly will be welcomed with more enthusiasm than was displayed at her departure'. Deasy adds: 'I may not see the end of this – my sentence is only suspended and I am here as a condemned prisoner.' Oddly, however, the letter – purportedly from someone under imminent threat of execution – also contains an offer: 'A suspension of executions until the 6th February [1923] is guaranteed. Your reply to the attached is expected by that date.'[28]

The Deasy letter represents one of the most bizarre incidents in the civil war period and it is hard to say whether his impending death sentence was genuine or whether he was put up to it by Mulcahy in a bid to get the anti-treaty people to lay down their arms. In any event, Deasy was not executed, but the civil war continued for a further five months. He became a lifelong friend of Mulcahy and, on the outbreak of World War II, rejoined the army, rising to the rank of commandant.[29]

The worsening tit-for-tat killings prompted Liam Lynch to issue a proclamation on 1 February 1923, describing the government as a 'junta' which had 'suppressed the legitimate parliament of the nation and usurped the government'. Lynch added that, in their endeavour 'to destroy the Republic', the government had 'resorted to the infamous practice of shooting republican soldiers taken by them as prisoners of war, and have already put to death 53 officers and men in this manner'. In fact, by the end of the conflict some 77 anti-treaty prisoners would be executed. But Liam Lynch himself had barely two months left to live. He was fatally wounded during a round-up in the Knockmealdown mountains, south Tipperary, on 10 April 1923. Three days earlier, Ernie O'Malley was in the hospital wing of Mountjoy prison, and wrote to fellow prisoner Jim O'Donovan – who had been arrested in Dublin on 15 March – complaining that 'one's life depends on the whim of an IRB clique'.[30]

Professor Tom Garvin notes that 'As long as he [Liam Lynch] lived, his attitudes, which were profoundly anti-democratic and authoritarian, dominated the anti-treatyite movement. His death certainly hastened the end of the civil war ... his attitude to politicians was one of deep arrogance and contempt.'[31]

Frank Aiken succeeded Lynch as the anti-treaty IRA's chief of staff. On 24 May 1923, he issued a ceasefire order to all IRA units instructing them to dump arms, thus effectively signalling an end to the civil war.

On learning of Lynch's death, O'Donovan penned the following poem from his prison cell, entitled 'In Memoriam':

> Heroes – now one more has left us.
> Jesu! We do feel the loss
> With great bitterness;
> Yet know we well the while his tomb is sealed,
> The glories of Thy Court have been revealed
> And Thy pure Hands, which can with potence wield,
> Hold now him in caress –
> Purest gold 'mid earthy dross;
> Soul of him Thou hast bereft us.

> Brave Liam, with his lastest breath
> (Jesu! Do not heed our tears)
> Surrendered but to Thee!
> Too filled with woe the poet is to weave
> The hero's image, how he learned to grieve
> His love's apostasy and how reprieve
> Nor infidelity.
> Through his pain, lay low thy fears;
> Repentance, hope, are born of death.[32]

There was certainly no shortage of death in the Irish civil war. Some estimates put government fatalities at 800, plus an unknown number of anti-treaty republicans, and civilian deaths for which no official figures are available either. The death toll for the earlier war of independence is put at approximately 1,200.[33]

Historian John M. Regan puts the civil war death toll in thousands. He contends that 'both treatyites and anti-treatyites could have prosecuted their civil wars with more violence to good effect for their respective causes. The fact remains that they did not. The policies of assassination and reprisal in early December 1922 witnessed both sides staring into the abyss and both sides preferred to take a step back. There was in time of civil war a greater consensus which few were prepared to step outside.'[34]

In the wake of the civil war, elections for the Fourth Dáil were held on 27 August 1923, resulting in a victory for the incumbent government of W. T. Cosgrave. Two days later, fifteen leading anti-treaty republicans, including Jim O'Donovan, were moved from Mountjoy to Arbour Hill military prison and all were kept in separate cells to avoid communication between them. The prisoners included Éamon de Valera. On 25 September, O'Donovan penned another poem, in English and Latin, entitled 'Quid Retribuam?' He must have been undergoing something of a spiritual journey at this time because the writing starts by quoting lines from a Psalm beginning 'What shall I give back to the Lord for all the things He has given me?' At the end of the poem, O'Donovan adds: 'Arbour

Hill, 25th September 1923. Written on the fourth day of absolute and solitary confinement to cell.'[35]

Some of the prisoners, including O'Donovan, were later transferred back to Mountjoy. Their names and addresses are recorded because he asked them to sign his copy of a book of poems entitled *Athens Aflame*.[36] O'Donovan's fourteen fellow inmates in B-wing of Mountjoy were (address in brackets):

Andy Cooney (Ballyphilip, Nenagh, County Tipperary), who later became IRA chief of staff, 1925–26, and later still qualified as a medical doctor.

Peadar O'Donnell (Donegal), was elected to the Fourth Dáil in September 1923. In the 1936–38 period he wrote articles for O'Donovan's literary journal *Ireland To-Day*.

George Oliver Plunkett (26 Upper Fitzwilliam Street, Dublin), brother of the 1916 Proclamation signatory Joseph Plunkett, who was executed as one of the leaders of the Rising. George became a member of the IRA's army council in the 1930s.

Frank Gallagher (Dublin), one of de Valera's closest confidants, in 1931 became the first editor of the Fianna Fáil leader's new *Irish Press* newspaper.

Tom Ketterick (Westport, County Mayo), quartermaster-general of the IRA's west Mayo brigade.

Tom Derrig (Westport, County Mayo), a 1916 veteran who served as a minister in various de Valera cabinets from 1932 to 1948.

Patrick Coughlan (Kilbritten, County Cork), served as a divisional engineer in the IRA's Cork brigade.

Gerry Boland (Clontarf, Dublin), another close ally of de Valera's, he later served as minister for justice. In that capacity, he interned O'Donovan in the Curragh camp in 1941.

Malachy Sweetman (47 Merrion Square, Dublin), held the post of O/C Policing with the IRA and also led a flying column in Cork during the war of independence. His father John Sweetman was Sinn Féin's second president. After the civil war, Sweetman (1900–69) ran a farm near Enniscorthy, County Wexford. He joined Fianna Fáil and was elected as a councillor, but later, as a director of the Central Bank, he fell out with the party over what he saw as Charles J. Haughey's inflationary 'spend, spend, spend' policies at the department of finance.

Andrew McDonnell (Rathmines, Dublin), though on the anti-treaty side, his brother Mick McDonnell had been a member of Michael Collins's 'squad'.

Frank Henderson (75 North Circular Road, Dublin), was a member of the Four Courts garrison in 1922. His brother Ruairí was aide-de-camp to President de Valera in 1959.

Patrick McCarvill (Lake View, Monaghan). Dr McCarvill was a TD 1922–27, first for Sinn Féin and later for Fianna Fáil.

Barney Mellows (21 Mount Shannon Road, Kilmainham, Dublin) was a brother of Liam Mellows, who was executed during the civil war.

Austin Stack (Tralee, County Kerry), the veteran republican, was O/C of the IRA's Kerry brigade in 1916 and later became minister for home affairs in the First Dáil. He died in 1929.[37]

By Christmas 1923, O'Donovan and twenty-six others were in Kilmainham jail where the director of chemicals was jocosely rechristened 'O/C Decorations' and put in charge of brightening up the surroundings for a festive feast, which included eight turkeys, a goose, four hams, eight plum puddings and thirteen Christmas cakes! On 1 January 1924, O'Donovan was on the move again, this time to Hare Park internment camp in the Curragh. His fellow internees included Andy Cooney, Seán Russell (IRA chief of staff 1938–39) and Peadar O'Donnell.[38] O'Donovan and his comrades would languish in captivity until their release in mid-July 1924. As they emerged into a post-civil war landscape in which their opponents ruled supreme, a difficult period of readjustment lay ahead of them.

5.
PICKING UP THE PIECES

In the wake of Frank Aiken's order to dump arms on 24 May 1923, the anti-treaty IRA men – many of whom were in prison – were left to lick their wounds and ponder their futures, which did not seem particularly bright. A general election was called for 27 August, which resulted in a majority for the existing government of W. T. Cosgrave. It would remain in power until Éamon de Valera's victory in 1932 with the new Fianna Fáil Party. On 13 October 1923, IRA prisoners in Mountjoy, including Jim O'Donovan, began a hunger strike. The protest continued until 23 November. In later years, O'Donovan boasted of having 'outdone Christ' by fasting for forty-one days.[1] The anti-treaty leaders, including O'Donovan, were released from internment in mid-July 1924.

But the mid-1920s was not a time for boasting, and particularly not by those who had been involved in the anti-treaty forces during the civil war. Their cause lay in tatters and they could only look on helplessly as the new government consolidated its position, ruling the fledgling 26-county Irish Free State. Tough times lay ahead.

O'Donovan's elder son, Donal, wrote that on 30 January 1928 he was

> ... born in Cherryfield Avenue [Ranelagh, Dublin] because my father was broke. He was a young master of chemistry who had invented two explosives during the war of independence and he had re-enacted the drama in the civil war. Those who fought on the losing side paid the price. Vae victis [woe to the vanquished]. Some went to America; some tried to make a living at home.[2]

Jim O'Donovan chose to remain in Ireland and, while some were beating swords into ploughshares, he was swapping explosives for other less deadly chemical compounds (although he would revert to active service in the IRA as a middle-aged man in 1938). In October 1924, he founded the City Chemical and Colour Company in Summerhill, Dublin, which produced paint products. The *Irish Builder and Engineer* magazine enthusiastically reported on the firm's progress, describing it as 'perhaps the youngest business venture of its kind in the country'.[3] A photograph of the company's founder/manager in the magazine showed an immaculately groomed O'Donovan sporting glasses, a high starched collar and his MA conferring robes from UCD. His stationery's letterhead bore the name James L. O'Donovan M.Sc. 'consultant and analytical chemist', with an up-market address at 31 Upper Merrion Street – ironically just a stone's throw from Government Buildings where his ex-IRA comrades were now running the affairs of state. O'Donovan, for his part, looked every bit the young entrepreneur destined for great things. The company boasted a healthy first year of operations, securing valuable contracts to supply its Fortuna range of paints to – according to the magazine report – government departments, railway and tram companies, the Dublin Port and Docks Board, Dublin Corporation, and Grangegorman mental hospital. The magazine's promotional puff continued: 'Mr O'Donovan is ably assisted by his works manager, Mr Cotter, who has had years of paint manufacturing experience in a well-known English factory'. Understandably perhaps, O'Donovan did not tell *Irish Builder and Engineer* that Jim Cotter was the same man who had worked as his assistant in a Dublin bomb factory five years earlier.[4]

The report cited the company's 'remarkable progress which has marked its development, and the reputation which it has built for itself amongst architects, building contractors, painters and decorators, ensures that it has now come to stay....' Despite the positive waxings of the trade magazine, however, O'Donovan's venture was destined to go bankrupt and he was left with large debts to those who had bankrolled the short-lived paint company. The warning signs came as early as mid-1925 when O'Donovan tried unsuccessfully to persuade his maternal uncle, James Brennan in Bandon, to provide fresh capital. Brennan had no intention of getting involved and told his entrepreneurial nephew: 'I am in a very tight corner for cash at present, never so straitened in my life ... in these circumstances, I could not at present invest a penny in your business'.[5]

O'Donovan's son Gerry recalls: 'With my mother's dowry he started the City Chemical and Colour Company in Dublin. It was doing very well. People like the ESB and Dublin County Council used his paint because there was a great buzz about buying Irish. But they didn't pay him. They kept putting it on the long finger and he went bankrupt. So his chief manager bought the firm from him and it went on until the 1950s, but under a different name – Devereaux's Paints – that was the name of the manager.' The foreman at City Chemical and Colour, Joe Tallon, described the company as 'All chiefs and no Indians'. According to O'Donovan's daughter Sheila, one of the creditors was Lady Conyngham who had 'helped him financially to set up the paint factory'.[6]

On 28 April 1926, Jim O'Donovan married Mary Christina Barry. He was twenty-nine, while she was only twenty. It was a marriage made in republican heaven. 'Monty' Barry was a sister of the republican folk hero Kevin Barry, who had been executed by the British in 1920. His death had prompted the eponymous rebel song which begins: 'In Mountjoy Jail one Monday morning, High upon the gallows tree, Kevin Barry gave his young life for the cause of liberty.' Yet unknown to those outside the O'Donovan/Barry inner circle, Monty strictly forbade the singing or playing of her dead brother's lament in the family home. Donal O'Donovan recalls that his mother 'taught me the words of all the songs – the Marseillaise and ballads like "The Boys of Wexford" – but she wouldn't teach me that one. It was totally forbidden to sing that. She thought it was dreadful, maudlin rubbish. Yet she had been the closest of the sisters to Kevin. She used to polish his shoes and iron his shirt, but she never said much about Kevin.'[7]

Monty Barry was born on 6 December 1905. Her father, Tom Barry, was a dairy farmer and shopkeeper from Tombeagh, Hacketstown, County Carlow. Her mother Mary's maiden name was Dowling. During the civil war, Monty and her sisters Kathy[8] ('Kitt') and Elgin were both active in the women's IRA wing, Cumann na mBan. The marriage proved to be stable, despite O'Donovan's many absences over the next 17 years on IRA business and as a prisoner or internee. At the time of Jim's death in 1979, they had been married for 53 years. They had five children – one of whom, Mary, died in infancy – Donal (born 1928), Gerry (1931), Sheila (1932) and Aedine (1937).

Somehow the family struggled through the late 1920s with little work and not a few changes of address around Dublin – all rented properties. O'Donovan was on the look-out for a steady job and at this time did not appear to seek out the company of his former companions in the anti-treaty IRA. But his old sparring partner, Seán Russell, 'happened to be passing by and dropped in' to the office in December 1928. It was apparently the first time they had met since their release from prison in July 1924. On 16 January 1929, O'Donovan ran into Russell again, this time in Parnell

Street. The latter confirmed that he was still active in the IRA, 'responsible for safely housing two escaped prisoners from Belfast jail' who had been on the run for eighteen months. Russell's home was raided by gardaí but no arrests were made because, according to O'Donovan, 'nobody, least of all Eoin O'Duffy [Garda commissioner] was willing to arrest them and hand them back'. He noted that 'Seán was worried by these [raids] and various offers of assistance and apparent attempts at rapprochement from these former adherents of the Republic, since defected to the Treaty'. O'Donovan suspected that both he and Russell were being watched by the 'CID' (Garda detectives) and learned that 'Liam Tobin reported to Seán Russell that it was known that he had visited me in my office'.[9]

O'Donovan made a point of keeping abreast of developments and noted that, on 10 August 1929, 'a memorial cross was unveiled at Dean's Grange cemetery, Dublin, in memory of the men executed in connection with the shooting of [Sir Henry] Wilson [in London on 22 June 1922].' During 1929, O'Donovan also began contributing 'A Current Commentary', a column for *The Irish Book Lover* magazine, under the Irish version of his name, Séamus Ó Donnabháin (he was known as Séamus within the republican movement, but was called Jim by family and friends). In the November/December issue he wrote:

> It is an extraordinary fact that the pictorial and other literature dealing with the civil conflict of 1922-1923 should be much more difficult to procure than that relating to the Rising of 1916. It is hard to explain unless such matter had been subject to confiscation; perhaps, some reader may be able to throw light on the relevant literature of this period. The National Library is incomplete in this section. This is to be regretted, as, historically, the period is one of vital importance to the country.

Further on in his column, O'Donovan invited readers to search out 'allusions to Ireland or Irishmen in fiction'. He commended certain titles, including Michael Arlen's *These Charming People*, from which 'a quotation may be forgiven: A newsboy yelled, "Execution of Erskine Childers", into his ear. "Boy,"'said Major Cypress, "you must not do that. You must not gloat on death like that, and before perfect strangers, too. And besides, though you may not have shared Mr Childers' political opinions, you must admit that he did not die meanly. Here's a shilling for you, and don't let me hear you talking so much about executions in future."'

So, in a relatively short column, comprising four items, O'Donovan had managed two swipes at the Cumann na nGaedheal government, first over Erskine Childers' execution by an army firing squad in November 1922, and then all but accusing the government of confiscating civil war literature. In the latter case, of course, O'Donovan was being deliberately disingenuous. He must have known that in 1929 there was no public appetite for studying or debating the recent civil war, which had left deep divisions that would last for generations. In fact, detailed historical accounts of the 1922–23 period would not emerge until half a century afterwards.[10]

The political atmosphere in the new Free State remained tense and there was unfinished business from the civil war period not long before. The worst episode occurred on Sunday morning, 10 July 1927, when a senior government minister, Kevin O'Higgins, was gunned down near his home on Cross Avenue, Blackrock, County Dublin.[11] The 35-year-old O'Higgins – who, unlike modern-day justice ministers, had no bodyguards – had a civil war record that did not endear him to radical republicans. He sanctioned a number of executions of anti-treaty prisoners in 1922–23, including, on 8 December 1922, that of Rory O'Connor who, just a year before, had been best-man at O'Higgins's wedding.

The identities of the three IRA men who killed Kevin O'Higgins eventually became public knowledge in the mid-1980s with the publication of Belfast republican Harry White's memoirs. The three, identified as IRA irregulars in George Gilmore's faction, were named as Timothy Coughlan, Bill Gannon and Archie Doyle.[12] But Jim O'Donovan had been much exercised by the circumstances surrounding the 1927 assassination, and initially sought to divert blame from the IRA to the Garda Síochána.

In mid-August 1929, O'Donovan came up with a memo entitled 'A theory of Kevin O'Higgins' death', as follows:

> The old IRA was being steadily weeded out of the F[ree] S[tate] army (e.g. Liam Tobin, Tom Cullen, etc.). O'Higgins' murder had humiliated Mulcahy, Gearóid O'Sullivan, etc. There was also the group of 'murder gangers', alleged by promoter of this theory, whom I understood to have been organised or at least assisted by Séamus de hAodha (connected with broadcasting station) who had been a Volunteer 1914–15 but had then dropped out and had no association with Volunteers or IRA until 1922 (post-Four Courts). These were responsible for murder of Lemass, Cole, Colley, Breslin, etc., and a dozen others. They are still alive, they have not gone to America, they are still in Dublin and mostly still in Dublin Castle [Garda headquarters in 1929]. While O'Higgins was away at Imperial Conference [London, 1926], the Waterford police brutalities were receiving publicity. Eoin O'Duffy was in charge temporarily of the army. There were almost 100 Republicans arrested. O'Higgins returned and amazed his subordinates by having all prisoners released and further deciding to punish the Waterford police. He was not exactly popular with this crowd, and would not truckle to their terms. He arranged his affairs with marvellous precision during the few hours of life after his assassination [attempt]. He surely had

> some information as to the identity of his assailants or the manner of their attack. It seems strange that after more than two years no light should be shed on a murder of a Minister of State. Hundreds of Republicans have been accused of the crime, but no evidence was forthcoming. In connection with O'Higgins' case, etc., in the 'Dáil', it will be recalled that Gearóid O'Sullivan stepped in by assuming the mantle of O'Higgins' prestige and glory.[13]

According to this somewhat convoluted motive for Kevin O'Higgins' killing, the 'promoter' of the theory – presumably not O'Donovan himself – seems to point the finger at disgruntled Garda personnel in Waterford. It is informative that, writing in August 1929, O'Donovan purposely puts the word 'Dáil' in inverted commas, thus questioning the legitimacy of the government and, by extension, the Oireachtas as a whole. O'Donovan seemed fond of conspiracy theories concerning the killings of his former comrades-turned-enemies. For example, in a handwritten note dated 3 November 1940, he wrote: 'Jim Hurley – alleged to be man who shot Michael Collins'.

Six months later, in a memo dated 19 February 1930, entitled 'A clue to Kevin O'Higgins' death', O'Donovan wrote:

> I learn today from a 'high-up' civil servant who is usually fairly well informed, of an interesting aspect of a recent court case. Archibald Doyle was sentenced to 10 years for robbery with arms, having held up the car bearing the wages, £1,600, of Messrs Kenny's builders staff, near their Donnybrook building scheme. Two others were implicated but acquitted. At the time, it was rumoured that A. Doyle was an IRA man and republicans were sorry at the man's apparent lapse. I now learn (for what it is worth) that Archibald Doyle was IRA and in gaol, but subsequently he

joined the CID. He was one of the mutineer group and is supposed to have driven the car used at the assassination of Kevin O'Higgins. At the trial, he stated that he required the money he stole for 'a very special purpose'. Had he been IRA he would undoubtedly have done one of two things: (a) refused to recognise the court or (b) declared that the money was for the IRA and he robbed under instructions. In neither case could the sentence have been more severe. As an addendum, my informant suggests that blackmail is very prevalent as between such types (thugs, mutineers, ex-active service unit men, etc., and responsible heads of government) and that much of the dread of disclosure of monies voted for Secret Service, etc. (files and facts of which are withheld even from the government's own auditor-general) arise from this unpleasant and unsavoury feature.... There are still not only at large, but in receipt of pensions and working on salary in the Custom House or Dublin Castle, men whose names are definitely associated with murders and the foulest atrocities. From the same source, I heard – again only for what it is worth – an explanation of Mr J. J. Murphy's resignation from the chairmanship of the Electricity Supply Board (last week). It is that Cosgrave was trying to push into lucrative jobs nothing less than paid members of the board itself, two cronies, Joe McGrath and Seán McGarry. Murphy, it is averred, could not and would not stomach this.[14]

The 'high-up' civil servant's reference to this court case is, of course, very relevant, as Archie Doyle was one of the three IRA men involved in the killing of Kevin O'Higgins two and a half years earlier. O'Donovan seeks to muddy the waters by using this note to distance Doyle from the IRA. The note further reveals

O'Donovan's loathing for the leaders of the Cumann na nGaedheal government, whom he places at the same level as 'thugs' and 'mutineers'. His swipe at W. T. Cosgrave's appointment of 'cronies' to 'lucrative jobs' in the ESB – while no doubt prompted by his own impecunious position at the time – is humorous in hindsight since he was soon to benefit from a post at the same state-owned company.

O'Donovan's change in fortunes eventually came in late 1930 when he applied for, and got, a job with the headquarters of the Electricity Supply Board in Dublin. The move effectively catapulted him from the status of unemployed to being a middle management figure in a semi-state company. Having just turned thirty-four years of age, he began working for the ESB on 19 November 1930. It is something of a mystery how O'Donovan managed to get such a permanent and pensionable state job during Cumann na nGaedheal's 1922-32 period in office, given that he was one of the high-profile anti-treaty men who had taken up arms against the incumbent government. The answer may lie elsewhere, however, since his wife's elder sister, Kathleen 'Kathy' Moloney (née Barry), was already working in the ESB at that stage and may have been able to help by pleading his case in the right quarters.[15]

O'Donovan's ESB career provided him with a stable income and later, in 1937, enabled him to buy his first home, 'Florenceville', a fine Victorian house on one and a half acres, beside the Shanganagh river near Shankill in south County Dublin. This is the house that would, in 1940, shelter a German spy, but for the moment it provided much-needed comfort to a family that had had its fair share of deprivation and disillusion.

O'Donovan worked for a time as the ESB's statutes and wayleaves officer, dealing with negotiations that paved the way for the erection of pylons across a mainly rural landscape, which would bring electricity to areas that hitherto had had to rely upon paraffin lamps and solid fuel cooking. Donal O'Donovan recalls accompanying his father on ESB trips:

> Our first car was a baby Ford as they used to call it. He was given that by the ESB, as far as I remember, because he was working on these power lines and he had to travel around the country. I went on a few trips with him before the war … one was certainly to Waterford where he had a great friend called Enright. He must have been in the [republican] movement. I think he was something in the ESB in Waterford…. We'd stay in grotty hotels but, I mean, they were all grotty then.[16]

The bulk of Jim O'Donovan's later career was spent in the ESB's secretary's organisation, specialising in legislative issues and their impact on the company. But early on in his new job, he seemed incapable of putting the past behind him and remained obsessed with the civil war whose ruinous outcome had cost him so dearly. In the following note, penned on 27 February 1932, O'Donovan embarked on a rant against some of his civil war adversaries:

> Joe McGrath (now the Hospitals Sweepstakes king) is by his own admission ingloriously associated with and deeply implicated in the murder activities of 1922–1924. Stopped recently to give a lift to Bridie Clynes – challenged with Lemass's murder (Noel's), denied it saying that he went out specially to try and stop that particular murder. Alleged today by 1.1x A214..0 [O'Donovan's code for name] to have been up to the neck in the murder of Bobby Bonfield, etc. Also, that these murders were directed by a definite group housed at 69 Merrion Square, with L. O'Brien as one of the heads.[17]

Two days later, on 29 February 1932, O'Donovan continued railing:

> 'Colonel' Joseph O'Reilly, till now 'aide-de-camp' to 'President' Cosgrave, has, according to today's papers, been appointed to 'a civil post in the Board of Works'

in view of the impending formation of a new (Fianna Fáil) govt. under de Valera. This Joseph O'Reilly was throughout the Tan time merely a glorified messenger-boy – confidential courier to M. Collins would perhaps be a fairer description. His education, as far as I know, was next to nil – his pretensions to cultural training absent. On the night of my arrest (15/3/23) when I was brought to Portobello [army barracks], he was one of the three who threatened to murder me, beat me about the head and body with revolvers, stuck the muzzle of same down my ears and mouth, etc. I was convinced he was not drunk, but his conduct was like that of a maniac: 'Are you glad that Mick is dead? (bang). Are you glad that Mick is dead? Eh, Jimmy?' (I can almost swear that between a liberal splattering of Shamuses and Jimmys, he actually used the latter endearment as described above.) 'Are you glad that Mick (bang) is dead? Are you glad, etc. – '. I don't know how soon after this Holy Thursday was in that year, but the chance arrival of a newspaper of that day or day following showed the rather nauseating illustration of the same man with Cosgrave doing 'the seven churches' like saints. And as some years rolled by, seeing him greeting the first diplomatic representative from the Vatican, Archbishop Paschal Robinson, in Cosgrave's name and escorting him 'mid the plaudits of the onlookers' in an open limousine. If Robinson but knew.[18]

Unsurprisingly, O'Donovan's recollections of his close brush with death as a prisoner in Portobello barracks still remained vivid eight years later.

As the Cumann na nGaedheal government's period in office drew to a close early in 1932,[19] O'Donovan turned his attention to the prospect of a change of government:

> Apropos of change of govt., rumours of meetings of IRB and resistance to a constitutional handover of the reins of govt. to Fianna Fáil, I might as well record, while I think of it, P. S. O'Hegarty's statement about one and a half or two years ago that when a defeat on a division in the 'Dáil' had seemed to point the way to a change of govt. there had been a holocaust of files and archives, something on the same lines (and with no doubt the same purity of motive) as had been followed by the British prior to their (physical) evacuation of 'the Castle'. Two Ministers were freely being rumoured as being opposed to giving up the reins of govt. – Mulcahy and Blythe, the latter because his finances won't bear examination. I hesitate to believe this on particular grounds such as misappropriation, etc., but on general matters, army pensions and gratuities, secret service and other votes during civil war, ultimate financial settlement with England, there may be much in it.

O'Donovan names two Cumann na nGaedheal ministers, Dick Mulcahy and Ernest Blythe, as 'being opposed to giving up the reins of government'. While O'Donovan may not have realised it, there was an element of hypocrisy in his comments, since preventing a handover of power (from the IRA's GHQ to the Dáil) is exactly what he had had in mind a decade earlier, in mid-January 1922. O'Donovan concludes his note with the following:

> P. S. O'Hegarty (Secretary to Minister of Posts and Telegraphs) was, by the way, one of several people who claimed credit for my not having been executed after my arrest on 15th March 1923. On the subject of keeping of records, it may be worth recording that Cosgrave alone (or more likely in conjunction with Diarmuid O'Hegarty, the Secretary to the Executive Council)

could destroy all Cabinet meeting minutes and other valuable records without let or hindrance from anyone. He alone holds key of strong-room attached to his own room except for one duplicate preserved with great care by the American manufacturers.

Just how O'Donovan knew about the layout of W. T. Cosgrave's private office, or the fact that there were two keys to the strongroom, is unclear. The IRA may have had a mole in or near Cosgrave's office.

When de Valera's new government took over following the general election of 16 February 1932, an olive branch was thrown to IRA men imprisoned under the previous administration, and they were released – most of them from Dublin's Arbour Hill prison in March 1932. Donal O'Donovan recalls his father boasting

> ... of having voted twice for Dev in 1932. Every university graduate had a vote, so he had a vote for the Dáil and the Seanad, and used both for Fianna Fáil. Then he saw de Valera wearing a top hat to go to [the League of Nations in] Geneva. And, of course, the IRA campaign began, the military courts were reinstated [in 1936] and the whole thing fell apart.... He absolutely detested de Valera from then on.[20]

In October 1932, O'Donovan received a chatty letter from Robert Barton, a signatory to the Anglo-Irish treaty of 1921, who was then living in retirement at St Edward's Terrace, Rathgar. Despite the fact that O'Donovan had fought against the treaty, both men appeared on good terms ten years on, although Barton mistakenly addressed the letter to Seán L. O'Donovan. The former Sinn Féin TD for Wicklow launched into a detailed description of his poultry farm before concluding as follows: 'Hope you are happy in your job and may long enjoy a sympathetic government.'[21] The treaty signatory seemed to be under the misapprehension that O'Donovan was on good terms with de Valera.

Regardless of his personal feelings towards de Valera, at the end of 1932 O'Donovan decided to open formal communications with the new government – something he would never have dreamed of doing with the previous administration. On 29 November 1932, O'Donovan contacted de Valera's finance minister, Seán MacEntee, essentially seeking jobs for the boys, i.e. his old IRA comrades who had fallen on hard times since the civil war ten years earlier. MacEntee – who had been IRA commander in the north during the war of independence – didn't seem too eager to meet his ex-colleagues but may have been persuaded to do so by Jim's younger brother Dan O'Donovan who had joined Fianna Fáil in 1927. Almost a year later, MacEntee eventually agreed to receive a deputation, including Jim O'Donovan, on 23 October 1933, at which the minister 'requested further particulars of the persons covered by the original application'. The day after the deputation had seen MacEntee, O'Donovan (who was careful to use his home address at 9 Fairfield Park, Rathgar, rather than his ESB headquarters one) wrote a detailed letter to the minister, which included a list comprising no less than twenty names of former comrades from the war of independence and civil war (twenty-one in total, including himself). But only seven on the list are denoted as people 'who would probably apply for, or accept, any post likely to be offered'. O'Donovan tells MacEntee: 'We are confident that it would be the desire of the Executive Council [i.e. the government] to do anything possible for all old army men who had participated honourably in the national struggle....' His argument was that since such people were 'old Dáil officials' supported 'out of Dáil funds', they should now be entitled to 'reinstatement into the Civil Service and in the case of moulders, fitters, etc., employment in the Board of Works or Post Office....' The letter informs the finance minister that former staff of the IRA departments of chemicals, munitions and purchases

> ... by virtue of their proficiency in a technical direction, were asked to give up their calling – a

serious step making resumption difficult if not impossible – and thus increasing the hardship of their circumstances when times became normal. But for their technical proficiency they would merely have carried on an ordinary civil occupation in the daytime with army duties when free, whereas they carried out army duties of the most difficult type during the day and ordinary military duties in their free time.

O'Donovan then adds to the pressure of his petition to MacEntee by referring to similar employment provided by the outgoing Cumann na nGaedheal government: 'It might be added that the late government, in placing the various members of the staffs of the munitions and chemical departments, appointed several to the Civil Service, others securing comparatively high army posts.'[22]

The letter refers only to ex-staff of three of the seven pre-treaty IRA departments: chemicals (of which O'Donovan himself was director), munitions (of which Seán Russell was director) and purchases (of which Liam Mellows was director). Mellows was executed on 8 December 1922. The list sent to Seán MacEntee contains the names of eleven members of the department of munitions (including Russell), nine members of the department of chemicals (including O'Donovan himself), and one member of the department of purchases (Miss Una Daly, who by that stage had already been reinstated in the civil service).

It is unclear what action, if any, the new Fianna Fáil administration took to provide state jobs for those named. O'Donovan had personally selected nine 'deserving' or 'pressing' cases to be considered for civil service, post office or other jobs in the government's gift. But others, including O'Donovan himself, were already 'comfortably placed' (his own choice of wording) by the time the finance minister received the petition. Whatever the outcome, the former IRA director of chemicals could content himself with the thought that he had tried his best to lobby the government on behalf of his former comrades-in-arms.

Some 12 months later, the ghost of Kevin O'Higgins reappeared to torment O'Donovan once more. Almost four years after joining the ESB, O'Donovan returned to, what for him remained, the vexed question of who had shot the minister for justice on 10 July 1927. In a note dated 22 September 1934, and entitled 'Kevin O'Higgins' Death', he wrote:

> On Thursday, 19th Sept. 1934, at a small party at Laurel Lodge, Ballybrack, at which 702 1:5.27 [a code to protect the visitor's real name] and Todd Andrews were present, the former confided to the two of us that to his certain knowledge the above death was at the hands of men of IRA (tho' all the evidence points the other way and such people as a Cumann na nGaedheal superintendent of police, Seán MacCurtain, give it openly as their belief that it was some of the disappointed police that 'did him in'). The startling information is that a meeting of 4th Battalion (only?) was being held in a Thomas Street house in 1927 to decide on attitude towards Fianna Fáil and entry to the Dáil; a man was present, largely to prove his alibi, who was actually one of those directly responsible for K. O'H's death. The meeting was held, as far as could be remembered, at 1 p.m. (very possible as after-last-mass meetings were very common). It was common knowledge at it [the meeting] of his death, altho' Stop-Presses announcing his wounded condition were not for some time after.[23]

On foot of this memo, it seems that O'Donovan was reluctantly letting go of his Garda conspiracy theory concerning the death of O'Higgins. He had also stopped writing the word Dáil in inverted commas. His 1934 informant – although cloaked by a mysterious code-name – was on the right track in saying that the justice minister's 'death was at the hands of' IRA men. But it would take over 50 years for the three assassins' names to come into the public domain.

By the mid-1930s, O'Donovan seemed to have settled into his ESB job and was less inclined to vent anger and frustration at his former civil war opponents. W. T. Cosgrave, Richard Mulcahy and others in the Cumann na Gaedheal party were destined to twiddle their thumbs in opposition until finally regaining office in 1948. They would have ample time to consider the vagaries of the democratic system they had fought so hard to preserve. For O'Donovan, these were years of relative comfort and he had time to turn his attention to other ventures. One major undertaking arose from his decision to publish and edit a new literary journal entitled *Ireland To-Day*. It would provide him with an outlet for his writings, albeit using several aliases – such as Thomas Fitzgerald and Laurence J. Ross – to avoid any clash with his employers.

Ireland To-Day, which sold for one shilling, appeared from June 1936 to March 1938, producing twenty-two monthly issues. Its offices were based at 49 Stafford Street, Dublin. The cover of its first issue was emblazoned with the magazine's logo, a phoenix rising from the ashes – a potent nationalist symbol of resurrection. Writing anonymously (his name never appeared in the magazine), Jim O'Donovan declared in the first issue: 'Greatly daring, we rise from the smouldering ashes to which so many of our predecessors had fallen'. The theme of renaissance was evident from the start. After a dozen or so years of relative political inactivity, O'Donovan may have felt the need for an outlet through which to express his opinions under the safe cloak of anonymity. Frank Shovlin found it was

> ... not clear what prompted O'Donovan ... to undertake a project on the scale of *Ireland To-Day*. Perhaps the example of his uncle, the novelist Gerald O'Donovan (author of *Father Ralph*, 1913), played some part in his decision. Equally, his friendship with a group of Dublin-based film enthusiasts may have convinced him of the need for a high-quality cultural

forum to combat the dominance of right-wing religious publications.[24]

A month after the literary periodical's first appearance, the Spanish civil war broke out and consequently much space was devoted to that conflict – most of it tending towards a defence of the left-wing Spanish government, rather than Franco's right-wing forces. Marking the 50th anniversary of *Ireland To-Day*'s demise, in 1988, Brian Kennedy noted that the journal 'was founded because of Jim O'Donovan's perception of the need … for a magazine that would be the voice of advanced opinions on political, sociological, artistic, religious and international affairs. It aimed to establish itself as the voice of all Ireland. Ten of its principal contributors hailed from Belfast'. O'Donovan was always keen on approaching matters from an all-Ireland perspective; partition was not part of his vocabulary. In later life he would pen a number of academic articles on subjects such as inland waterways and peat resources, thus promoting the benefits of what would now be termed all-island initiatives. The contributors to *Ireland To-Day* included Patrick Kavanagh, Frank O'Connor, Peadar O'Donnell, Ernie O'Malley, Seán Ó'Faoláin, Owen Sheehy Skeffington, Bulmer Hobson, James Hogan and Michael Tierney (the last two were Blueshirt members). It made for an eclectic mix of left- and right-wing opinion. But O'Donovan had a tough editorial policy and did not see eye to eye with either Ó'Faoláin (who left after only five issues of the magazine, following disagreements over the magazine's 'ideological and aesthetic thrust') or Sheehy Skeffington, who quit after the March 1937 issue – O'Donovan objected to his continuing anti-Catholic Church articles, which he felt were harming the journal's circulation (the print run was 3,500).[25]

Writing six months after the journal's launch, O'Donovan's friend Todd Andrews took issue with his editorial on Irish and European heritage when he said: 'Dating our European heritage only from Christian times, it is evident that until the French Revolution, almost all human endeavour in Europe occurred under a totalitarian regime in the form of a despotic monarchy. There is no evidence that I know of, and I have a sort of an idea that you have no evidence, that art, music, science, etc. flourish less under the Nazis (to take the worst possible case) than in former times.' Andrews went on to attack O'Donovan's editorial style as 'half-baked, sentimental and quite unworthy either of yourself or the paper'. But Andrews' ire may have been prompted not so much by the editorial as by a review in *Ireland To-Day* of a new book entitled *Up Dev*, 'at which I really and sincerely feel very annoyed'. Andrews told O'Donovan that 'this attempt to debunk de Valera … is very offensive to a lot of people'. He felt particularly annoyed at the reviewer's suggestion that the Fianna Fáil leader was 'a seeker of publicity' and 'a poser', and made clear that the review did not 'add to the reputation of *Ireland To-Day*'.[26] While the two men did not fall out over this incident – Andrews began the letter 'Dear Jim' – it is worth noting that while Andrews revered de Valera, the same could not be said for James L. O'Donovan. And given their differing views, particularly on domestic politics, such clashes were inevitable during the journal's two-year lifespan.

Donal O'Donovan recalls that *Ireland To-Day* 'was very broadly based in terms of its contributorship but its editorials [mostly written by his father], while they weren't communist or socialist, they weren't [pro] establishment anyway. It was mainly because of Sheehy Skeffington that the campaign against it began. Priests were asking people to tell shopkeepers to "take that red rag" off their shelves'.[27] *Ireland To-Day* tended to be more left-wing than right-wing, particularly when it came to dealing with the Spanish civil war. For example, O'Donovan allowed the noted left-winger Peadar O'Donnell to recount his experiences of the war, but none of Eoin O'Duffy's right-wing supporters who fought for Franco ever wrote in the magazine.

In the October 1937 issue, O'Donnell launched a stinging attack on the Fianna Fáil government, accusing it of 'making an unbelievably bad fist of rural unemployment'. As a result, copies of that issue were circulated to all Cabinet members. The following month's issue contained an article entitled 'Spain – Prospect and Retrospect', penned by Jim O'Donovan under the pseudonym John Fitzgerald, which 'espoused the Republican cause'.[28] This may explain why *Ireland To-Day* received a postcard from a Basque separatist radio station in December 1937 thanking the magazine for its 'sympathy for our Basque Country [which is] warmly appreciated'. The postcard, acknowledging receipt of a letter dated 14 December 1937 – by which time the Spanish civil war had been going on for almost eighteen months – was from station EAJ8, which styled itself as 'The voice of the Basque country's anti-Franco popular front'. O'Donovan or O'Donnell had presumably sent a copy of the November issue to the Basque radio station.[29]

Historian Frank Shovlin notes that a column entitled 'A Foreign Commentary' (written by Sheehy Skeffington and others) was 'used to subvert the right-wing interpretation of the Spanish situation'.[30] O'Donovan's sacking of Sheehy Skeffington in March 1937 came too late to save the magazine, whose list of advertisers had dried up. But it managed to stagger on for another twelve issues, largely because of some American contributions and O'Donovan's own financial backing, which he put at $650 a month. Those who tried to assist the ailing magazine, financially or otherwise, included: Dublin businessman Joe McGrath, who later backed *The Bell* magazine, and Dr Patrick McCartan and John Caldwell-Myers, from the USA. In February 1938, just a month before the magazine folded, O'Donovan estimated that *Ireland To-Day* needed an injection of between $1,250 and $2,500 per annum to survive.[31]

A month after the closure of *Ireland To-Day*, the Dublin-born millionaire philanthropist Albert Bender wrote to O'Donovan from San Francisco, as follows: 'I am deeply sorry that the paper is discontinuing because it has a real place in the Ireland of today.' Bender refused a refund of his annual subscription, asking O'Donovan to use the money 'for postage or any other requirement'. He added: 'I congratulate you on the way in which you have faced your difficulties. It is most honourable on your part'.[32] Bender (1876–1941), the son of a rabbi, had spent years donating antiques to the National Museum in Dublin, unaware that its Austrian director, Adolf Mahr, was a member of the German Nazi party. Bender was also unaware of Jim O'Donovan's feelings towards Hitler's resurgent Third Reich, which would lead to him becoming the IRA's chief liaison officer with Nazi Germany nine months later.[33]

His editorship of *Ireland To-Day* from 1936 to 1938 adds yet another jigsaw piece to the enigma that was Jim O'Donovan. Under his stewardship, the magazine appeared deliberately to steer clear of overt criticism of the Soviet Union or Nazi Germany where Hitler had been in power since January 1933. In his article of resignation – spiked by O'Donovan, who considered it too provocative to publish – Owen Sheehy Skeffington complained that the editor [i.e. O'Donovan] had suggested toning down his 'A Foreign Commentary' column, avoiding observations on communism, fascism, Russia and Spain. Sheehy Skeffington added: 'A Foreign Commentary which succeeded in avoiding such vital topics in the world outside might just as well call itself Home Notes.'[34] Skeffington had a valid point, of course, because while the outside world was being polarised between extreme left- and right-wing elements, O'Donovan seemed keen to keep *Ireland To-Day*'s focus on a narrower basis. Nonetheless, one study describes *Ireland To-Day* as 'the only publication … daring to include in its contents the essays, poems and stories of Irish sympathisers with the Republican government in Valencia'.[35]

As to why O'Donovan chose to publish foreign-interest articles primarily on Spain, rather than also including events unfolding in Nazi Germany and elsewhere, Frank Shovlin comments:

> It's true that Spain remains the focus and I suppose that's for two primary reasons: years of publication and the Irish involvement with the Spanish conflict

on both sides. Jim O'Donovan may also, perhaps, have been thinking about the possible usefulness to Irish republicanism of such a powerful enemy to the British empire as a resurgent Germany. But I can only be speculative about that. I found nothing in researching *Ireland To-Day* to make me think that O'Donovan had any fascistic sympathies. Quite the opposite, in fact.[36]

It is hard to fathom how an editor whose magazine's columns were 'used to subvert the right-wing interpretation of the Spanish situation' – and which avoided exploring events unfolding in the Third Reich – could, within a year of the publication's closure, be actively forging close links with the Nazi regime whose weaponry had helped to instal Franco's dictatorship. The following chapter will explore how this extraordinary sequence of events came about.[37]

6.
A CALL TO ARMS

The collapse of *Ireland To-Day* was a setback for Jim O'Donovan, who had obviously relished his role as editor with a wide brief to comment, albeit through anonymous editorials and pen-named columns, on a variety of issues. But he was not someone to stand still for very long and, just as one door closed, another yet far more dangerous enterprise beckoned. The ex-publisher and current state employee was about to receive an old comrade's call, which he would find impossible to refuse. It would entail turning the clock back and reverting to an earlier guise. He would soon start work on drawing up the blueprint for a widespread bombing campaign in England.

O'Donovan recalls that

> ... early in August 1938, Seán Russell[1] had enlisted my aid in launching the bombing campaign in England ... he became responsible for personnel, organisation and finance, whereas I evolved the whole

details of the sabotage campaign (hence the S-plan, which was erroneously interpreted as the 'Séamus' plan or the 'Seán' plan), conducted the entire training of cadre units, was responsible for all but locally-derived intelligence, carried out small pieces of research and, in general, controlled the whole explosives and munitions end. When I took over, the balloon-type incendiary or bomb was in the experimental stages, Paddy McGrath (later executed for shooting a policeman in Dublin) having done excellent work in correlating time and fabric thickness; the alarm-clock electric fuse mechanism had already been perfected, too, by Jim Ryan.[2]

In fact, problems persisted with the incendiaries, which were meant to be triggered by acid eating through a small rubber balloon inside the explosive device. According to Joseph Collins from Dunmanway, County Cork – a central figure in the S-plan in Manchester – the assembly of such devices was fraught with danger and he narrowly escaped being blown up on one occasion:

> ... the premature explosion was caused by a leak in the rubber acid container, which was part of the fuse ignition. At the start of the campaign we had good quality rubber acid containers, but these had now been exhausted and we were now using halfpenny balloons which we purchased in Woolworths. These sometimes had impurities in the rubber, tiny specks of grit or dirt. Whereas it would take three hours for the acid to burn through the rubber, it would penetrate any of these defects in a matter of minutes. Even the smallest trickle of acid was sufficient to ignite the outer chemicals and the fuse. The police were well aware of the use to which we were putting balloons and had instructed stores to scrutinise customers

> purchasing them, especially customers who bought them in quantities. We began to use heavy quality rubber contraceptives as acid containers after a while, and these worked very well. Often a man had to walk for half an hour with a bomb to reach a target. I had done this myself and it was a far from pleasant exercise, with one's life depending on a halfpenny balloon of cheap rubber. Before now men had been killed with these devices. Experienced volunteers such as Jimmy Joe Reynolds had been killed.... When alarm clocks were used to detonate an explosion they were usually of the cheapest type because money was scarce with us. These were frequently unreliable and alarmed before their time.[3]

It is not clear whether Jim O'Donovan, Paddy McGrath or local commanders in England recommended IRA bombers to use condoms rather than Woolworths balloons as acid containers. But even when writing his memoirs of the S-plan campaign some 25 years later, O'Donovan appeared unaware of these difficulties encountered during 1939. His memoir continues:

> Then followed the dispersal of the trained units, the working out of individual plans in each area and finally the documentary exchanges – if one-sided action can be so termed – with the British government, failure to deal with which by agreeing to evacuate the whole of Ireland, was to be met by appropriate action on our part within four days. Needless to say, nothing happened and this was our zero hour: January the fifteenth 1939.[4] What happened startled the British government, but fell sadly short in magnitude of what had been planned. The campaign developed in a desultory manner, with odd spurts of effective action here and there. The

British government made numerous arrests and very early secured a copy of the S-plan, which was published *in extenso* in the *Daily Telegraph* and *Morning Post*.[5] The discovery of the S-plan put them on their toes and already by drafting enormous numbers of special police, 50,000 was stated, they had the situation well in hand. It [the bombing campaign] was characterised as obviously the work of a trained military staff (hinting at German connivance) and this was very gratifying to me as the document was entirely my own in conception and execution. It was accepted *in toto* by Seán Russell as being 'the goods'. When playing a fairly dangerous game, in absolute secrecy and as anonymously as possible, it is little sops to one's vanity such as this that afford the daily spur to greater and still greater effort. This is not to confuse ambition with patriotism. But hitches are encountered daily, friction and disagreement are not always absent and, even from the physical strain alone, nerves are increasingly on edge. Fear of capture, disappointments at failure, especially when caused by gross carelessness, the strain of accepting responsibility for the incidental damage and casualties of the campaign are all heavy psychological burdens that are made bearable only by the sure approach of ultimate success.[6]

But did any of O'Donovan's children realise he had resumed active service in the S-plan's preparatory period, from August 1938 to January 1939? The answer appears to be yes. His elder son Donal, who turned eleven in January 1939, recalls realising 'very early' that his father was involved in the IRA:

> I remember wondering about cars coming up the drive to us [one] with 'Dark Rosaleen' in chrome letters on the bonnet and dark strangers going in to

meetings and things. They [his parents] would go out to meetings, too, and they'd just say they'd be going out and would be back later, and 'You're to be in bed and asleep by the time we come back'. But one night they came home and my mother came in to say good night to me. I said, 'Was tonight anything to do with the IRA?', and she said, 'I might have known you'd guess' [laughs]. That's all she said.[7]

Jim O'Donovan's memoirs, written almost 25 years after the S-plan, reveal that in the early stages he felt it was still possible to achieve the objective of a British withdrawal from the Six Counties. His optimism may have been sparked by a combination of self-delusion and a natural effervescence at being at the centre of IRA activities once again. Yet O'Donovan was in an extraordinary situation: at forty-two years of age he had virtually turned his back on family life to concentrate all his free time on IRA affairs – essentially launching a war on English soil in the name of a 'government' of a non-existent 32-county Irish republic. Added to which, he was simultaneously holding down a full-time job with the state Electricity Supply Board, where he had clocked up just over eight years' service. Some twenty-five years on, though, O'Donovan still finds it impossible to mask his feelings of pride that Seán Russell had described the S-plan as 'the goods' – a 'little sop' that spurred him 'to greater efforts'. And the ESB man is only too willing to accept authorship of the S-plan document as being 'entirely my own in conception and execution', which indicates that he did not intend these personal memoirs to be published in his lifetime, which they were not. When he refers to the 'strain', 'fear' and 'disappointments' involved in the campaign, he is more likely than not referring to such emotions being felt by IRA commanders and volunteers on the ground in England, rather than by himself. By his own admission, he was incapable of much emotion; he once told his son Donal, 'Beneath that rough exterior there beats a heart of stone'.[8] In addition, his reflection that 'the strain of accepting responsibility for the incidental damage and casualties of the campaign are all heavy psychological burdens that are made bearable only by the sure approach of ultimate success' is a rather Jesuitical way of saying that the end justifies the means. Reading between the lines – and given O'Donovan's undisguised pride in having devised the S-plan – it is hard to escape the conclusion that when he refers to 'casualties', he means IRA men, rather than members of the public in England.[9] Overall, O'Donovan's semi-detached comments on the effects of the bombing campaign – which, apart from his four 1939 trips to the continent, including the unplanned return through London that August, he witnessed from the safety of Dublin – leave the impression of someone living in the realms of fantasy.

Did O'Donovan have any regrets about the S-plan campaign? His memoirs tend to put a glossy spin on things, but his last word on the 1939–40 campaign appears in an additional memoir he drew up in 1965, which was part of an unfinished history of the Irish Republican Army. In that document he describes the run-up to the S-plan:

> Despite the warnings of the more prudent element, he [Seán Russell] and his closest supporters favoured a sabotage campaign in England which was expected to re-unite the Republican elements of the country before former ideals were entirely forgotten and possibly even to interest Germany in making her decision, if it were at all her intention to engage England in a showdown. The more prudent elements pointed out that at least two years' preparation and considerable expenditure would have to precede such a campaign. (Years later, even so sober an historical analyst as Professor James Hogan admitted to the author that, if government backed and spending say £100,000 per annum, and really infiltrating the English scene, such a campaign could go a long way

towards success.) The bombing campaign was briefly prepared for and launched in January 1939 by four days' notice demanding withdrawal of the British forces from Ireland, served upon Lord Halifax, then Foreign Secretary. There was virtually no plan, no leadership and both trained personnel and funds were in short supply. The suggestion that the move was German-inspired was completely wide of the mark, and was indeed a poor tribute to German efficiency. Naturally, when it burst upon a surprised England, Germany took cognisance of it and subsequently sent over an agent or two to report what was happening, and later, when war had been declared [i.e. on 3 September 1939], to explore the potential situation from a military angle. This whole misguided development ended with some thousand internees and several deaths and executions, between the years 1940 and 1945.[10]

According to this account, O'Donovan's main regret appears to be that the bombing campaign was not better organised and better funded. O'Donovan's lack of reaction to deaths and injuries in the bombing campaign he drew up indicates, at best, an inability or unwillingness to accept a link between cause and effect. In any event, it is certain that he was hardened – brutalised might be a more accurate term – and possibly traumatised by his IRA activities both during the war of independence and the subsequent civil war. In this respect, the maiming of his right hand in an explosion in May 1922 and his near brush with death at the hands of his captors in Portobello barracks a year later are significant.

Despite O'Donovan's old-soldier status, historian J. Bowyer Bell thought the IRA's 'acquisition' of him in 1938 'was particularly valuable for he was not only a skilled explosives expert but he had a far broader vision of both military and political realities in Europe than did any of the men surrounding Russell'.[11]

Whether O'Donovan's 'broader vision' of political realities in Europe extended to Ireland, however, is a moot point. On 8 December 1938, Russell had announced that the IRA was taking over 'the authority of the "Government of the Republic of Ireland" from the "Executive Council of Dáil Éireann". This meant that those who had recognised the Second Dáil as the *de jure* government of Ireland now recognised the [IRA] army council (and Seán Russell as its head) as the legitimate rulers of Ireland.'[12] In fact, it was the same point O'Donovan had haggled over with Mulcahy in January 1922, and a bugbear he would return to intermittently for the rest of his life.

Soon after Seán Russell's S-plan request in 1938, the American writer James T. Farrell found IRA men Moss Twomey,[13] John Dowling and Andy Cooney gathered at Jim O'Donovan's home on 22 August. Farrell considered the IRA group to be 'curiously insular and eccentric in their political attitudes', adding that 'O'Donovan is very quiet and shy, but probably the most intelligent of the lot'.[14]

According to Jim O'Donovan's wife, Monty, Dr Andy Cooney (IRA chief of staff, 1925–26) was the first person to suggest that the IRA should collaborate with Nazi Germany. Cooney's son, Dr Seán Cooney, takes up the story:

> I recall Moss Twomey and Jim O'Donovan coming to our house almost every week to spend an evening closeted privately in the drawing room with my father, in 1939. I recall years later, Donal's mother, Jim's wife (a sister of Kevin Barry) telling me casually that my father was the first person she ever heard suggesting that the IRA should collaborate with the Germans against Britain. My mother spoke German and she and my father were in Germany in 1936 (on the way to a conference in Czechoslovakia). Pop and my mother knew many of the German spies during the war.[15]

A CALL TO ARMS

By the end of 1938, O'Donovan had spent five months working on the forthcoming bombing campaign. It was now time to put the S-plan into action. Just before Christmas, twelve IRA men crossed over to Britain (to join others already *in situ*): two to Glasgow, three to London, two to Manchester, three to Liverpool and two to Birmingham.[16] Despite the despatch of two operatives to Glasgow, it is worth noting that Russell and O'Donovan had determined that Scotland and Wales, as Celtic countries, would be excluded from the bombing campaign, which would focus solely on targets in England.[17] This did not stop Welsh or Scottish people falling victim to the campaign, however. One of the fatalities in the 25 August 1939 bomb in Coventry, for example, was Welsh. In addition, the IRA targeted King's Cross railway station in London (the scene of another fatality), which was used by people travelling to and from Scotland.

The first time anyone outside the IRA knew anything about the S-plan project was on 13 January 1939 when a formal letter landed on the desk of the British foreign secretary, Lord Halifax. The letter, dated 12 January 1939, and on a letterhead bearing the words 'Irish Republican Army, General Headquarters, Dublin' (in Irish also), bore all the hallmarks of O'Donovan's inimitable style of threat cloaked in courteous formality. The IRA ultimatum, addressed to 'His Excellency, The Rt Hon. Viscount Halifax, GCB',[18] read as follows:

> Your Excellency, I have the honour to inform you that the Government of the Irish Republic, having as its first duty towards its people the establishment and maintenance of peace and order here, demand the withdrawal of all British armed forces stationed in Ireland. These forces are an active incitement to turmoil and civil strife, not alone in being a symbol of hostile occupation, but in their effect and potentialities as an invading army. It is secondly the duty of the Government to establish relations of

friendship between the Irish and all other peoples and to achieve this we must insist upon the withdrawal of British troops from our country and a declaration from your Government renouncing all claim to interfere in its domestic policy or external affairs. The Irish people have no cause of hostility to any European nation, even those nations whose natural development may bring them into conflict with British interests, and we are desirous of making it clear that we shall in no event take part in a war of aggression against any people or permit the nation to be regarded as having any community or identity of interest with Britain that would make us liable to attack by British enemies. The occupation of our territory by troops of another nation and the persistent subvention here of activities directly against the expressed national will and in the interests of a foreign power, prevent the expansion and development of our institution in consonance with our social needs and purposes, and must cease. Neither the Government of the Irish Republic nor the Irish people are actuated by any feelings of hostility to the people of Britain. Rather would we welcome a better understanding but this can be brought about only on the basis that each of the two peoples is absolutely free to pursue its own course unhampered by the other. We shall regret if this fundamental condition is ignored and we are compelled to intervene actively in the military or commercial life of your country as your Government are now interfering in ours. The Government of the Irish Republic believe that a period of four days is sufficient notice for your Government to signify its intentions in the matter of the military evacuation and for the issue of your Declaration of Abdication in respect of our country. Our Government reserve the right of appropriate action without further notice if upon the expiration of this period of grace, these conditions remain unfulfilled.

The letter was signed 'Patrick Fleming,[19] Secretary ... on behalf of the Government and Army Council of Óglaigh na h-Éireann (Irish Republican Army)'.

Jim O'Donovan was not only adept at formulating IRA statements, he was also good at covering his tracks. In this particular case, for example, he had provided the perfect alibi by attending an air raid precautions course for ESB staff at Griffith barracks in Dublin. The department of defence course ran from 9 to 31 January 1939, thus covering the period when his S-plan campaign was unleashed on an unsuspecting British public. An old black and white photograph shows O'Donovan at the barracks in the company of senior Irish army officers. The top brass could hardly have guessed that their companion was also a senior military officer currently waging war on England.[20]

In retrospect, the IRA ultimatum appears breathtaking in its audacity. The idea that a small armed group could style itself as 'the Government of the Irish Republic' – ignoring the existence of an elected government in Dublin – was stretching credulity to the limit. And this point can hardly have been lost on the authorities in London. But what appeared to be a fanciful gesture by a handful of unelected republican leaders in Dublin would soon turn into a deadly menace. The IRA had set the deadline and would now have to stick to it by unleashing the bombing campaign O'Donovan had designed. The IRA volunteers were in place in English cities, ready and waiting for the green light. One of them, Joe Collins, recalls the mood at the time:

> I had been working in Dublin when this current campaign in England began. On Sunday, 15 January

1939, posters were appearing all over Dublin and in the main cities of England calling upon Britain to withdraw her armed forces, officials and institutions from every part of Ireland … at 6 a.m. [on 16 January] the campaign was launched and selected targets were bombed in many parts of England. Over half a million pounds worth of damage was caused on that first night. Enfield arms factory was left without power. In Manchester, sewers and gas mains were blown open and gas flames shot twenty feet into the air.[21] I had known about preparations for this campaign of course, and had earlier volunteered to join in the campaign in England. I knew that, for some reason I could not then fathom, Seán Russell was selecting many inexperienced volunteers for this campaign.[22]

A 1946 Irish army intelligence (G2) assessment cast fresh light on Russell's *modus operandi* during the S-plan period:

During the IRA campaign in England in 1939, Michael Fitzpatrick and Maurice [Moss] Twomey organised the resident IRA in England into battalions and had them located in the larger towns of England. Seán Russell, on the other hand, organised a second fighting unit in this country on the same lines as the old IRB [Irish Republican Brotherhood], and these men were transferred in groups to England but were told to keep clear of the resident IRA in England. This method soon became known to the British authorities, and practically all personnel who left this country were picked up and imprisoned…. Russell's arrangement was the cause of the collapse of the whole cause.[23]

Joe Collins's memoir also reveals that 'At the general army convention [in 1938], I had opposed, along with all Cork city and county delegates, Seán Russell as chief of staff, and when the attack on Armagh was called off I left Ireland in disgust to work in Scotland.' A short time later, however, Collins rejoined 'the IRA and was working in Dublin at the erection of a farm building at the Kerry Cow dairy in Cloghran. This dairy was owned by a Kerry man, Jerome O'Riordan, a well known republican.' Collins appears to have patched up his differences with Russell, who arrived at the dairy

> ... accompanied by Stephen Hayes and Sam Kennedy; this latter was at that time O/C in Glasgow. Seán knew that I had volunteered to join the campaign in England and that Sam Kennedy had recommended me. He enquired if I was still of the same mind and I assured him that I was most anxious to go. 'Are you in full agreement with this campaign?' 'Of course I am. Without some action the army will become moribund.' 'Good. Stephen here will notify you in a day or so where you are to go for training. I know that you are good with a machine gun, but this will be a bombing mission.' I felt elated and had been fearful that the stand of the Cork units in opposing this venture would be held against me. Sam Kennedy's recommendation had been an important factor in my selection for this mission.... After a few days I had a note from Stephen Hayes asking me to meet him in the Castle Hotel where I was instructed to attend a training class at a premises [the Green Lounge] in Stephen's Green. Our instructor there was Paddy McGrath who was an expert in explosives. Paddy, a 1916 veteran, was to be later executed by the Free State. There were four classes each day, each lasting for about three hours, and there were anything up to nine men at every class. The training was very thorough, and this was later to be shown in the

campaign where there was not to be one fatal accident in all the hundreds of bombs assembled and laid in England.[24]

Something of the IRA mindset is revealed in Joe Collins's memoir, written thirty years after the S-plan campaign. As with O'Donovan's unpublished memoirs, they similarly contain no hint of regret or remorse over death or injury caused to members of the public in England. When Collins states that 'there was not to be one fatal accident ... in England' during the 1939–40 campaign, he is of course referring only to fatalities concerning IRA personnel. A total of seven members of the public were killed in that campaign, five of them in a single explosion in Coventry. Two IRA men were hanged for the Coventry bombing, but Collins does not refer to them either.

In conjunction with the bombing campaign, the IRA in Dublin kept producing a steady stream of propaganda, examples of which survive among O'Donovan's papers. One such bulletin, from January 1939, states:

> We stand twenty years beyond a glorious day in 1919 [initial sitting of First Dáil on 21 January 1919] when the Proclamation of 1916, from being a heroic and historic document, passed into the history of our country as the basic code and constitution under which the Government of the Republic of Ireland elected to function. The regime of that Government – the First Dáil and the Second Dáil – represented the golden age of Irish Nationality.

After lashing out at 'the puppet parliament' in Dublin, which 'operates under an English-made law', the IRA statement called on Irish people to support

> ... the noble efforts of our Expeditionary Force in England to-day [by giving] sympathy, publicity, propaganda, money, help to Prisoners' Dependants,

recruits ... be proud to link up with us in this final drive to overthrow England's domination of this country and assert our full and unfettered independence under the same Almighty God, reverently invoked by the heroes of 1916.[25]

One of the IRA's top men in London at the time was Dan Keating from Kerry. Like Seán Russell and Jim O'Donovan, he was also a veteran of the war of independence and had decided to remain in active service after joining the anti-treaty forces in the civil war. In a rare interview in 2006, just a year before he died, Keating filled in part of the background to his S-plan activities:

> I went to London around 1935 or '36 and I worked there until 1939 [as] a barman in Mooney's – Mooney's of Dublin. They had nine [public] houses that time in Dublin and they had nine houses in London.... I was sent back in charge. I had a number of men there – three or four active men. We kept ourselves small and we laid bombs whenever we got the chance, you know. You would have to say we were very successful for a long time.... You would select places [to bomb] and one of the places we selected was the Grosvenor Hotel in Park Lane. The bomb was laid at the back of a flowerpot.

Asked if he was concerned about killing people, Keating replied:

> Oh Jaysus, to kill a lot of people – 'twas timed to go off about 11 o'clock but it didn't go off until 2. But if it went off at 11 it would have killed a lot of people.... At the time now we didn't mind.... The only thing was to try and cause as much confusion as we could. But as time went by, what we were doing was nothing. The great war was on, and in the meantime supplies ran out for us as well and I went back to work again in Mooney's. I was working away in 1939.

Keating also revealed how some of the targets were chosen: 'There was a very big firm in London, I forget the name, but [among] the people that owned the firm was a judge. But he was very ruthless when he met Irish men and that firm got it. Everywhere we'd see it we'd lay a bomb.' Keating claimed that his IRA unit escaped injury and arrest, and that while the bombs caused a lot of damage 'no one got killed'. He narrowly escaped capture in 1939 when Scotland Yard detectives came to arrest him at Mooney's in The Strand. Keating had gone back to his guesthouse on a lunch break and was phoned there by a barman who tipped him off. He decided to return to Ireland by ferry from Liverpool. Avoiding the railways, Keating recalls:

> I got a Green Line bus to Leeds and got a bus from Leeds to Liverpool. There was a man just outside Liverpool, Con O'Connor, who I knew well and he'd be a supporter of ours. There was a Kerry man who used to be a night security man in the boat now and again. Lynch was his name. And the night he was on anyway I got into the boat and I got back quite safe.

Back in Dublin, Keating 'got a job in the Butt Bar', resuming work as a barman.[26]

In the course of 1939, a special order was issued to all IRA members, exhorting them 'to fulfil the national purpose – the absolute independence of Ireland'. The statement, seemingly designed for broadcast on the IRA's secret radio transmitter, bears the following introduction in O'Donovan's handwriting: 'The following is a special order issued to all our forces recently. As an indication of the spirit in which the present campaign is being conducted, it speaks for itself.' The statement recognises IRA volunteers' 'hearty and generous co-operation in times of stress and difficulty that have [sic] enabled the Volunteers to achieve the great national advance that has been made ... to consolidate our gains and extend the influence of our movement your continued help and disciplined action is essential, and we rely confidently upon you for this.' O'Donovan further rallies the troops with the words: 'The nation is on the march; it is yours to guide it to victory ... when we are again in complete control of the country from Cork to Belfast.'²⁷

But O'Donovan's stirring rhetoric belied the chaos on the ground in England as a haphazard campaign staggered on amid inevitable mishaps. Joe Collins recounted one such hair-raising incident in Manchester:

> I had a room in Temple Street where I assembled bombs. It was a tenement house where the tenants were mostly unemployed men or old people. The rent was six shillings a week, there was no gas and no electricity. The room was illuminated at night time by a paraffin lamp which hung from a nail in the wall. The landlady was an Irish woman, named Mrs Murphy, who did not live on the premises. That suited me, as she didn't know whether I was working or not. At that stage of the campaign any Irishman renting a room might well be reported to the police, especially if he didn't appear to have any job. This house had been recommended to me before I arrived in Manchester by an IRA man from Belfast, Bernard McGuinness, who also stayed there. He was known to the occupants of the house and they took little notice of his comings and goings. I had a report of a bus depot where anything up to two hundred buses were parked at night, so I decided that these were a suitable target. Six men were detailed to place incendiaries under the rear seats of six buses as they made the last journey of the evening back to the depot. I assembled the bombs in my room and Bernard took them out one by one in small attaché cases, passing them on to the IRA men waiting in a public lavatory to receive

them. Bernard had left with the second bomb and I was stooped over an open attaché case working on a third when there was a knock on the door. I knew it was Bernard returning and went to open door, and just as I opened it there was a sudden explosion behind me in the room. Bernard took off down the stairs without a word. I turned back, the room was filled with black smoke, the glass was smashed in the window and the smoke was pouring out onto the street. My oil lamp had gone out, my bed was on fire, as was the carpet. Underneath the bed was a case containing gelignite, detonators and a bottle of sulphuric acid. The room was in complete darkness. If the explosion had taken place about six seconds earlier I would have lost my head. Some detonators with short lengths of fuse attached had been lying on the floor and I could see the fuse on one sparking in the darkness. I didn't know that the detonator had already exploded and that the fuse was burning back. On impulse I picked up the fuse to throw it into the fireplace and the burning fuse stuck to my hand. I used the other hand to pull it off to get rid of it. The palms of both my hands along with my fingers were black with the sticky substance of the burnt fuse. Searching around for my jacket, I found it and put it on. There were a number of old people who had rooms in this house; I had seen them from time to time. I thought of them and the case of gelignite under the bed. I poked around for the case, found it and started off down the stairs with the case. By now the stairs was almost blocked with people and I had to force my way through. Nobody tried to stop me, though some of them looked hostile. I'd say that most of them were no friends of the police anyway. 'What happened?' somebody asked aggressively. 'The paraffin lamp exploded' I explained. 'Where are you going now?' 'To get the fire brigade.' When I got to the street the black smoke was still pouring out from the broken window and a crowd was beginning to gather.

Collins made good his escape aboard a tram and, cleaning up at a friend's house later, he reflected 'at least I had salvaged the gelignite for another day'. Joe Collins's personal memoir also reveals that not all his targets were purely economic – at least one was sparked by revenge. After the explosion in Temple Street, his Manchester landlady gave Bernard McGuinness's name to the police (she did not know Collins's identity) but the Belfast man had taken the first boat to Dublin. Collins recalls:

> Bernard's mother and sister both lived in Manchester. His mother was old and dependent on Bernard and her daughter for support. His sister worked in a department store in the city and after questioning by the police she was sacked. I resolved to burn the place. One of our girls, a Volunteer from New Ross, went in to buy a coat. She succeeded in placing a number of incendiaries in the pockets of a lot of coats. At twelve noon the place went up in flames and I stood among the crowd on the street watching it burn. Bernard's mother and sister returned to Belfast.[28]

The start of the S-plan campaign in mid-January 1939 had alerted the authorities to what the IRA had in mind. Things now got tougher for IRA units on the ground, as houses were raided and arrests were made. Joe Collins was eventually captured in Charlton-on-Medlock, Manchester, on 12 May 1939, in a room that had been rented for him by a sister of Tralee IRA man John Joe Sheehy. A day earlier Collins and his unit 'blew up six of the biggest shops in the two main streets in Manchester, Market Street and Piccadilly'. Collins was the IRA's operations officer in Manchester, and recalls: 'this was also my rank in London before I had to get

THE DEVIL'S DEAL

out of there. The operations officer before me was Ritchie Goss, who was later shot dead [in 1941] by a Free State Army firing squad in Portlaoise. The operations officer after my capture was Jackie Griffiths, who was shot dead, on sight, by the Free State Special Branch in Holles Street, Dublin [in 1943].'

After his trial, Collins was imprisoned in Parkhurst gaol, Isle of Wight, from 1939 to 1948. His memoirs provide a glimpse of the long years of incarceration, including a visit from

> ... Father Brady, a Cavan man. Brady looked me up and down in a hostile manner. 'How did you come to be mixed up in this business?', he asked aggressively. 'I am a Volunteer in the Irish Republican Army', I answered. 'What bloody army? You are a gang of bloody gunmen. You should all be shot. There must be some terribly evil driving force behind you to send stooges like you to a place like this for twenty years. There is no cure for your kind; you should all be shot' ... 'Get out!', I shouted. I was so mad that I almost hit him.

Long terms in jail took their toll on the IRA men, especially those who were married. Collins recalls that one such prisoner, Denny Duggan from Tipperary, 'his eyes filled with tears, once showed me a letter from his wife in which she apologises for a small delay in writing. She said that her fingers were so sore from thinning turnips on Tipperary farms that she couldn't hold the pen. She was earning half a crown a day, and the money was sorely needed.'

Though based in Manchester, Joe Collins's memoirs disclose that 'the main explosives dump we were to draw from was in Liverpool, and was accessed through a bookshop in Scotland Road'. Collins and other IRA volunteers in Manchester regularly made the trip to Liverpool by bus or train, returning 'with a suitcase filled with explosives'. The IRA's commanding officer in Liverpool at the time was Joe Deegan (1914–94) whose memoirs were published, in Irish, in 1962.[29] In his book, Deegan recalls that he

> ... was one of the eight who left Dublin before Christmas 1938 in order to initiate the campaign begun by the IRA the following year in England. Towards that end, we resigned our jobs in England when the IRA sought volunteers who knew England and the English way of life. We were from Glasgow, Liverpool, Manchester, Birmingham and London. Three of the eight were born in Britain. In 1938 we attended a training course in Dublin. Some of us, including myself, did an intensive course after that. We were called Operation Officers, and each had a knowledge of explosives, [tear-]gas bombs and incendiary bombs, as well as revolvers, rifles and machine guns. We could make certain types of mines.... We were willing to share our expertise with other volunteers in Britain if necessary. Above all, we were able to measure the strength of explosives accurately. We had a specific instruction from Russell to be on guard lest an explosion would kill anybody.[30]

Deegan's version of events suggests that civilian casualties were to be specifically avoided. Yet the choice of targets – including railway and tube stations, buses, bridges, cinemas, pillar boxes, litter bins (and, as Dan Keating recalled, hotels) – increased the likelihood of death and injury among the general public.

As to the reasons for the 1939–40 campaign, Deegan notes that:

> Russell and his advisors believed that a bombing campaign in England would be the best way to arouse an awareness amongst the English public about the partition of Ireland.... People often said the fight should be taken to the Six Counties also at that time, and not to bother with England, and to concentrate all efforts on destroying Stormont. It's quite a debatable point, but Russell himself had a specific

view on this. I heard him say that he didn't want the IRA to do any fighting in Ireland at all, as nothing would come of that but damage to our own country …. My understanding in those days was that the *Ard-Chomhairle* [army council] of the IRA would not sanction any campaign in the Six or the Twenty-Six Counties, since, as Russell put it, 'that would be tantamount to Irish people fighting each other'. Another reason for taking the fight to England was that this was the period before the German Luftwaffe visited much destruction on England. Up until then, the English were used to waging war in faraway lands and conflict never took place on their doorstep.[31]

Deegan's book boasts that 'The campaign undertaken by the IRA in 1939 was the biggest and best organised of any campaign until then. It lasted for over a year. There were about 200 explosions'. But he also acknowledges the backlash it triggered, including the execution of two IRA members for the Coventry bombing and the imprisonment of ninety-four others. Deegan adds:

On the 28th July 1939, the Prevention of Violence (Temporary Provisions) Bill came into force, conferring power on the British Home Secretary to deport suspicious persons. People were deported and many others left voluntarily. Many of them lost their jobs and the property they had acquired over many years. They came to Ireland – men, women and children – with nothing in store for them but poverty and hardship.[32]

Deegan managed to leave Liverpool on the evening of 27 July 1939, the day before the Prevention of Violence Act came into force. According to his own account, he had been under close surveillance for some weeks before and managed his departure only with the help of a friend, Tom Martin, who surreptitiously booked a ticket for the Liverpool–Dublin sailing purportedly on his own behalf, then handing on the ticket to Deegan. They both sauntered about in the vicinity of the Liverpool docks in the hour or two before the sailing, giving the impression of being out for a walk. Shortly before the gangway was raised, Deegan made a dash for the boat and managed to get on board, presenting the ticket. Police officers followed, but the ship's officers refused to allow them to make an arrest on board and they left the ship, warning Deegan not to return to Britain.

In the early 1940s, Deegan ended up in the Curragh internment camp with Jim O'Donovan. The Liverpool IRA man's memoirs refer to Séamus Ó Donnabháin and himself spending two days discussing the policies of Ailtirí na hAiséirí (Architects of the Resurrection) while 'walking about in circles on the broad plain of Leinster' – Deegan's cryptic reference to the Curragh camp.[33]

A less high-minded account of the S-plan period comes from Liverpool-born IRA man Tom Byrne (aka Tomás Ó Broin) who recalls that the secret army was not that well organised and also fell foul of informers.[34] His father and grandfather had both been active in the republican movement. Byrne joined the IRA's Liverpool brigade as a 17-year-old in 1936 and took part in the S-plan campaign in 1939:

> The O/C of Liverpool brigade was Joe Deegan. When the IRA declared war on Britain and sent this letter to Lord Halifax, the foreign minister at the time, we stuck all these notices about the Irish Republic all over Liverpool. When you think of it, how daft it must have been. In January 1939 when the bombing campaign started, the police must have known something because they were able to pick up practically everyone who was connected with it. They must have had an informer of some sort ... there was a Dublin man, a fellow called O'Neill, who they said was responsible, but I wouldn't know. I wouldn't be

> sure. I tell you, they [the police] were able to pick up practically everyone who had anything to do with the IRA, or any of the organisations like that. But they didn't do anything about it. In other words, where I lived [Crosby Green] I had a special branch guy sitting on the wall outside. So every time I went out of the house anywhere they would follow me.... Mind you, I was pretty fit then. They had trams in Liverpool and very steep hills, so he'd be sitting a few seats away from me on the tram, and the minute I wanted to go I would wait until the tram was speeding down the hill and I'd jump off. And he'd never be able to do it because he was a bit too fat or too big. I'd shoot off ... and disappear.... Then they would have me in the next day for questioning. They used to beat me up but not badly. What they used to do was sit you in a stool and three of them would pummel you in the back of the neck, but not making it so obvious that they would mark your face.... If I went to the cinema, there would be a special branch man sitting on either side of me.

Byrne recalls that on the way home from the cinema the policemen would punch him with their gloved fists:

> I have always had trouble with this ear from one of the clouts I got.... Mind you, we got away with things considering we tried to blow up – Jesus, when you think of it now – the wall in Walton jail because there were a couple of IRA fellows there.... Our job was to blow a hole in the wall so they could get out. We did not realise the fecking walls were about that thick.... all we succeeded in doing was to make a little hole in it. We did not get caught. Oh Jesus, it's a gas.... You'd go to the Gaelic League on a Saturday

night ... you'd say you were going for a dance or whatever and you could also have a meeting at the same time and be told what to do the next day.

Byrne recalls how an average bombing mission would unfold:

> If there was a job to be done we had to meet at a certain place, but we were told also that we could not wait for more than five minutes. You couldn't hang around waiting. It was always more or less the same place, in the street outside a hotel. I think it was the Exchange Hotel ... it was a place you could actually stand outside without making yourself too obvious.... Whoever you had to meet had to be punctual. There couldn't be any mess up about waiting half an hour or anything like that.... The person would hand you a parcel of gelignite which would be primed with a timer. If the timing device was sulphuric acid it would probably go off within a few minutes of my taking charge of it. It was a bit hair-raising, I know.... The one I did that day was the outside of an Owen Owens [department store]. You could just flop it in, the same as you'd put it into a letterbox. They had a receptacle in the window that you could just drop it into. It went off; I heard it a few minutes later. No one was injured. It was around midnight. I wouldn't do anything like that in the daytime. It caused minor damage. The bomb was light, easy to carry. It wasn't very nice. I wasn't terribly keen on any of those jobs. I don't think any people were killed or injured in Liverpool.

As 1939 dragged on, Tom Byrne began to express doubts about the effectiveness of the S-plan campaign and said so to two senior IRA men in Liverpool, Joe Deegan and Martin Staunton (aka Máirtín Standún). Byrne recalls:

> There was nothing scientific or well organised in any of the jobs that were done. It was amateurish. It was a sort of campaign I wasn't too happy about. I didn't feel it was doing anything. I told them many times … I told Standún myself – I said, 'this is not warfare'. He said, 'You're not very keen'. I said, 'Well, I'm not very keen. You can tell.' Mind you, it wasn't a question of being keen. If you were told to do it, you did it and that was the end of it.

According to Byrne, the Liverpool IRA was short of manpower and weapons:

> In the period from January to August 1939, you'd be lucky if there were ten people in the IRA unit. A lot of people who were actively talking about it before they started, suddenly disappeared. You know what I mean? They got less and less. We got support from one or two of the catholic clergy in Liverpool.… At its greatest there were about 15 people in the unit in Liverpool. I mean, 15 to 17 people and it was whittled down to about half when it started, so what would a handful of people do?

In addition, the IRA had access to only 'small amounts of gelignite' which 'was pinched from British Rail or wherever they could lay their hands on it. They stole it from demolition jobs or quarries.' Guns were few and far between, and Byrne remembers, 'I couldn't get my hands on a rifle'. Despite the shortage of weapons, IRA training seemed to be well organised: 'The people who were training us had been in the officer training corps in Liverpool University. They knew what they were talking about as regards an army, but this [Liverpool IRA] wasn't an army.' The trainers included Séamus Mangan, who was O/C of the Liverpool Fianna – the IRA's youth wing, which Tom Byrne had joined as a 13-year-old in 1932.

A CALL TO ARMS

Discussing the events more than sixty years later, Byrne recalls that Joe Deegan and Martin Staunton were 'knocking my ideas on the head. They thought I was educated I suppose. I probably was a young hothead.' Byrne wanted to attack a prison van taking IRA volunteer Seán Hannan for trial in Manchester: 'I wanted them to attack the van, like they did in Fenian times, and get him out … it could have been done but they [the local IRA leaders] would not allow it. It was considered to be silly warfare.' Byrne also wanted to blow up the liner *Queen Mary*, then in dry dock pending her maiden voyage:

> I wanted to blow the bloody ship up…. As a shipping clerk with F. J. Callaghan and Company – ships providers for the Cunard line – I had access to the nine miles of docks in Liverpool. I wanted the IRA to do something like that. You see, I didn't believe in putting bombs in letterboxes and silly things like that…. I wasn't too keen on those jobs at all because I didn't like the idea of killing innocent bystanders…. I would have been happier with military targets or something like the *Queen Mary*. If we had sunk the *Queen Mary* we would at least have made the headlines…. If you're going to terrorise people, you could terrorise them far better than by dropping a bomb in a letterbox. You could go and look for some bloody fellow like Lord Halifax and shoot him. It's not the first time it was done in London…. The S-plan would have been all right if they had had both the gear and the proper way of doing it. If you're going to do it you could have the stuff in, use it and blow up half the bloody town hall. If you actually see what was done, however, there was really nothing done. The idea that this was going to force the British out of the North is ludicrous, isn't it? I was only 20, I probably wouldn't have had the courage to talk to

them, never mind argue with them. These people, like Séamus O'Donovan and Seán Russell, had carried on guerrilla warfare in Ireland; it is a different thing altogether. You have to be organised to do a proper job.... Practically none of us were really organised.

But time was running out for the IRA's operation and Byrne recalls that 'public opinion in Liverpool was against the IRA. The Gaelic League and the GAA ceased to operate once the campaign started because public opinion was anti-Irish.' In August 1939, the authorities decided to swoop:

> In one night the entire unit was arrested. They were taken straight to the boat. The Scottish Borderers took me away. You were stuck in a van and they took you down to the boat and that was it. They came for me at my house. My parents weren't very pleased – my mother was very upset – but they knew what was going on.... The other guys were all on the bloody boat. I don't think we had any money; we certainly weren't in the bar having a drink. Half of Liverpool's Irish were on the boat as well. They were all going back to Ireland. It was at the end of August 1939, just before the outbreak of war.

The decision to deport Tom Byrne and others from Liverpool in late August 1939 was most probably prompted by the Coventry bombing on 25 August, but special deportation powers had in fact been introduced a month earlier. The minutes of a meeting at the War Office in London on 4 July 1939 (in preparation for a cabinet meeting the following day) disclose that while the Home Secretary, Sir Samuel Hoare, favoured deportation, the head of MI5, Sir Vernon Kell, wanted internment to be introduced. Kell's wish was rejected, although internment was brought in two months later on the outbreak of war.[35] The Prevention of Violence (Temporary Provisions) Bill was introduced in the House of Commons on 19

July 1939 and provided a range of tough new anti-IRA measures, including expulsion, police search powers, registration and prohibition on entry to Britain. According to press reports at the time, the British government rejected the idea of banning the IRA 'for practical reasons'.[36]

Even allowing for a certain cynicism when looking back on the events of over half a century before, Tom Byrne's account reveals the shambolic nature of the Liverpool IRA's activities in 1939. The personal recollections of young IRA personnel caught up in Seán Russell's S-plan bear scant resemblance to the grand designs encapsulated in Jim O'Donovan's verbose and haughty statements on behalf of 'the government of the republic of Ireland'. Even with the bombing campaign well under way, IRA leaders were no nearer to forcing a British withdrawal from Northern Ireland than they had been before the sabotage plan was conceived. But while the bomb attacks in England prompted a clampdown on extreme republicans both by Dublin and London, they were to have a positive result for the IRA in one important respect, for they had begun to attract the attention of a crucial third party – Nazi Germany.[37]

7.

THE GERMAN CONNECTION

As the bombing campaign got under way in England in January 1939, the new IRA leadership was poised to forge closer links with Hitler's regime, which at that time had chalked up six years in power. According to one historian, the IRA's pact with German military intelligence (the Abwehr) was 'a partnership doomed to disaster'.[1] At this pre-war stage, however, both the IRA and the Nazis were on a roll and eager to do business together. In fact, the forthcoming contacts between both sides would not be the first to have occurred in the 1930s. Andy Cooney (IRA chief of staff, 1925–26) visited Nazi Germany with his wife in 1936 and was the first to suggest an IRA collaboration with Hitler's regime against Britain. According to post-war MI5 files, a leading Breton nationalist, Olier Mordrel, met IRA man Frank Ryan in Paris in 1937 'while the latter was on leave from the International Brigade during the Spanish civil war'. Mordrel sent a report of this meeting to the Abwehr. Also in 1937, Tom Barry – who led the flying columns in Cork during the war of independence and was IRA

The remains of the IRA bike bomb which killed five people in Coventry on 25 August 1939.
Photo courtesy of Coventry Police Museum

Leo Whelan's unfinished group portrait of the IRA's general headquarters staff, 1921.

Back row, standing, left to right: J.J. 'Ginger' O'Connell, assistant chief of staff; Emmet Dalton, director of training; Séamus O'Donovan, director of chemicals; Liam Mellows, director of purchases; Piaras Béaslaí, director of publicity.
Front row, seated, left to right: Michael Collins, director of intelligence; Richard Mulcahy, chief of staff; Gearóid O'Sullivan, adjutant general; Eamonn 'Bob' Price, director of organisation; Rory O'Connor, director of engineering and O/C Britain; Eoin O'Duffy, deputy chief of staff; Seán Russell, director of munitions; Seán MacMahon, quartermaster general.
Photo courtesy of National Museum of Ireland

German spy Hermann Görtz is buried in a Swastika-draped coffin at Dean's Grange cemetery, Dublin, on 26 May 1947. Three days earlier, he had committed suicide at the Alien's Office in order to avoid deportation to Germany. Jim O'Donovan can be seen in centre of the archway at top left of picture. *Photo courtesy of The Irish Times*

Above: A war of independence era grenade designed by Jim O'Donovan. Mobile phone for scale. *Photo courtesy of Defence Forces Press Office*

Left: Donal O'Donovan holds his father Jim's portrait, painted in 1922 by Leo Whelan. *Photo: author*

Jim O'Donovan (back row, fifth from left) attends an ESB managers' air raid precautions course at Griffith Barracks, Dublin, mid-January 1939. At the time this photograph was taken, O'Donovan's S-plan bombing campaign was just starting in England.

Photo courtesy of National Library of Ireland

Jim O'Donovan pictured (centre row, on left) as a prisoner at Hare Camp, County Kildare, in the aftermath of the civil war in 1924. *Photo courtesy of Michael MacEvilly*

Below: Jim and Mary 'Monty' O'Donovan pictured in Dublin in the 1950s. *Photo courtesy of Donal O'Donovan*

Jim O'Donovan, aged 22, at his M.Sc. conferring ceremony in University College, Dublin, 1919. A year later he joined the IRA's GHQ staff as director of chemicals. The photograph was used to promote his paint manufacturing business in the mid-1920s, which later went bankrupt.

Photo courtesy of Gerry O'Donovan

Jim O'Donovan's daughter Sheila holds the crucifix O'Donovan made in the Curragh internment camp in the early 1940s. The wooden cross is made from matchsticks, while Christ's figure is made from a lead toothpaste tube. *Photo: author*

A young Jim O'Donovan in 1909, aged 12, at St Aloysius' College, Glasgow (front row, third from left). He was consistently one of the top students in his class at the Jesuit school and did particularly well in English and mathematics. *Photo courtesy of St Aloysius' College archives*

Clockwise from top: Jim O'Donovan pictured at the Bridewell Garda Station in Dublin after his arrest on 26 September 1941. He spent the following two years as an internee in the Curragh camp, County Kildare. *Photo courtesy of Irish Military Archives*

IRA chief of staff, Seán Russell, pictured at an Easter commemoration in the late 1930s. *Photo courtesy of Irish Military Archives*

A *Sunday Express* exposé of Seán Russell on 30 July 1939, six months into the S-plan bombing campaign in England. Jim O'Donovan was not publicly linked to the S-plan until 1961, the year before he retired from the ESB. *Photo courtesy of National Library of Ireland*

Jim O'Donovan's parents in Drumcondra, Dublin, c. 1920.
Left to right: Margaret O'Donovan (née Brennan), Jim's sister Mary and Daniel O'Donovan.
Photo courtesy of Donal O'Donovan

chief of staff 1936–37 – had travelled to Germany accompanied by Jupp Hoven, a German intelligence agent, to seek support for IRA attacks on British military installations in Northern Ireland. (But back in Dublin, Barry's plan – proposed at the IRA convention in April 1938 – was rejected in favour of the Russell/O'Donovan S-plan to bomb England.) While Oscar Pfaus is generally taken to be the first Abwehr agent sent to Dublin (in February 1939), another person acting for German military intelligence had arrived in Ireland a year earlier. MI5 files reveal that Henri Le Helloco, head of the pre-war Breton intelligence service, was sent to Ireland in spring 1938 (by a senior Abwehr official, Friedrich Carl Marwede) 'to contact IRA leaders and report on details of their organisation'. The files note that 'it is more than probable that he [Le Helloco] used [Leon] Millarden, the Breton greengrocer in Dublin, as his main point of contact'. In his subsequent report for German military intelligence, Le Helloco named 'about six persons believed to belong to the IRA'.[2]

An immediate post-war assessment of Jim O'Donovan's links with Nazi Germany, prepared by Irish military intelligence, G2, revealed that:

> From 1937 on, O'Donovan was in touch with the Germans and was closely involved in the Held-Görtz incidents. While he was not an actual member of the IRA, he was in close contact with the heads of the organisation and acted as their intermediary with the Germans. He tried to indoctrinate the IRA with the Nazi ideology but met with little success as the outlook of the leaders of that body did not lend itself to the acceptance of Nazi doctrines.[3]

As late as February 1939, Hoven and his colleague Helmut Clissmann (both men were from Aachen and served with the German army's Brandenburg regiment during World War II, as well as acting for German military intelligence) were still in touch with Tom Barry in Dublin and also met with Moss Twomey, who had been IRA chief of staff from 1926 to 1936.[4]

Seán MacBride – who was briefly IRA chief of staff in 1936, between the Twomey and Barry leaderships – could be said to have initiated the IRA's post-World War I links with Germany. In 1929, MacBride travelled to Frankfurt-am-Main with Donal O'Donoghue to represent the IRA at the world congress of the anti-imperialist league. Hoven and Clissmann also attended the same event as representatives of the left-wing Prussian youth league (both men later joined the Nazi party).[5]

More IRA-German contacts were established by Seán Russell (IRA chief of staff, 1938–39) who was in contact with German diplomats while resident in New York in 1936. In fact, Russell's opportunistic attitude towards Nazi Germany is encapsulated in a letter he wrote to the German ambassador to the United States, Dr Hans Luther, on 21 October 1936. Writing from the Seville Hotel in New York City, Russell says:

> Your Excellency, The Government of the Republic desires me to call to your attention a news item reporting refusal by the Irish 'Free State' government of landing rights in our country for your international air service. As special Envoy to the United States and Quartermaster General of the Irish Republican Army, I am asked to express to you on behalf of my government the sincere regret of our people that the German nation, in return for past friendships to us, should be refused a right apparently conceded without question to England, the traditional enemy of the Irish race.

Invoking the memory of 'Pearse and Casement', Russell assures the German ambassador that:

> The government of the Republic and the people of Ireland are, and will continue to be, mindful of the

debt they owe to the German people and their government for assistance calculated to rid our country of that foreign rule that now uses the so-called 'Free State' as its domestic agent. That this is true is attested by the fact that our Chief of Staff [Moss Twomey], many senior officers and our best men are in jail....

Russell then gets to the nub of his missive to Dr Luther: 'Republican Ireland is disposed to, and shall be glad of the opportunity when she may, make return to her friends in Germany for valued assistance in the early days of the present phase of our fight.'[6]

In retrospect, Russell's letter takes on the appearance of an insurance policy for, or down-payment on, future German aid to the IRA in the form of arms, money, radio equipment and agents – the last three commodities were, in fact, supplied in the 1939–43 period. A cynical observer may point out that the letter had little or nothing to do with criticising de Valera's refusal to grant landing rights to German aircraft, but everything to do with establishing Russell's *bona fides* with the German administration – a sort of *laissez-passer* for future dealings with the Nazi regime. Russell probably guessed, rightly, that Ambassador Luther would forward the note, via the diplomatic bag, to Berlin. The letter resurfaced decades later in the archives of the German foreign ministry.

Just over two years later, in early February 1939 – i.e. seven months before Britain and France declared war on the Third Reich – Germany was beginning to sit up and take notice of what was happening in Ireland and more particularly the bombing campaign in England. But while the Abwehr acted swiftly in sending Oscar Pfaus to Dublin, the Nazi leadership reacted more slowly to the IRA's S-plan campaign. The Reich propaganda minister Joseph Goebbels's first mention of it came in his diary entry of 28 November 1939, over ten months after the campaign had started.[7] Jim O'Donovan, however, thought that even the Abwehr was slow off the mark:

THE DEVIL'S DEAL

It was only early in February that Germany cocked up her ears, heard something and decided to investigate. An ordinary contact [Oscar Pfaus] was sent over whose steps led him first to General O'Duffy,[8] the somewhat discredited leader of the pro-Franco Irish brigade in the [Spanish] civil war. Thence he was directed to Maurice Twomey and finally, making progress through such intermediaries, about the third of February he met Seán Russell and myself in Pete's [Kearney] house in Clontarf. He explained that his principals would be glad to meet a representative from us and discuss the possibility of assistance or at least investigate to what extent there was any community or aim or interests between us. German participation in Spain, and Guernica, were still fresh in our memory and I think the general feeling was one of caution and lack of enthusiasm. However, Germany's perennial friendliness to our country and her undoubted ability to be of enormous assistance to us in our weakness, should her aid or interest be secured, could not be overlooked. Oscar Pfaus – the toughly-built dark-haired agent who had been sixteen years in America, had an American passport and wore in his buttonhole an enamelled American flag – was invited to call back in the afternoon for our reply. It was typical of our attitude at that stage that we extended very scant courtesy to Pfaus and in a strange city let him fend completely for himself. He was a most agreeable fellow and performed his task with commendable tact and restrained friendliness. When he returned we had our answer ready. Seán Russell had said there was only one thing to do, accept the invitation as it certainly could not do harm and there was obviously only one person to go, if I would signify my willingness. Complications as to family, job or leave of absence submitted to dissolution under pressure of the circumstances and after memorising a couple of addresses in Hamburg, I said Auf Wiedersehen to Pfaus.[9]

Having been entrusted by Russell to reciprocate Oscar Pfaus's visit, O'Donovan wasted no time in preparing for his trip to continental Europe – it would be the first of no less than four such voyages in the coming seven months (his wife, Monty, would accompany him on the first and last visits). O'Donovan's hand-written timetable of this initial visit to Nazi Germany was 'reconstructed from timetables, to be filled in and confirmed from ESB records'. The outward journey took Mr and Mrs O'Donovan by bus to Dún Laoghaire where they caught the mail boat to Holyhead, then on to London and via the Dover–Calais ferry to Brussels, Cologne and Hamburg. O'Donovan's recollections of this vital first meeting with his German hosts are instructive:

> To cover my unwonted travels at this time of the year especially [February 1939], I arranged that my wife, feeling run down, should be medically advised a complete change. What better tonic than a return to Brussels where we had spent a large part of our honeymoon? The passports, of course, covered entry to Germany also, but this deception that we were going no further than Brussels precluded my purchase of Traveller's Marks so that I was horrified to find the cost of rail alone from Cologne to Hamburg was nearly £12. An uneventful journey terminated in Brussels where, at the Grand Hotel, we had a memorable meal, in which cream played such a distinguished role that one remembered it by pitiful contrast with the cream substitutes or other creamlessness of our subsequent stay in Germany [in August 1939]. In Cologne, which was en fête for a

carnival, there was only an hour or so wait between trains, but we saw groups of gaily bedecked youths, lustily harmonising, marching on the pavements, breaking against one round corners. One also preserved the last impression of the Cathedral in its perfection, never to be seen again in our lifetimes. Arrived in Hamburg, we secured very comfortable quarters in a suitably modest hotel, the Basler Hof, at which Pfaus had said he would contact me. Having effected contact at Hamburg I had to wait till next day to meet Herr Pfalzgraf [a cover name for Abwehr officer Friedrich Carl Marwede], obviously the head of a very considerable Department. So Pfaus suggested meeting Herr Kessemeir [*sic*][10] a principal in Propaganda (and the Auslands Organisation)[11] and arranged to call upon him that evening. I learnt of his connection with the Fichtebund at 30 Jungfernstieg, which was pointed out to me in the course of the day, and also the offices of amalgamated publishing houses. We arrived by car and soon had quite warmed to dapper and droll Herr Kessemeir [*sic*] and his charming blonde young wife. We discussed many matters of common interest and even got so far as to arrange for certain faked documents for use in a certain eventuality, which would have supported a political hoax of great significance. By adroit juxtaposition and the skilled application of scissors and paste, it would be possible with certain captured documents to produce photographic reproductions that would be devastating when used politically. I mention this to record that such things were done and had been brought to a very fine art indeed. I had no scrupulous hesitation in agreeing to adopt such methods. Deception in war is wholly admissible, deception of the enemy, deception even of your own people and deception of yourself as the highest consummation of the art, whereby you finally believe everything that it is expedient to believe. As it turned out, no such device was ever employed by us.[12]

After discussing 'matters of common interest' with his Nazi hosts, it was time to relax, as the IRA envoy recalled:

Herr Kessemeier proposed as a diversionary activity that we should go to the Munchan [i.e. Münchener] Brauhaus and see Hamburgers enjoy themselves. Tyrolean cabaret turns were proving popular with the vast crowds in the lofty, gilded room. There was some dancing on tables, but mostly just singing all the old folk-songs, the occupants of every table linking arms with their fellows in the famous 'Hamburg roll'. Beer flowed in abundance and as the absorbent pads [beer mats] piled up or received additional pencil ticks from the 'Ober', our self-consciousness melted away and we linked and swayed with the best of them. Before parting that night, we sobered up very correctly to put finishing touches to what we had been earlier discussing, and Kessemeier wrote out for me – I still have the slip of paper – the address under which I was to communicate with him: the name O. Leiter, being a simple disguise thought of on the spur of the moment – 'Leader'.

From the behaviour in the bierkeller, it is clear that Hamburg residents had no idea they were a mere six months or so away from a catastrophic world war. Given O'Donovan's description of the revelry, one can only guess at what Seán Russell's attitude might have been, since the IRA chief of staff was a teetotaller who attended mass daily. A 1941 MI5 document contained the following advice for identifying 'true IRA' personnel: 'Irishmen who, when they have had a glass or in the heat of an argument, say "Up the IRA" or "Down with Britain", are not likely to be members of the IRA. The true IRA do not drink and do not talk. They are religious fanatics.'[13]

O'Donovan's memoirs do not record whether he suffered a hangover the morning after when he had more Abwehr agents to meet. He recalls:

> The next morning, Pfaus and I walked from my hotel to the Esplanade Hotel, where we were immediately joined by at least two others: one tall, perfectly groomed in the most impressive of official black, and stuck to a black briefcase, pressed protectively to his side; the other small, not old but wizened as though screwed up from short-sight and with a humorous sparkle. I always thought of him later as very closely resembling my old friend Barney Mellowes. These were Herr Pfalzgraf and Prof Fromme,[14] both becomingly bespectacled: Pfalzgraf in wide dark tortoiseshell; Fromme, the interpreter and language expert, in misshapen, small-lensed, steel spectacles that occupied varying positions on his nose ... Introductions over, and Pfaus gone, we adjourned to an upstairs room having two telephones, which were immediately checked by Pfalzgraf. To my growing curiosity, he also checked about the next rooms on either side and their locks and keyholes. In the ensuing months, when my respect and regard for the Germans I had to deal with grew as I got to know them, I nevertheless had to live down and stifle the slight feeling of disappointment and unease that such precautions should be necessary.[15] I dealt with the whole IRA position as given to me by Seán Russell. I passed on in good faith what events proved to be a very roseate appraisal of their strength in personnel and

equipment, and their prospects as an organisation. As my mission was to find out the extent of German interest and, with plenary powers, to arrange if possible for co-operation and help by arms and money, I naturally said nothing that would depreciate the organisation in German eyes. The interest of the English press certainly made it easy to enhance its prestige and by many examples with which I had come equipped, Herr Pfalzgraf was duly impressed. They were not unfamiliar with the situation, however, as was obvious from their establishing the first contact, not we [sic]. Fromme knew Dublin quite well, he had even been as near to me in Shankill as Cabinteely where at a friend's house (Connaughton's) he had met various Dublin people, including Peadar O'Donnell. He was over writing a book[16] on Ireland's struggle for independence, of which – as a simple code communication by which any two books reaching me meant 'Come, we would like to see you' – I subsequently received two copies. We arranged initial co-operation and means of communication. Our radio was soon to be ready but even by letter, a complete series of forms of letters of ostensibly simple purport were arranged to convey important elementary messages. These, and the associated names and addresses, were given to me orally by Pfalzgraf, and there and then memorised. I was to keep them fresh in my own mind by frequently committing them to paper and then immediately destroying them by fire. This was probably only my own way of doing it, but it was certainly successful and, as I did it, quite safe.[17]

Jim O'Donovan's 1960s' memoirs are, as always, revealing. Whether he intended them to be taken at face value or read between the lines is a moot point. In the piece just cited, for example, he admits that during his first face-to-face contacts with the Germans in Hamburg, he conveyed 'a very roseate appraisal' of the IRA's strength. In other words, he left his Abwehr hosts with an excessively optimistic impression of the secret army's capabilities. O'Donovan was exaggerating the IRA's position, rather in the same way as he used official IRA bulletins to paint a rosy picture of the S-plan campaign, which would lead 'to victory'. He was in a difficult position at the initial meeting in Hamburg because a precipitate request for arms would expose the IRA's lack of weaponry. O'Donovan appears therefore to have played a cagey cat and mouse game with the Abwehr in order to, as he put it, 'find out the extent of German interest', while saying 'nothing that would depreciate the organisation [i.e. the IRA] in German eyes'. Russell's shopping list for arms, ammunition and money would have to await a subsequent meeting – and there would be two more such tête-à-têtes in Germany before the outbreak of World War II in September.

Kurt Haller's version of the first O'Donovan-Marwede meeting, as related to MI5 interrogators in 1946, is also revealing. He noted that

> ... both parties seem to have acted with reserve. Marwede was not convinced of O'Donovan's bona fides, and O'Donovan constantly stressed the 'democratic nature' of the IRA [Army] Council, which made it necessary for him to refer back to his Council before a definitive decision on collaboration could be reached. He emphasised from the beginning that, while the IRA would welcome German assistance, they would consider themselves only temporary allies of Germany and reserved unconditionally their freedom of action. Under those circumstances it was clear that the members of the IRA could not, as Marwede had hoped, be regarded as Abw[her] agents directed and controlled by Abw II. The IRA would not be prepared to place individual members or groups

> at Germany's disposal to carry out military sabotage operations as instructed by Abw II. Collaboration with Germany would be limited to German supplies of arms and ammunition and money, while the IRA would undertake to throw its whole weight behind Germany; operational plans would be worked out by the IRA leaders; O'Donovan further stressed that the IRA's one and only aim was the conquest of Northern Ireland; it had little interest in other military or political operations against the UK.[18]

Jim and Monty then headed homewards the same way they had come, by rail and ferry. He noted that they travelled from Dover to London on the 'morning of selection of Pope' (Pius XII was elected Pope on 2 March 1939). As he pored over the newspapers on the train, his mind must have been awash with thoughts stemming from the key meeting in Hamburg that had effectively established formal links between the IRA and Hitler's regime. Alighting from the mail boat at Dún Laoghaire, O'Donovan noted 'car not used'. In a move that would gladden the hearts of twenty-first-century environmentalists, the top IRA man and his wife took the bus home to Shankill. It had been an eventful journey, but now it was time to revert to their respective day-jobs as electricity board official and housewife.

O'Donovan's main task was to report back to Russell and the other IRA headquarters staff in Dublin. But other things were rankling in his mind too, particularly Fleet Street's claims that Germany was financing the S-plan. Looking back on these events a quarter of a century later, O'Donovan commented:

> From this first authentic account [i.e. his own memoirs] of our contacts with Germany, it is abundantly clear that the charges against Germany of having inspired and organised and equipped the bombing campaign are groundless. In fact, the

campaign was on the wane by the time the first meeting took place. Hence the sensational, pseudo-political press of England such as *News Review* and *Cavalcade* uttered the most insubstantial tales and forged the most fantastic top-secrets, but it was all grist to our mill, as the name of [the] IRA acquired almost an international status and was on everybody's lips. We, who realised our failure, were only too bitterly conscious of our shortcomings and weakness. Yet perhaps recovery might be possible under certain circumstances and it was good to have our prestige featured at inflated values. It was more surprising to find the staid and militarily well-informed *Daily Telegraph* and *Morning Post* guilty of such an error of fact and judgment as to think that Germany had had anything to do with the IRA (up to that stage).[19]

In hand-written notes detailing his first crucial visit to Germany, O'Donovan refers to the 'miserable progress' of the S-plan, adding that '… in terms of war, the advantages of the "bombing campaign", paradoxically enough, rested almost entirely with England rather than with Germany'. He admits that 'the campaign was on the wane by the time the first meeting took place' in Hamburg in early February – that is, just over a fortnight after the bombings began. Essentially, this means that despite the rousing republican rhetoric of his propaganda output – and the excessively optimistic ('roseate' was the term he chose to use) picture he painted for the Abwehr of the IRA's personnel, equipment and prospects – O'Donovan's S-plan was going nowhere fast.

It is something of a miracle that the campaign managed to continue for another year – the last recorded incidents being in London on 18 March 1940 when an unexploded bomb was found in a litter bin at Grosvenor Place, and rendered harmless. On the same day, an explosion occurred at Westminster city council's refuse depot when street litter was being dealt with.[20]

THE GERMAN CONNECTION

With no immediate prospect of money from Germany to sustain the campaign in England, the IRA decided to send Seán Russell on a fund-raising trip to America where he would liaise with Joe McGarrity, the powerful leader of the Clan na Gael organisation. Stephen Hayes from Wexford was appointed to take over as the new chief of staff when Russell left Ireland at Easter 1939. In fact, Russell would never set foot on Irish soil again and had less than 18 months to live.

To coincide with his colleague's departure for the United States, O'Donovan drafted a 'Message to America' from the IRA army council, designed to elicit much-needed funding from IRA supporters in New York, Boston and elsewhere. The opening lines are as follows: 'We are nearing the end of the war with Britain and are confident of complete success. In a few months we shall have compelled the evacuation of enemy forces from every part of our country and will be free to undertake the work of national and social reconstruction'. But O'Donovan was unhappy with the wording and rewrote the introduction to read as follows: 'The conflict with Britain is pursuing its scheduled course and we are confident of a successful outcome to our efforts. Our continued pressure will ultimately compel the evacuation of the enemy forces....' The rewording suggests that, rather than sell the idea to American supporters that 'complete success' was approaching as the IRA neared the end of its war with Britain, the party line would instead opt for a longer-term scenario whereby 'continued pressure will ultimately compel' Britain to pull out of Northern Ireland. O'Donovan must have calculated that, given 'the miserable progress of this campaign' – i.e. his assessment almost twenty-five years later – it would be more advisable not to promise McGarrity's people instant victory, but get them used to accepting a longer-term strategy instead. The 'Message to America' concluded by expressing 'the nation's deepest gratitude' for the co-operation 'of our people in America'.[21]

At around the same time, O'Donovan was busy drafting another IRA statement, this time for domestic consumption.

Entitled 'German Gold and the IRA', it was designed to counter claims by the British press that Nazi Germany was financing the bombing campaign in England. O'Donovan used the 'official pronouncement' (broadcast on a secret IRA transmitter on Easter Sunday, 9 April 1939) to take a swipe at all the usual suspects. He said the 'Expeditionary force of the IRA operating in England … is merely reversing history for a change. England had got so used to coming over to Ireland and bombing and terrorising our people, setting fire to our creameries and industries, and our public buildings, such as Cork City Hall [in 1920] etc., that it has come to her somewhat as a shock that the tables should be turned.'

O'Donovan also used the IRA broadcast to criticise the Taoiseach, Éamon de Valera – whom he describes as 'the former leader of the Irish people'[22] – and what he terms the 'discredited Twenty-six County Parliament'. O'Donovan acknowledges receipt of financial backing from Britain and Clan na Gael of America, adding: 'without the fund they have transferred to us we should hardly have been able to embark upon our present policy and certainly should not have been able to sustain it'. He then uses the broadcast to give a 'solemn assurance' that 'not one penny', 'technical help', 'personnel', 'materials' or equipment' have 'been directly or indirectly obtained from Germany' before or during the present campaign in England.[23]

O'Donovan seems to have been stung by UK press reports linking Germany to the S-plan. The IRA's Easter statement, which he penned, refers to an 'examination of seven British Sunday papers of last week', i.e. 2 April 1939, which 'reveals complete unanimity in attributing to German gold and German agitators blame for IRA activities in England'. For example, a *News Review* story referred to 'members of the IRA [as] innocent dupes of the Gestapo'. In his rebuttal, O'Donovan writes: '… in the ranks of the IRA it is safe to say that not one per cent had even heard of the Gestapo'. Whatever about his tussle with Fleet Street's line, readers of the *News Review* would no doubt have been fascinated to discover that the author of the IRA statement had met with German military intelligence agents in Hamburg just over a month earlier. They might also have been interested to learn that a fortnight after the IRA's Easter broadcast, O'Donovan would be heading to Hamburg yet again for another clandestine meeting with his Nazi hosts.

In early April, Jim O'Donovan received the prearranged 'book in the post' signal summoning him to a second meeting in Germany. This time he would travel without Monty and would also forego the train-ferry voyage, opting instead to travel in grander style aboard the Hamburg-America line's cruise ship *SS New York*. Arranging ten days' holiday from his ESB job, O'Donovan caught the liner at Cobh on Monday, 24 April 1939. It called at Cherbourg and Southampton the following day, docking at Hamburg on Wednesday, 26 April. Before his arrival in the German port city, O'Donovan had perused a lavish breakfast menu printed in German and English, which he kept as a souvenir. Years later, the menu, along with O'Donovan's travel tickets and other papers, were purchased for £100 by Seán O'Mahony, a collector of republican memorabilia, to whom the author is grateful for photocopies of these items. The menu offered virtually every breakfast combination from cantaloupes and sauerkraut juice to German pancakes, fried sea bass and smoked country sausage. It could all be washed down with coffee or English breakfast tea – but, given the nature of his mission and his republican sensibilities, O'Donovan presumably opted for the coffee.

Once the liner had docked, the IRA man had work to do, linking up once more with his principal contact, Oscar Pfaus. O'Donovan's notes on this, his second trip to Nazi Germany, do not seem to have survived, apart from the names and addresses of those he met, which he recorded as follows: 'Oscar C. Pfaus (Steindamm 22, Hamburg and Lange Reike 86, Hamburg); Dr Kessemeir [*sic*] (Jungfernstieg 30, Hamburg)'. The historian J. Bowyer Bell notes that the short visit was 'to discuss potential agents, the supply of arms in the event of war, radio sets and courier communication. The only firm result was a courier route between Brussels and London using an exiled Breton.' O'Donovan's scant notes for this period disclose that the Breton was Paul Moyse, with an address in Brussels.[24] Having completed this brief mission, O'Donovan returned to Cobh aboard another liner, the *Washington*, on 'May 2nd or 3rd'.

In addition to being furnished with the names and addresses of agents in Hamburg, the Abwehr also supplied their Irish visitor with the names of contacts in Holland, Denmark, Belgium and Portugal. Bullfrog was the codename to be used for Portugal, Bulldog for England, and Mackerel for Ireland. In his notes on the second Hamburg trip, written in the early 1960s, O'Donovan records the names of Abwehr agents, couriers and contacts as follows (addresses in brackets): Fraulein Paula Schlimbach (Goethe Strasse 4, Hamburg 21, Germany); Mrs Gerda de Fries (c/o Kiosk Rembrantsplatz, Amsterdam C, Holland); Stenild N. Moller (Brostedgaard, Kirstrup, Randers, Denmark); Edwin La Grange (Sarphatistraat 125, Amsterdam); Jacob Brinknielsen (Strandbygade 45, Esbjerg, Denmark); Paul Moyse (4 rue des Paroissiens, Bruxelles); R. S. Stamer (Lisboa, Estoril Villa, Arriga).[25]

The month of May 1939 saw over forty IRA incendiary, tear-gas and bomb attacks in thirteen English towns and cities. By mid-May, O'Donovan was making arrangements to meet his Breton contact in Brussels face to face, primarily to collect an Abwehr code needed to establish secret radio contacts between the IRA and Berlin. This time he would again travel alone, leaving Monty at the family home in Shankill. In his brief memoirs of this period, O'Donovan notes that he did not have to take leave for this weekend trip, thus keeping his ESB employers in the dark as to his clandestine IRA activities. He recalls that he 'left office for mail boat on Friday [19 May], 5.30 p.m.' From Holyhead in Wales, he caught the train to London Euston, transferring to Victoria station for the journey to Dover to board the ferry to

THE GERMAN CONNECTION

Calais. He reached Paris 'on Saturday afternoon early' and 'went to Brussels Sunday morning' to see the man whose address the Abwehr had supplied. Paul Moyse was a member of Breiz Atao, an underground movement seeking independence for Brittany; he acted as a courier for the Germans, bringing secret messages to London and elsewhere. Having collected the secret Abwehr codes, O'Donovan immediately left Brussels, returning via Lille, and taking the Boulogne–Folkestone ferry 'caught Irish mail [train from Euston to Holyhead] at about 10.30 p.m. Car garaged at Dún Laoghaire. Into office early Monday morning [22 May].'[26]

Back at his desk at the ESB head office in Dublin, Jim O'Donovan could follow the progress of his S-plan attacks in both the British and Irish newspapers. In addition to a limited use of tear-gas bombs, planted mainly in cinemas, IRA volunteers like Joe Collins and others were continuing to use the penny balloon/condom incendiary devices. In June alone, fire-bomb attacks occurred in London, Leicester, Lincoln, Birmingham and Manchester. Pillar boxes were a favourite target as mail vans inadvertently carried the bombs to sorting offices. Bridges, railways and power lines were also hit. But despite the continuing attacks, O'Donovan knew – as he revealed in his 1960s' memoirs – that 'the campaign was on the wane'. Nonetheless, he was adamant in defending his S-plan against all criticisms. These included a condemnation of the IRA campaign by the Catholic archbishop of Westminster, Cardinal Arthur Hinsley. On 29 June 1939, O'Donovan – acting 'for the staff of the army' at 'IRA general headquarters, Dublin' – wrote:

> May it please Your Eminence, We have read with pained surprise your condemnation of certain incidents in England. As a Prince of the Catholic Church we expected that, if in the assumed interests of your own country you found it necessary or desirable to use the prestige of the Church to defend your country's aggression in Ireland, you would have

> refrained from reducing religion to the level of political diatribe. We are quite certain you are aware that the Cardinal Primate of Ireland has expressly stated that the occupation of our country by the armed troops of your country is an unwarrantable act of war.

Spurred on, no doubt, by his memories of how the Irish Catholic hierarchy had sought to excommunicate anti-treaty IRA volunteers in 1922, O'Donovan goes on to lecture Cardinal Hinsley as follows:

> The Catholics of Ireland have been subjected to recurring campaigns of murder, arson and despoliation beside which the London incidents you condemn are insignificant.... We are, however, sure that you have been malignantly misquoted in your references to the 'cowardly' activities of our expeditionary force in England ... you might with better effect have used the dignity of your position to say the simple truth – 'Our country, England, has no right or title to employ its army to occupy the territory of another Nation and in our interests subsidise the subjection of its people'. [27]

O'Donovan the wordsmith was in his usual effervescent form and did not shirk from taking on the head of the Catholic Church in England, if it meant defending his 'expeditionary force' against 'vulgar altercation', including what he called 'cheap' and 'offensive' adjectives like 'cowardly'. As well as bringing the cardinal up to date on IRA thinking, O'Donovan also offered Hinsley a history lesson, citing 'the example of Cardinal Mercier when his country, like ours, was occupied by a foreign soldiery in the interests of another empire'. (Belgium's Cardinal Désiré-Joseph Mercier had spoken out against the German occupation of his country during World War I.)

One can only guess at Cardinal Hinsley's reaction to the IRA's missive. But had his eminence known of its author's upbringing, he might have had mixed emotions on learning that the Jesuits in Glasgow had produced someone who could write such an eloquent rebuttal of his episcopal pronouncements. Nevertheless, O'Donovan was stretching the argument to claim that 'the London incidents you condemn are insignificant'. He was speaking in a comparative historical context, but Cardinal Hinsley's condemnation was sparked by a series of bombings in London on 24 June. These included attacks in Piccadilly Circus and at three banks. In addition, two pillar boxes were hit and three bombs went off at Madame Tussaud's waxworks. On the same day, unexploded bombs were found at Piccadilly and in a public toilet at Oxford Circus. On 26 June, an unexploded bomb was found near a petrol dump in Coventry. As well as causing injury, the campaign had already claimed one life, and another person would die in an explosion a month later.[28]

As IRA bombs were exploding across England, the German ambassador to Ireland, Dr Eduard Hempel, was on an official trip to Berlin in June, which would prove to be his last pre-war visit to Germany. While there, he met Colonel Erwin von Lahousen, an Austrian aristocrat who was Admiral Canaris's deputy in the Abwehr. The diplomat took the opportunity to ask the spy chief 'about stories which had appeared in the Irish and British press that the German secret service [i.e. the Abwehr] was backing the IRA. Lahousen blandly assured Hempel that there was no foundation in such rumours'. Lahousen was, of course, pulling the wool over Hempel's eyes because – unknown to the diplomat – Henri Le Helloco had met IRA personnel in Dublin on behalf of the Abwehr in 1938 and, just four months beforehand (in February 1939), Abwehr agent Oscar Pfaus had met the IRA leadership in Dublin.[29]

Meanwhile, Seán Russell was arrested on 5 June in Detroit – on the basis of having made false declarations when entering the USA – and held in prison during a visit by King George VI and Queen Elizabeth to nearby Windsor, across the Detroit river in Canada. The arrest helped to raise Russell's profile among IRA supporters in the United States, where he was trying to raise funds for the S-plan. One account notes that the IRA's GHQ staff in Dublin were delighted by 'the refusal of some fifty members of the House of Representatives to attend the meeting of American legislators and the British royal couple. Protests and petitions had barely begun when Russell was released [on 8 June].'[30] The FBI had tracked Russell and Clan na Gael leader Joe McGarrity across America, staking out hotels in Los Angeles, Chicago and Detroit. One report, based on the release of US archives almost sixty years later, hinted that Seán Russell was plotting a bomb attack on the royal couple.[31] Russell would eventually leave the United States a year later, bound for Berlin.

The summer of 1939 dragged on, with the newspapers reporting IRA explosions in railway stations and pillar boxes. Wires were being cut regularly in phone kiosks and, on 26 July, one person was killed in an explosion at a cloakroom in London's King's Cross railway station. Ironically, given the decision to exclude Wales and Scotland from the S-plan, King's Cross handled most rail traffic to and from Scotland.

Jim O'Donovan's summer reading that year included a book from Germany, the signal that meant 'Come, we would like to see you'. It was time for him to pack his bags yet again and set sail for Nazi Germany. It would prove to be his last trip to the Third Reich.

8.

'OUR FRIENDS' IN BERLIN

The middle-aged man (accompanied by his wife) advanced slowly in the queue at Croydon airport, south London. It was 21 August 1939 and he was in a hurry to return to his desk job in Dublin, so that nothing would appear amiss. The British officials were checking passports as the passengers got off a flight from Rotterdam. The immigration officials were taking extra care to check the paperwork because an IRA bombing campaign in English towns and cities had been continuing at that stage for seven months. Just four weeks earlier, one person had been killed in an IRA explosion at London's King's Cross railway station in London. Tensions were running high.

The uniformed passport controllers could not have guessed that the smallish, brown-haired man approaching them was a senior IRA leader who had devised the sabotage plan that was currently causing death and destruction across England. Jim O'Donovan's name did not appear on any wanted list in either Britain or Ireland, and there was nothing that marked him out from the other passengers, apart, that is, from the fact that he wore a glove to hide his badly maimed right hand. Twenty years earlier, O'Donovan had been the IRA's top explosives expert, fighting in Ireland's war of independence as a leading member of the secret army's headquarters staff. And, as far as he was concerned, he was still fighting the same fight in 1939, but this time on English soil.

Given the friction that existed in late 1939 between the colossal tectonic plates that were the British empire and the Third Reich, the IRA leadership was ever keen to enlist the help of Nazi Germany as a useful ally against England, the ancient enemy. To this end, O'Donovan was on that very day returning home from a top secret meeting in Berlin, where he had discussed matters of common interest with agents of Germany's military intelligence service, the Abwehr (specifically Abwehr II, which maintained links with disaffected minority groups within nation states, including Bretons, Flemish, Scottish and Welsh nationalists, as well as the IRA). Unbeknownst to the authorities in either Dublin or London, O'Donovan had, since February, made three clandestine trips to Nazi Germany and a fourth to Brussels to meet a Breton courier working for the Germans. But he had sailed close to the wind, returning home just ten days before Hitler invaded Poland on 1 September, thus provoking World War II (Britain and France declared war on Germany on 3 September 1939).

O'Donovan was becoming nervous as he approached the immigration desk, worried that he might be asked to sign something, in which case the officials would notice the glove that masked his deformed right hand, which still contained old shards of shrapnel and from which two and a half fingers were missing. If the British had records of old IRA men and their disfigurements, the cat would be out of the bag.

Three days earlier, on Friday 18 August, Jim and Monty O'Donovan had begun their outward journey to the continent in Cobh, boarding the transatlantic liner *Washington* which had sailed from New York. It was hardly a coincidence that the head of Clan na Gael (the IRA's main benefactors in America) was also on board, as O'Donovan recalls: 'via *Washington* with Joe McGarrity and daughters on board, but without recognition except when I walked to Le Havre (leaving M[onty] on board) and passed him on a dock bridge making salutation only.'[1]

In fact, the Clan na Gael leader and the ESB man were both heading for Germany. Historian Seán Cronin notes that McGarrity 'went to Germany on a holiday with some of his children, reforged old links, made new friends, and slipped across the Baltic to Sweden as the invasion of Poland began. From Gothenburg he sailed to America.'[2] But another historian, Mark Hull, hints that McGarrity was also heading for a meeting with German military intelligence. Professor Hull notes that aboard the liner O'Donovan and McGarrity 'pretended not to recognise each other though they were, in fact, representing two symbiotic factions in the meeting with Germany: the IRA and the Clan na Gael.' Professor Hull also notes that, on his return home, McGarrity wrote to one of his German hosts: 'A great country and a fine people, hope all are tending to their task. Now is the day and now is the hour.'[3] Professor Eunan O'Halpin notes that: 'Between February and August 1939 Jim O'Donovan made three trips to Germany to meet the Abwehr. Clan na Gael's Joe McGarrity attended one of these.'[4]

As it happened, O'Donovan's last meeting with the Abwehr agents almost failed to get off the ground. This was owing to a heavy-handed approach by German customs officers at Hamburg when the O'Donovans disembarked from the liner. Donal O'Donovan recalls that his mother 'had a row' with the customs people. 'She was a smoker and she had concealed 20 cigarettes in her bag. They strip-searched her which annoyed both of them very much. It turned her off Germany.'[5] Jim O'Donovan's anger over the strip-searching incident (which is never referred to in his memoirs) boiled over when he met his Abwehr contact Oscar Pfaus, who remembered that the IRA man 'mocked the swastika flag, the brown party uniform, ridiculed the "cadaver-like obedience" of the

German Wehrmacht and doubted that such soldiers could be fit for war. Everything about Germany got on his nerves.' Their German hosts tried to repair the damage by booking the O'Donovans into a luxurious Berlin hotel and presenting them with gifts.⁶

After travelling by rail from Hamburg to Berlin, Jim and Monty checked in at the exclusive Rüssischer Hof hotel in the city's Georgenstrasse. The middle-aged couple did not attract any undue attention as they made their way to room 307. The hotel, which did not survive the wartime bombing, was a giant five-storey edifice with hundreds of rooms. Guests were luxuriously accommodated and could avail of coach tours of Berlin by night, as well as the former royal palace, Sans Souci, in nearby Potsdam. But O'Donovan would have no time for sight-seeing in Berlin because he had a round of meetings lined up with his contacts in the Nazi regime. He identified two of the Abwehr men in notes written twenty-five years later as Herr Neumeister, 10 Wichmann Strasse, Berlin, and Dr Schwendy, 2 Heinrichstrasse, Berlin.

The German military intelligence officers considered O'Donovan to be a prime acquisition. Documents discovered after the war – most notably the Abwehr war diaries of Admiral Canaris's deputy, Major-General Erwin von Lahousen – describe the ESB official as the *Haupt-V-Mannes der Abw. II in Irland:* Abwehr II's chief agent in Ireland. Lahousen's war diary rather injudiciously names the agent, in brackets, as Jim O'Donovan. Others are also named, including Seán Russell, who is described as *der Irenführer Shen Russel* [sic], i.e. the Irish leader, Seán Russell. Jim O'Donovan's diplomat brother Colman is indirectly mentioned in the diary, though not by name.⁷

In March 1940, Abwehr agent Franz Fromme was preparing to arrange the transit of Seán Russell from America to Berlin for a face-to-face meeting with Hitler's foreign minister, Joachim von Ribbentrop (the meeting took place on 5 August 1940). At the end of March, Fromme made contact with Colman O'Donovan at the Irish Legation in Rome to enquire about his brother Jim. The diplomat was unaware of his brother's involvement with German military intelligence, still less the fact that ex-IRA chief of staff, Seán Russell, was about to arrive in Italy in four weeks' time.[8]

Colman O'Donovan was later posted to Portugal as Ireland's first ambassador there. According to his nephew, Donal O'Donovan, 'the secretary of the department [of External Affairs] Joe Walshe didn't want Colman O'Donovan in Dublin any more, so he sent him packing to Lisbon…. He was given some money and told to arrange his own legation premises, as well as hiring a secretary.' In the event, O'Donovan paid his own daughter to do the secretarial work.[9]

The Abwehr II chief, Erwin von Lahousen, presumably never envisaged a German defeat or that his secret diary would fall into Allied hands, hence the liberal use of agents' names, including Jim O'Donovan's. But despite the high rank his Berlin hosts accorded O'Donovan, the IRA man considered himself to be on an altogether higher plane. Far from being a German agent, O'Donovan saw himself as a 'plenipotentiary' with 'plenary powers' to negotiate with Hitler's regime on behalf of the 'government and people of the republic of Ireland' (the terms he uses in his unpublished memoirs). His son, Donal O'Donovan, considers the plenipotentiary tag as 'pretentious', adding: 'Plenipotentiary, my God … he was deluded because he certainly wasn't anybody's plenipotentiary. It's very strange.'[10]

O'Donovan may have been living in cloud-cuckoo land but his personal perspective of his role was deadly serious. He had never accepted the 1922 handover of power from the IRA HQ staff (of which he was a member) to the new government and, thus, did not accept the notion of civilian control of the army. In addition, he claimed that the second Dáil had never met, as intended, on 30 June 1922 to dissolve itself and formally transfer powers to the third Dáil.[11] But such nit-picking would have been lost on the Abwehr agents, whose only interest was in manoeuvring rebel groups – in Ireland's case, the IRA – and, where possible, using them to instal puppet regimes. The Nazis were adept at playing a double game, anyhow; they had a diplomatic mission in Dublin which dealt with de Valera's government on a daily basis. But German military intelligence was quite prepared to deal with O'Donovan and Russell as quasi-official Irish representatives. (German foreign office trouble-shooter, Kurt Haller, told MI5 in 1946 that 'the Germans, by playing a double game – supporting the IRA on the one hand and wooing the Irish government on the other – made both policies half-hearted in execution'.)

A year after O'Donovan's final visit to Berlin in August 1939, Seán Russell was in Berlin and met the German foreign minister, Joachim von Ribbentrop – the highest level meeting ever held between IRA representatives and the Nazi regime. On 4 August 1940, the Abwehr reported that Frank Ryan had arrived in Berlin (having been released from prison in Spain shortly before). On the same day, unknown to Ryan, a conference was held by Foreign Minister Ribbentrop, which was attended by Abwehr chief Admiral Wilhelm Canaris, his deputy Erwin von Lahousen, Edmund Veesenmayer of the foreign office and Seán Russell representing the IRA. (On 7 August, Russell and Ryan were to sail from Wilhelmshaven aboard a U-boat bound for Ireland.)[12]

Meanwhile, O'Donovan was in a fairly strong position in Berlin because his German hosts were fully aware that the IRA's bombing campaign in England was still ongoing. Later that year, Hitler's propaganda minister, Joseph Goebbels, would note the IRA attacks in his private diaries. Meanwhile, Goebbels instructed his radio teams to play up the attacks in English cities, as well as highlighting the treatment of IRA prisoners in British jails. But the treatment of IRA prisoners in the 26 Counties, including executions, never merited any mention. This was because Irish neutrality suited the German war aims at that time, and so the Berlin propagandists tried to avoid upsetting de Valera. In late August 1939, Germany and Britain had little time left before both countries would be at war. In theory, this should have been to the IRA's advantage.

The plush surroundings of the Rüssischer Hof hotel in Berlin belied the reality of what was going on. The O'Donovans had travelled far to get there, but the Germans made no allowances for a lie-in on Sunday morning, 20 August.[13] Leaving his wife to enjoy 'breakfast in bed, as her arrangements were purely social and less exacting', Jim O'Donovan chose to have his 'breakfast alone in the cool, green brilliance of the trellised and open-air court, which is one of the attractions of the Rüssischer Hof'. At 9 a.m. a 'spruce and youthfully moustached' German diplomat called Neumeister called to collect the Irishman. Neumeister had worked in the diplomatic service in Japan and O'Donovan found his English to be 'impeccable … he was never stuck for a word'. When O'Donovan complimented the German on his command of English, Neumeister replied: 'Helped no doubt by my American wife.'

O'Donovan may have felt ill at ease because he told the German, 'I envy you your facility in languages: Japanese, English, French and the rest. It is galling to me, in a mild way, to have to use and propagate the language of the very country whose bonds with us we are trying to loosen rather than make fast.' Neumeister offered to speak German to O'Donovan 'supplemented by whatever other languages you have,' but O'Donovan declined the idea, adding that he was 'afraid it would slow up our exchanges too much. Besides it is not right to use you on this occasion for a mere language lesson.'[14] So the IRA man and the Nazi chose to use the language of their common enemy, with Neumeister endorsing its usefulness: '… the desire to acquire languages can be an exaggerated one. Waiters, hotel managers acquire what appears to be a fair grasp of a language, but analyse it and you'll find it never can become a medium of thought exchange. Such language knowledge is worthless when you possess an international language such as English.' The two men drove to Neumeister's flat in Wichmannstrasse and from there to the Heinrichstrasse flat of another Abwehr agent called Schwendy.

O'Donovan's pen-pictures of the agents he met are instructive. Neumeister's viewpoint was 'always very definite yet always posed with the most agreeable insistence, a smile always hovering unformed but ready to disarm and humanise his smooth urbanity.' Schwendy, by contrast, had an 'enormous neck and fine head almost devoid of hair'. The five[15] men in the room included 'a young Nordic of magnificent figure, with perfectly drilled blond hair, pale handsome face (nothing gross) almost ascetical, with the most exquisite light grey suit, perfect tie, white shirt with just the correct amount showing gold cufflinks – altogether the most elegant person I have met in my life.'

O'Donovan could spot style when he saw it and was no stranger to cutting a dash himself. (The IRA men who were to be incarcerated with him in the Curragh internment camp from 1941 to 1943 recalled in later years that he cut a 'dapper' figure, often wearing an expensive overcoat and silk cravat.) But this was Berlin in the balmy, pre-war August of 1939. The IRA leader had stepped into the lion's den to do business that he and his IRA headquarters colleagues considered might be of benefit to them. The Nazis, for their part, were keen to talk to him, and O'Donovan was in ebullient mood. After all, he still had two years to run before he would, in his own sardonic words, pay 'the inevitable price of all this fun'.

As Neumeister took his leave, O'Donovan joined the Germans at a table near the window and recalled that with the 'politeness over, we settled down to the most serious discussion, their attitude so unrelievedly sober and earnest that I cannot recall one single pleasantry during the course of over three hours' discussion.'

O'Donovan detected a certain 'tension' in the room which he could neither define nor explain, but he was glad that the Abwehr men's

> ... sympathy with my objectives was obvious and sincere.... All my previous discussions [i.e. on his earlier two visits to Hamburg in February and April] had been academic and leisurely by contrast with the immediacy which seemed to invest this morning's talks. I did not know the rank or status of those with whom I talked so freely but felt ever so much nearer

the operational stage as distinct from intelligence and propaganda.

O'Donovan could not discern the reason for the tension at the secret meeting in Berlin, but noted that 'factual issues alone were discussed and it was left to Neumeister later, merely on the conversational level, to sound me [out] … as to England's probable reactions in the event of war'.

For three hours, O'Donovan faced a continual 'bombardment of questions and queries, all deadly apposite and knowledgeable' from the German agents whose faces appeared 'strained and flushed'. The IRA/Abwehr conference

> … was continuous over the whole morning. There were constant comings and goings [and] occasionally a strange face would come in for a few minutes and earnest rapid conversation ensue. Occasionally one or two would be absent from our round table while a particular individual was discussing a certain point with me in a specialised way … telephones were busy in the next room but I was definitely the centre and focal point of this room – for that day it was definitely the *Irland* room.

It was with some relief that O'Donovan saw Neumeister return to take him to lunch. Monty O'Donovan had spent the morning sight-seeing in Berlin. Now Mrs Neumeister would join them to make a foursome for lunch at their Berlin flat. O'Donovan noted the lunch protocol in detail:

> Grace before and after the meal was a very formal matter. Everything was simple and the serving maid deft and neat.… [The lunch] consisted of a dish of fresh green beans, a very small length of porksteak or veal, and baked potatoes, followed by a cup of coffee, somewhat *ersatz*, without trimmings. This was the one-course meal adopted for Sundays. It was the

principal meal, in this case of the highly salaried class. One felt it was being consumed with a quiet pride – a meal that was a gracious offering. The sacrifice was conscious, well directed and not over-laboured.

After lunch, the quartet strolled 'in the sunshine to the Tiergarten which presented a perfect picture of crowded colour, animated and gay, in the many tiers of seats spread round in front of the bandstand.' O'Donovan listened to four trumpeters performing with a band: 'Their silvery blare in a perfect synchronism attained a maximum effect. The perfection of the performance was arresting.' He recalls 'listening to the music, caressed by the sun and watching the people – some solidly enjoying the music, others frankly ignoring it or using it as a background, children eating ices and in constant motion, the time passed pleasantly until the hour of my resumed conference approached.' O'Donovan noted that Mrs Neumeister had a limp and made slower progress than the others. Then it was time for the IRA man to rejoin the Abwehr agents, bidding goodbye to the ladies and 'arranging to meet at a café on Unter den Linden at the Friedrichstrasse crossing at about 6 o'clock. We were then to dine and catch the train homewards.'

On the way back to Schwendy's apartment, both men discussed the possibility of war and England's reactions. '"Do you think England will fight us?" asked Neumeister. I replied at once, not pontifically but because I was saturated with this whole subject at the time: "She will undoubtedly not undertake it lightly or with enthusiasm but I should think her reaction would be, if war is to come sooner or later, then it had better be now rather than in five years' time, because by then Germany will have consolidated her position and prestige in Europe and will have ironed out internal opposition by her solidly established security."'

Even allowing for the fact that these words were penned approximately twenty-five years after the events they describe, O'Donovan's words are revealing. He is virtually telling his Nazi hosts that Britain will not stand idly by and will take up the cudgels against Germany in the event of war. He contends that if war is delayed until August 1944, Germany would be a harder, almost unassailable, opponent. He could not have guessed that in five years' time Hitler's regime would be only eight months from total defeat and that the Third Reich would lie in ruins. But O'Donovan was hardly being prophetic in predicting that in five years' time Germany would have ironed out its internal opposition, since by August 1939 all political opponents – including socialists, communists and Röhm's SA faction within the Nazi Party – had been effectively eliminated.[16]

The top level IRA-Abwehr meeting resumed at 3 o'clock but O'Donovan recalls that 'only one outstanding incident merits recording. That incident was the highlight of my whole visit. One of our number rejoining us, sat down and gravely announced: "There is to be war. Probably in one week".' The IRA man was nonplussed:

> Why I, a stranger, due to leave Germany in a few hours, should be included in this confidence I have never fathomed. The news seemed to click in my brain and from all the proximate and immediate talk about war and war preparations there was a sudden startling pressure in this switch over to reality. That was all I heard – no details were vouchsafed and, from the general conversation in German, I gleaned nothing.

What had prompted the Germans to reveal their war plans to O'Donovan, if, indeed, they had? He may have misheard a comment made in German, or the Abwehr might have wished to gauge his reaction. They may also have wished to mislead their Irish guest, hinting at war with Britain, whereas the tanks would be heading for Poland on 1 September, just 12 days later (not 'in one week' as they told O'Donovan).

For his part, the Irish state employee knew that in meeting secretly with Abwehr personnel in Berlin, he was playing for very high stakes. If Germany pulled off a blitzkrieg invasion of Britain, O'Donovan and Russell could stand to reap the benefits, perhaps acting as pro-German quislings in a forcibly united Ireland – always assuming that de Valera could be toppled in a coup d'état and that the Irish army would not put up a fight (two major assumptions that the IRA leadership could not count on). It can have been no coincidence that the man behind the plan to bring Seán Russell and Frank Ryan to Ireland aboard a U-boat just twelve months later was none other than Dr Edmund Veesenmayer, Ribbentrop's coup d'état specialist at the Berlin foreign office.[17]

O'Donovan spent almost four hours in conversation with the German agents who, he noted with relief, were picking up the tab for his visit to the Fatherland:

> It was nearly 7 o'clock when we broke up and again with Herr Neumeister I rejoined the ladies but so late that we had to abandon thought of dinner. After a short farewell chat over a snack, we made tracks for the hotel, which was just opposite the station. I was relieved of all concern over the hotel bill, our luggage or booking; one or two unobtrusive people having done everything for us. We were shown to a twin-bedded stateroom on the waiting train, the guard handled all our tickets and passports so that we should not be disturbed at the frontiers and after final benedictory words we said goodbye to all our German friends through Herr Neumeister.

O'Donovan's thoughts were agitated as his train pulled out of Berlin's Friedrichstrasse station. The events unfolding outside the carriage windows now took on a fresh perspective, given what the Germans had revealed of their war plans:

> What I saw acquired a new significance in the light of the momentous news that still surged through my brain. Emerging past the marshalling yards we passed

whole train loads of artillery on the move. The trucks seemed only bare, low-slung chassis of forty or fifty feet in length, upon which were mounted, snout to the sky, long slender guns, with armed soldiers on guard at each corner of the trucks, silhouetted against the now greening sky. They were on the march already and seemed headed east!

When Jim and Monty O'Donovan began their long journey home to Dublin, the IRA man had much to ponder. As dusk descended, he remembers

> ... sinking back after a tiring day and luxuriating in the comfort provided, but my thoughts were riotous. My mind refused to grasp the reality of what I had heard. I was due to return via London. What would the English not give to possess just that much definite information? With my background, they could not fail to accept my story as being completely genuine, and what an advance it would represent on all the reports from their agents and foreign representatives.

As his train sped through the night, O'Donovan could not resist indulging in some fanciful projections, visualising what might lie in store if England was the loser in a war with Germany:

> And so my mind played with one facet after another of the tremendous significance of it all. I had then no doubt in the world that my own country at last would become a place worth living in and living for, a virile entity, freely functioning in a noble European federation, instead of the miserable, misshapen land of decay and hopelessness that we knew and still know.

O'Donovan's words amount to a damning indictment of his erstwhile comrades, Cosgrave and de Valera, and their stewardship of the country for the past seventeen years. Clearly, he thought that he could have done a better job and, given half the chance, would seize an opportunity to do so. In retrospect, his desire to see Ireland 'freely functioning in a noble European federation' appears prescient since the Republic of Ireland eventually joined the European Communities in 1973. However, Hitler's vision of a 'new European order' – a recurring theme in Nazi propaganda – which is what O'Donovan may have been thinking of in 1939, was of course a recipe for Nazi domination of the continent. In such circumstances, Ireland could possibly have achieved unification, but only as a satellite of Berlin. Therefore, O'Donovan's admission that, in August 1939, he 'had no doubt in the world that my own country would at last become a place worth living in and living for, a virile entity', can be seen principally if not exclusively in the context of a German victory. Given his background, one can appreciate O'Donovan's desire to see a united Ireland free of British influence, but he fails to explain how this could be achieved in 1939 or 1940 without Nazi influence. A casual observer could be left with the impression that he was being disingenuous and, as such, had no objection to some German influence in Irish affairs if it delivered a united Ireland and a defeated England. Since his memoirs were written in the 1960s, a person of O'Donovan's intellectual capacity cannot have been unaware of the nature of Hitler's dictatorship and what had transpired in Nazi-occupied Europe from 1933 to 1945.

With war looming, O'Donovan knew that his moment of destiny could be approaching. But he had some hurdles left to jump if he was to return to his desk by Tuesday morning without attracting suspicion that he was something more than a humble employee of the Electricity Supply Board. His problems began when the Berlin train arrived at the Dutch port of Flushing and O'Donovan found that the 'only shipping connection would miss Irish mail [train] at Euston and land me in a day late for office return date'. This was the overnight train from London to Holyhead, which connected with the mail-boat to Dún Laoghaire.

'OUR FRIENDS' IN BERLIN

He had used the same route to return from Hamburg in February and from Brussels in May. O'Donovan now had to do some quick thinking since nothing must seem untoward when he got back to his desk at the ESB. With the air of a schoolboy on a precarious weekend pass, he coyly wrote, 'It was imperative that I should be back in my office upon the expiry of my leave.' Did the IRA man suspect that he was under surveillance by the gardaí or by his employers? Whatever the case, he now had to cut corners to get back to Dublin on time and so headed by rail from Flushing to Rotterdam to catch a cross-channel plane.

O'Donovan recalls his angst, as he had never flown before, in vivid detail:

> It was raining when we reached Rotterdam and selecting one of the buses that seemed littered round the circle in front of the station, we made our way to the KLM offices in the city where we joined a cosmopolitan crush of baggage and intending passengers. By this time, a thunderstorm had broken and a torrential rain was mirrored in the frequent lightning flashes. Reports were coming in of planes late and delayed, and altogether the prospects were most discouraging. Soon we transferred to the airport, however, and after a further brief wait we were the guests of KLM and climbing rapidly. I had always pledged myself that I would not travel by air without being first heavily insured. Yet here I was on my first flight, uninsured and taking off in the midst of a violent thunderstorm. So much for peace-time planning and war-time action. After some minutes, the storm broke and brilliant sunshine revealed to me one unforgettable picture, just as we left land behind – the colour of the bulb fields and canals of Holland fringed by the lacy-edged blue of the sea. A couple of years later when I was paying the inevitable price of all

this fun, I painted a watercolour of that memorable glimpse.

O'Donovan's reminiscences are revealing in a number of respects. Firstly, it is clear that he considers himself to be operating in wartime, even though his return trip predated the outbreak of World War II by thirteen days. He was of course referring to the state of war that existed between what he termed his 'government' and England. Secondly, his concern for his own safety and the need for travel insurance contrasts with his lack of concern – there is not a single word of regret in any of his written material – for the victims of the IRA's 1939–40 bombing campaign that he had devised. Thirdly, his phrase 'paying the inevitable price of all this fun' is a reference to his internment in the Curragh camp from 1941 to 1943. The wording suggests that, having heeded Russell's call to resume active IRA service in August 1938, he fully expected to be caught eventually.

As it turned out, O'Donovan's frustration about things German – which he voiced privately to Oscar Pfaus but not in his post-war memoirs – had a grain of truth in it. Despite the day-long talks in Berlin, the Abwehr agents forgot to provide their Irish guest with a code for exchanging secret radio messages when he got home. As a result of this oversight, the Brussels-based Breton courier Paul Moyse – whom O'Donovan had met earlier in the year – was dispatched to London with the code. O'Donovan began his secret radio transmissions to Nazi Germany on 29 October 1940.[18]

Kurt Haller's recollections of the final IRA-Abwehr conference in Berlin are somewhat different to O'Donovan's – but it should be recalled that the German's date from 1946, while the IRA man's were written in the early 1960s. According to Haller's MI5 file:

> The meetings were held at Neumeister's flat in Berlin, and the atmosphere was more friendly than had been the case during the first meeting. The IRA man again asked for German support for the occupation of Northern Ireland, while Marwede [a top Abwehr

officer] requested concentration, for the time being, on smaller military targets in Northern Ireland and Great Britain. The Germans tried to stall O'Donovan over Northern Ireland, but did not refuse point-blank, nor did O'Donovan altogether refuse IRA participation in attacks on military targets, but no real agreement was reached on this fundamental point. A large part of the discussions dealt with tech[nical] details. It transpired that O'Donovan was ordnance offr [officer] and QMG [quartermaster general] of the IRA and seemed most interested in obtaining delivery of weapons, amn [ammunition] and explosives. In particular, he requested amn for a certain calibre Colt revolver. His demands were on a very large scale and could not be met from the limited supplies available to Abw[ehr] II.

Haller told his MI5 interrogators that 'the following agreement was eventually reached' at the final IRA-Abwehr meeting:

> In principle, co-operation between IRA and Abw II.
> No operations would be undertaken until war between Germany and Great Britain had broken out. Until then the IRA was to remain in a state of readiness. Operations were to be started only on receipt of express instructions from Germany, and would be concentrated on strictly military targets in Northern Ireland and Great Britain. In the political sphere, subversive activities would be undertaken by the IRA. No detailed targets were given to O'Donovan, but he was told that the British aircraft industry should have priority whenever possible.
> Germany promised to deliver weapons, amn and explosives. The exact quantity was not defined. It was intended to land a cargo on the south or north Irish coast, but arrangements were to be left to the IRA. As

additional explosive, potassium chlorate was to be smuggled into Eire, being shipped from Hamburg, disguised as flour, to a bakery or flour-mill in Limerick.

The IRA would receive financial support from Germany. The exact amount was not laid down.

An immediate WT [wireless telegraphy] link between Germany and the IRA would be instituted.

It was agreed that a courier service should be arranged. For purposes of identification, about five or six slips of paper, torn irregularly through the middle, were exchanged, each party retaining one half.

O'Donovan demanded that the Germans should use his address as the only point of contact with the IRA. They were not to attempt to penetrate the IRA by other agents.[19]

And so we return to the man moving cautiously towards the immigration desk at Croydon airport in late August 1939. O'Donovan now had to pass his sternest test, coming face to face with the enemy; it put the Abwehr meeting in the shade. Could he pull it off and slip through the net undetected? The presence of Monty at his side surely helped to portray the picture of a middle-aged couple on their way back from a holiday break on the continent. The police and other officials had no way of knowing that the person approaching them was the very man who not only had masterminded the bombing campaign currently causing havoc in English cities, but also that he was hot-foot from a top secret meeting with German agents in Berlin. To cap it all, those same Abwehr agents had disclosed that war was due 'probably in one week'.

This was a test of nerves for O'Donovan. Could he make it back to the safe cover of his day job in Dublin? He recalls:

> At Croydon, lining up with the British subjects, as opposed to the aliens, I anticipated some sticky moments passing under the surveillance of the Scotland Yard men. It was so soon after the Coventry

incident,[20] the airports were being so well watched and all Irish more or less suspect, I had a queasy feeling. Besides, for two reasons I was somewhat passport conscious. First, on account of the repeated German visas within the previous few months, and secondly because through no effort of mine, but merely due to police indifference or negligence, the entry for physical defects was left blank. Had I then any document to sign or any reason to remove my right glove under observation, the defect of my right hand might arouse suspicion as though mine had been the responsibility for concealing it.

O'Donovan's hair-raising progress through passport control at Croydon continued:

What should happen but that when my passport was opened, my photograph fell out! The explanation was simple. In a justifiable excess of patriotism, the home officials had used locally-made paste but, unfortunately, used one of the spurious brands which always spring up to crash the high tariff protective wall. However, the photograph was as like me as passport photographs ever are and so, with a smiling injunction to me to 'better get it fixed', the blue-coated official handed it back to me. I told my knees to brace up for the onward march.

On the train up to London, O'Donovan devoured the morning newspapers, which brought matters into sharper focus:

The daily papers furnished all the answers. What I had been puzzled by all through that memorable Sunday was nothing less than the minute-to-minute progress of the German-Soviet pact filtering through I do not know how many channels. So Herr Hitler *had* [O'Donovan's emphasis] swallowed his words!

> How would it all end? By what a coincidence, out of
> all the hotels, that the Rüssischer Hof should have
> been selected for us.

The so-called Ribbentrop-Molotov non-aggression pact – signed on 23 August 1939 and lasting until Germany invaded Russia on 22 June 1941 – effectively sealed Poland's fate, dividing the country between Hitler and Stalin. Poland had been sold down the river, as it would be again in 1945. O'Donovan might have guessed that he could not trust the Germans but his hatred of England – born of his experiences in the war of independence – blinded him to the dangers involved in fostering close relations with the Nazi regime. For example, when the Germans occupied Brittany and Flanders (from 1940 to 1944), they never granted those areas any measure of regional autonomy or independence, although they relied on the support of local nationalist groups. O'Donovan probably did not fully think through the logic of pursuing the Nazi gamble. It would have been sufficient for him to see England weakened or even beaten by Germany, along with a consequent decline in unionist power in Ulster. And if de Valera could be forced from office in Dublin, so much the better from O'Donovan's viewpoint, as he considered the Irish leader to be a traitor, having accepted partial independence in lieu of a 32-county republic.

For now, however, the top IRA man had slipped the British net and lived to fight another day. It was time for him to report back to work, and he would also have to brief IRA chief of staff Stephen Hayes and the other headquarters staff on his meetings in Berlin. On Wednesday, 23 August, a day after returning to his desk at the ESB, O'Donovan wrote to the head office of Dutch railways seeking a rebate for part of his and Monty's rail tickets, unused since they had flown from Rotterdam to Croydon. It was typical of O'Donovan's attention to minutiae, and he didn't seem to realise the risk involved if the Irish or British authorities had been monitoring his mail. Meanwhile, the IRA bombing campaign would continue in England, and just two days later the worst atrocity of the S-plan would unfold in Coventry.

9.

CARNAGE IN COVENTRY

Coventry's police museum is not on the normal tourist trail. Most visitors make a bee-line for the city's impressive cathedrals. The old cathedral lies in ruins as a result of a Luftwaffe raid that flattened two-thirds of the city on 14 November 1940. The empty edifice has been left as a testament to the horrors of war, and its basement hosts a blitz museum with wartime exhibits and a video showing the devastation of 1940. Right next to it is the impressive new cathedral where visitors are invited to take part in a Church of England communion service at midday. Catholic visitors opting to attend would find little difference between this high Anglican service and the Sunday Mass – certainly in terms of the language used. But one striking difference on my visit (in June 2007) was that the ceremony was presided over by a statuesque blonde deaconess, something the Catholic Church has not yet envisaged.

The city's police museum is housed in a dark basement of the police station at Little Park Street. Admission is by appointment only. A retired sergeant, Tony Rose, is the curator and warns visitors that 'It's a bit gruesome'. He's right. Nothing can quite prepare you for this museum, particularly if you are not used to confronting death. To begin with, there is the death mask of Mary Ball, the last person hanged in Coventry, in 1849 – she was found guilty of poisoning her husband. Farther on, glass cases covered by black curtains reveal a host of bizarre exhibits. There's a colour photo of what is left of a human head – someone who jumped off a tower block in despair. It's unrecognisable as a body part, more reminiscent of a squashed melon. And if you can steel yourself for more, there's always the contorted face of the man who hanged himself after a row with his wife. The visage resembles a medieval gargoyle, and the strong flex he used is still tight round his neck in the photo. The horror show continues, including the headless corpse of an Asian girl whose head was found in a dustbin. There's even a miniature guillotine constructed by a deranged man to amputate his penis. He was rushed to hospital and subsequently locked up in a mental asylum, but committed suicide on his release. It's a wonder that school children are allowed into the museum, but they are; and they get souvenir handcuff keyrings as a memento of their visit. Maybe these school trips are aimed at toughening up the youngsters for adult life.

Strangely, however, the exhibit in Coventry's police museum that claimed most lives and caused most injury is seemingly the most innocuous one. Preserved in a glass case just above the curator's desk are the tangled remains of a bicycle. It's the delivery bike whose metal front carrier was used to transport an IRA bomb through the West Midlands city on Friday, 25 August 1939. Tony Rose gingerly opens the glass case and lets me touch the bike; 'I've got your prints on it now,' he laughs. Amazingly, the smell of potassium chlorate is still strong seventy years later. An IRA man left the deadly cargo leaning against Astley's hardware store in Broadgate, the city's busy main thoroughfare. Shortly afterwards, at 2.30 p.m., the bomb exploded, killing five people and leaving seventy-two injured. The five killed were: John Arnott (16), who worked at W. H. Smith's newsagents; Laura Ansell (21), who was to be married two weeks later; James Clay (82), a widower; Gwylim Rowlands (50), an employee of the corporation highways department; and Reginald Gentle (31), who also worked at W. H. Smith's, and was a native of Newtown, Wales. Laura Ansell was identified by her engagement ring. She was buried in her wedding dress five days after the blast.

By 28 August, five people were still detained in hospital with serious injuries. They included 14-year-old Muriel Timms, who underwent surgery to remove a piece of steel from her leg. She walked with a limp for the rest of her life. The outrage led to a crackdown on IRA suspects by police across Britain. It also sparked anti-Irish feeling in Coventry and beyond. For example, the 28 August edition of the *Midland Daily Telegraph* carried banner headlines reporting 'Widespread feeling against Irishmen' and 'Factory requests for dismissals'. The news story pointed out, however, that 'the vast majority [of Irishmen in Coventry were] entirely innocent of any sympathy with the IRA'. The newspaper also reported that some Irish people had been asked to leave their Coventry lodgings; the number of Irish workers in the city was put at 2,000. The previous day, 27 August, the sung Mass at St Osburg's Catholic church in the city 'was offered for the unfortunate victims of the murderous outrage'.[1] As one American study of the period reveals, Irish prisoners in Dartmoor were attacked on 30 August 1939:

> Eleven of the IRA inmates were so badly beaten that they were hospitalised and, from that point on, the Irishmen were separated from their fellow prisoners … the Coventry bombing increased the amount of abuse they had to endure at the hands of their fellow inmates and prison guards.[2]

Police later learned that the bomb had been assembled in a house at Clara Street, Coventry, and the delivery bike used to carry the device had been purchased locally. By the time the device exploded, however, the bomber (Joby O'Sullivan from Cork) was on a train to Leicester and would take the mail-boat from Holyhead to Ireland that same day.

On 14 December 1939, at Birmingham crown court, Peter Barnes and James Richards were both found guilty of murder in connection with the Coventry bombing. Three co-defendants were acquitted. The men's appeal was turned down on 23 January 1940. On 7 February 1940, both were hanged at Winson Green prison in Birmingham.

One of the first rescuers on the scene of the Coventry bombing was St John's ambulance driver Ted Cross, who recalls:

> On that particular day, I didn't hear the explosion. I was actually inside our office building, reporting in from doing a removal. I went out to the ambulance and just as I got to it a police motorcyclist said 'Are you the driver of this ambulance?' I said 'Yes'. He said 'Well, follow me.' I got into the ambulance and followed him at a fair speed down Jeston Street and up White Street, up Trinity Street into Broadgate where we picked up the first of the casualties, an elderly gentleman [James Clay] that had part of the bike actually embedded in his intestines. We got him on board straight away and got him to hospital as soon as possible. He was semi-conscious and greatly shocked. Therefore, although he was moaning and groaning, he was not coherent in other ways. All I was interested in was getting the injured away from the scene and getting them to hospital for treatment. This was the most important part of my job. It was a matter of getting them to hospital as soon as possible because of their injuries ... mainly cuts from glass, shrapnel wounds from parts of the bike, bruising, people being blown over and things like that.... The

first gentleman we took, I know he passed away, although he was still alive when we got him to the hospital. I was into Broadgate less than ten minutes after the bomb had gone off. There was nothing more we could do in that way. Other people were killed but I did not see them because as soon as I got the patient to the hospital I was away, back to the scene and during that time, other ambulances had come in. They were commandeering cars to move people around if it was possible. The police kept the way clear for us to continue going round to pick up.... There was glass everywhere, and people were going around picking up rings, trays of rings and other jewellery that had come out of the window of the jeweller's shop which was next door to Astley's. They were taking them to a gentleman with a sack, just putting them all in. It was one of the things that struck me: nobody thought of pocketing anything, it was just all going into this sack.[3]

Ted Cross continued to drive his ambulance through Coventry during the Blitz and later served with the British Army in North Africa and Palestine.

Another eye-witness is Mrs Joan Cook, who narrowly survived the bomb, along with her mother and grandmother. Some seventy years later, she can recall the events vividly:

The 25th August 1939 was granny's birthday, that's why I remember it so well. I was born in 1934, so I had just had my fifth birthday and was due to start school in September, a matter of a fortnight after this happened. My granny would have been in her fifties, mother was about 32. We had all gone into town to celebrate granny's birthday. I can remember this bit very plainly: we parted company in High Street; my mother went down what is now High Street to have her hair done, while granny and I walked to the post office in Hartford Street. I can actually remember walking past this bike and obviously the bomb had got to be in it at the time.... I definitely remember seeing this bike. I must have heard it go off but at that age you wouldn't understand would you? I'm very lucky not to have been blown up really. When you think about it, a few minutes either way and I could have been gone, couldn't I? I've survived a few things, including the IRA and the Luftwaffe [laughs].... There was a lady in Green Lane, where we lived, who always walked with a stiff leg after that. My grandmother used to say she was very fortunate to be alive. She had been a teenager when the bomb went off. I can't remember her name but she had a limp. As a child growing up, I was told that happened to her on that day.

A year after surviving the IRA bike bomb in Broadgate, Joan Cook witnessed the Luftwaffe blitz of Coventry:

> I wasn't evacuated because my parents thought 'Well, if we're going to go up, we'll all go together'. I was here for all of the blitz bombs and everything. I missed an awful lot of school. I remember the big air raid on 14 November 1940. It started at 7 o'clock in the evening and we were bundled down to the air raid shelter in our back garden where we spent the rest of the night. Of course, you came out and found that everything had disappeared. That's when I was picked up on my father's shoulders to look straight across the memorial park to see the flames of the cathedral burning. I can hear my dad saying 'Joan ought to see this'. I can remember going into the cathedral – I

don't know how long afterwards, weeks I suppose – and all the rubble was still on the floor. They had a service and I can remember standing on one of the pillars that had fallen so that I could see what was going on. It was all among the rubble that had come down from the roof. My mother had taken me in there about a fortnight before, so I can remember what the cathedral looked like before it happened. She walked me all the way round and told me about this and that. They had a little corner, I think it was a children's corner, where somebody had left a child's red umbrella. I was worried to death about that umbrella. When the cathedral was burning, I kept saying 'Daddy, there's a girl's umbrella in there'. That stuck in my mind for years. I was glad that I saw the cathedral before it was bombed…. We lost the roof and the windows in our house. We went to live in Sutton Coldfield for a while, with my grandfather's brother. I lost some school friends during the war. They lived in Beechwood Avenue and a bomb dropped on their house. We used to be at school together. They were two sisters. The whole house went up; all four of them died. I was about ten years old at the end of the war. The atmosphere was totally different and food started to appear. We'd never seen oranges or bananas during the war and all that started to come back. By 1945, things started to get a bit normal. People still shared things with each other: 'I've got some butter, if you want it you can have it' – that type of thing. My dad, John Brook, was in the ARP [air raid precaution service]. He was from York and my mother was from Coventry.[4]

According to retired police sergeant Tony Rose, the original target of the IRA bike bomb may have been Coventry telephone exchange. Alternatively, the target could have been the city's power station. Jim O'Donovan's S-plan specifically refers to Coventry's 'own generating station.'[5] Sergeant Rose recalls:

> If we look at other bombings in Coventry, they all seemed to happen around telephone kiosks or round those type of buildings – either that or in Royal Mail post offices and that is what made me think this is possibly what he was targeting. In Hartford Street you have actually got what used to be the main Royal Mail sorting office for Coventry, and that used to be also the main post office in Coventry where all mail was sent out and received. This is the reason why I think he aimed for the Royal Mail place. He must have realised that, although he didn't know Coventry well from what we can gather … you could see the post office in Hartford Street from where he placed the bomb in Broadgate. The telephone exchange was behind the post office and the Royal Mail sorting office used to be behind the telephone exchange. The object of the attack may have been to knock out all the phone systems so there'd be no way of communicating to get help or assistance.… One of the five killed was a young girl who was identified by her engagement ring. She was actually buried in her wedding dress. She was only twenty-one. Four other people were killed in the blast, and over seventy were injured – some of them had horrific injuries, while others had minor ones. On show in the museum is a piece of metal that travelled two and a half miles from the city centre and went into somebody's knee bone. That shows the force of the blast; it landed up in a place called Wyken.… There were horrific sights following the explosion. Some of them had arms and legs missing. It was devastating. They picked Friday, being a busy shopping day in

Coventry. The injured were taken to the Coventry and Warwickshire hospital. People were being ferried to every single hospital where they could find somewhere to take them.[6]

On 6 July 1969, 30 years after the Coventry bomb attack, the *Sunday Times* published an anonymous interview with the man who, the paper claimed, had planted the bike bomb in Broadgate. (On the same day, Barnes and Richards were being reburied in Mullingar.) The unnamed interviewee claimed that he had worked with Frank Richards (alias McCormick, one of two people hanged for the Coventry bombing) on the bomb plot. He also claimed that Peter Barnes (the other man hanged) was innocent and had nothing to do with the affair. The newspaper reported:

> After a mere fortnight's instruction [in making explosives] he was ordered to travel to Coventry alone. 'As a soldier of the Irish Republican Army, there was nothing I could do but carry out my orders to the letter', he insists. Two days later he kept a rendezvous outside Coventry post office with his director of training. 'We strolled down the street smoking cigarettes as if we had not a care in the world. Outside Montague Burton's tailoring shop in Broadgate the other fellow stopped. 'This is where you will place the bomb', he said. 'It will be in the carrier of a messenger boy's bicycle and you'll put the bike against the kerb at 2.30.' ... The significance of the operation sank in. 'Leaving the bomb in a crowded street and killing innocent people is nothing but cold-blooded murder', he said. Coldly again he was told, 'You'll do it because if you don't you'll be court martialled and shot the minute you set foot in Ireland again.'

The 1969 newspaper article described the IRA man taking the bike bomb into Coventry:

After the cycle ride, which still gives him nightmares, the bomber dismounted gingerly opposite Montague Burton's and lodged the rear pedal hard against the pavement. It was almost 2 p.m. The alarm clock was ticking loud enough to give the game away. 'I walked off down the street as if I had a message to deliver', the bomber recalls, 'looking neither right nor left. It was 2.15 when I got to the station. The train was due to leave at 2.20 p.m.' The bomber then describes changing clothes aboard the train to Leicester. When he got to Holyhead, the police were only checking those with tickets from Coventry or Birmingham.[7]

The return of the Coventry bombers to Irish soil got somewhat different treatment in Irish newspapers. Under a banner headline 'Barnes and McCormick come home', the *Irish Press* reported the return of the bombers' remains to Dublin airport on 4 July 1969: 'An eight-man guard of honour of young men dressed in black berets, black gloves and black polo-neck sweaters flanked the hearses'. The paper noted that the chairman of the repatriation committee was Sinn Féin president Tomás MacGiolla.[8]

In its issue of 7 July 1969, the *Irish Press* was already countering the thrust of the previous day's *Sunday Times* story, which appeared to be aimed at discrediting the reinterment ceremony in Mullingar by suggesting that the Coventry bomb had deliberately targeted civilians. Under the headline 'Coventry bomber panicked', the newspaper reported that members of the republican movement were highly sceptical of the *Sunday Times* report, insinuating that the bomb was deliberately placed in a busy Coventry street. The paper quoted a 'high-ranking member of the republican movement' as saying: 'The person who was in charge of moving the explosives, which were to be used against a military installation, panicked and ran away.' The unnamed high-ranking republican also told the *Irish Press* that the *Sunday Times* report was 'full of minor inaccuracies'.[9]

Commenting on the *Sunday Times* 'bike-bomb' report some thirty-eight years later, Ruairí Ó Brádaigh told this author:

> We were all very busy on Sunday, 6 July 1969, burying Barnes and McCormack [*sic*]. I was chief marshal on that day. The attendance was estimated to be 20,000. I never read the account in the *Sunday Times*, although we heard about it. No one appeared to take it seriously. I cannot name this alleged bomber. Under its constitution no one can be a member of the IRA until aged at least 16 years. There has been no 'oath' since 1925. A simple promise or word of honour is all that is required. A 'director of training' would not be in an operational area. The alleged conversation following the meeting outside Coventry P[ost] O[ffice] is unbelievable. The instruction alleged to have been given was totally at variance with the declared policy of the IRA and was *ultra vires*. For the record, the penalty for refusing to obey an order is dismissal from the ranks of the IRA. The threat to shoot is nonsense. Members of the IRA are 'Volunteers'. Any of them can resign at any time. No one would be a member if required to carry out such instructions. The allegations made in the article would besmirch the good names of Séamus O'Donovan and Seán Russell. I understand that if there were a disregard for civilian life, much more effective sabotage could have been carried out. I do not know and never heard the true account of the Coventry explosion. One version I heard was that it (the bomb) was intended for an electricity plant and that time ran out, the person panicked and abandoned it with disastrous results. You have the list of the operations in England 1939–40 and know the record. In 1867, the Clerkenwell explosion was wholly unintended by the Fenians. In the Dynamite

Campaign of the 1880s the only casualties were the Fenians, 'Captain Mackey' and two comrades losing their lives. In 1938, three Volunteers were killed on the Donegal-Tyrone border when a mine intended for a British customs post exploded prematurely.... With fifty-seven years of experience in the Republican Movement, no one I met would have joined it if such instructions were being given. The general view of the *Sunday Times* article at the time among Republicans was that the person interviewed was either a looney or a chancer.[10]

Ruairí Ó Brádaigh's suggestion that the intended target was 'an electricity plant' is supported by O'Donovan's S-plan document which, under the heading 'Electricity', states:

In selecting these [power stations for attack] consideration should be given to the size of towns and the degree of dependence for industry on electricity.... Of all towns, Coventry would seem to be the most dependent in relation to its population.... It is not wholly dependent on the Grid as it has its own generating station.[11]

While appearing at first sight to be a blunder, it is noteworthy that the bomb exploded at 2.30 p.m. in a city centre street thronged with shoppers. If, as has been suggested, the real target was the city's power station, the attack could have been carried out at night, thus minimising the risk to the public.

On paper, the S-plan appeared to target 'commerce' and 'key industries', it also specified 'public services' including pillar boxes, postal sorting offices, buses, railways and tube stations. Refuse bins were also blown up. In addition, tear-gas bombs were planted in cinemas and incendiary bombs in hotels and department stores. All such targets involved danger to the public, as did the manufacture and transportation of explosives in cities.[12]

CARNAGE IN COVENTRY

The American historian J. Bowyer Bell notes that IRA leader Seán Russell 'sought to inflict an atmosphere of terror ... on the entire British public'.[13] The IRA's officer commanding the English Midlands region in 1939 was Belfast man Dominic Adams, an uncle of the current Sinn Féin president, Gerry Adams.[14]

In a bizarre twist of fate, the Provisional IRA bombed Coventry again on 14 November 1974 – thirty-four years to the day since the Luftwaffe had destroyed two-thirds of the city in 1940. Tony Rose was on duty that night and recalls:

> History repeated itself here when James McDade[15] tried to blow up the telephone exchange. Coventry was the main link for the telephone system in the West Midlands, so we had all the lines coming in for the West Midlands into Coventry. The reason they tried to put the telephone system out of use was because a week after this happened the Birmingham pub bombings took place, when they wrecked Birmingham city centre. There were horrific scenes over there. There were over twenty people killed.

A week after the Coventry bombing, on 21 November 1974, 21 people died and 183 were injured in two pub bombings in Birmingham. Four months earlier, Provisional Sinn Féin president Ruairí Ó Brádaigh was quoted in a republican journal as saying: 'It was inevitable that the war situation would be carried to Britain ... it is inevitable that the poison would spread – this is what happened in the Algerian war. It spread to France.'[16]

Sergeant Rose adds:

> McDade had an accomplice with him called Raymond McLaughlin. He escaped from the scene and was later captured in a place called the Bull Yard, which is about a five-minute walk from the telephone exchange. When he left the telephone exchange, he had got a gun with him, which he threw in the

bushes. The gun was later recovered and used as evidence in his trial. James McDade blew himself to pieces. His head was found outside the council house, which is just up the road from our police station. Bits of his body were round the city centre. I was on duty that night and we were going around picking up body parts and putting them in black bags. Then they came to collect what parts were left in the coffin, which had the Irish flag on it. Some 5,000 people assembled outside the mortuary at Coventry and Warwickshire Hospital. As the coffin left, it was stoned by these people. It took them two and a half hours to get the hearse out of the mortuary.

10.

THE ROAD TO INTERNMENT

After the outbreak of war on 3 September 1939, there would be no more personal visits to Germany for Jim O'Donovan. But the lines of communication would remain open via couriers, coded postal messages, a succession of agents (who were landed in Ireland by U-boat and parachute from 1939 to 1943) and, last but not least, the radio set O'Donovan kept hidden in his study. In January 1940, the IRA leadership in Dublin got a chance to send their very own personal courier to Berlin. Francis Stuart had been part of the anti-treaty IRA side since the civil war days and was familiar with Germany, having taught English there in the summer of 1939. Fleeing a failed marriage to Iseult (the daughter of Maud Gonne), the writer was happy to take up a lecturing post at Berlin University, even though the war had been under way for over four months. Stuart's new job had been arranged by Helmut Clissmann, who ran the German academic exchange office in Dublin. The German was a key link between the IRA headquarters staff and Nazi Germany, but Clissmann was not working alone.

According to MI5, files he was assisted by Jupp Hoven, a German student who had visited Ireland 'regularly since 1931' and who made 'several visits to Northern Ireland' from 1938 to 1939. MI5 noted another link in the chain was 'Theodor Rehmann, the organist of Aachen cathedral, who visited Eire early in 1939'. Clissmann was a native of Aachen.[1]

O'Donovan knew Clissmann personally and both men had met regularly during the 1930s.[2] But half a century later, Francis Stuart had a somewhat jaded view of his 1940 New Year visit to O'Donovan's south County Dublin home, 'Florenceville' in Shankill, where chief of staff Stephen Hayes was also present. Stuart recalled that the IRA shopping list comprised money, a new radio transmitter and a German liaison officer to be sent to Ireland. The writer was given a torn piece of paper to take to Berlin where the other half, held by the Abwehr, would identify him as a genuine IRA courier. Iseult sewed the piece of paper into the lining of Stuart's coat but he ripped open the lining and disposed of the paper when he reached London, nervous and angry at what he called the IRA's 'playacting like you read about in the old spy books'. With no identifying paper, the Abwehr had to summon their trusty 'Irish expert', Professor Franz Fromme, to identify the mystery visitor. In fact, Stuart had his invitation to lecture at Berlin University plus an introductory letter from the German ambassador to Dublin, Dr Eduard Hempel, but he chose to disclose neither of these documents to the Abwehr, commenting: 'Either they believed me when I got to Germany or they didn't. I couldn't care less really.'[3] Fromme was, of course, the same man who met Jim O'Donovan in Hamburg in February 1939 and who would escort Seán Russell from Genoa to Berlin six months later. Fromme also met O'Donovan's brother, Colman, in Rome in March 1940, having made his acquaintance some years before when the Irish diplomat was posted to Berlin from July 1933 to April 1935.

Despite Stuart's laid-back attitude, the writer did the IRA's bidding, carrying messages to German military intelligence, including useful information for Hermann Görtz, whom the Abwehr were planning to send to Ireland within a few months. Stuart confirmed to an American researcher that he had met the German spy in Berlin before his mission to Ireland: 'I used to meet him in Germany and I remember sitting with him in Kurfürstendam.'⁴

In fact, the IRA sent a second messenger, Stephen Carroll Held, to Hamburg in April 1940 – just weeks before Görtz's mission in May – where he met Oscar Pfaus. Held produced the matching strip of torn paper to identify that he was an IRA emissary and said he had been sent by O'Donovan. Pfaus then took Held to Berlin where he was interviewed first by Kurt Haller and later by Major-General Marwede. Held did not meet Görtz on this trip, but he did deliver an IRA plan suggesting 'a joint IRA-German military operation for the conquest of Northern Ireland', including the use of flying boats to land German troops at Carlingford Lough and other areas from which British garrisons could be attacked. The IRA's message anticipated that such a German move would be supported by 'some' of the Irish army and 'the Irish people as a whole'. Haller later dismissed the plan because 'it seemed to show the IRA as unpractical dreamers with an obstinate single-mindedness'.⁵

A month after Stuart's departure for the Third Reich, IRA men Peter Barnes and Frank McCormick (aka Richards) were hanged, on 7 February 1940, in Birmingham for the Coventry bombing of 25 August 1939. With a world war on its hands, the British government paid little heed to a letter to war secretary Anthony Eden from Taoiseach Éamon de Valera pleading for the men's lives to be spared. Dev argued that 'If these men are executed, the relations between our peoples will almost certainly deteriorate.'⁶

Hitler's propaganda minister, Joseph Goebbels – for whom Francis Stuart would begin broadcasting on St Patrick's Day 1942 – noted in his 8 February diary entry, 'Eight Irishmen executed in Birmingham. We seize on this with all our might. This gives us ammunition for several days. I keep impressing my people with one basic truth: repeat everything until the last, most stupid person has understood.'[7] Goebbels had first referred to the bombing campaign in his diary entry for 28 November 1939 as follows: 'The Irish are carrying out bomb attacks in London.'[8] The propaganda minister's diary had ignored the S-plan for the first eleven months, presumably only seeing its wider significance for Germany once the war was under way. But German military intelligence was quicker off the mark, having dispatched its agent Oscar Pfaus to Dublin in February 1939.

The day after Barnes and McCormick were executed, a U-boat arrived off Killala, County Mayo, carrying a German agent, Ernst Weber-Drohl. The 61-year-old arthritic spy had been to Ireland before, performing under his stage name of Atlas the Strong. But this visit was more unconventional because he was carrying cash, a radio transmitter and instructions for the Abwehr's chief Irish agent, Jim O'Donovan. Weber-Drohl lost the radio set when his dinghy overturned, but managed to reach O'Donovan's home 100 miles away in Shankill, County Dublin, handing over $14,450 'and passed along the request for an IRA liaison officer to be sent to Germany'.[9]

By March 1940 O'Donovan's S-plan campaign was on its last legs, petering out with a few damp squibs in London. In any case, with World War II under way, the IRA leaders no doubt reflected that the Germans would soon be doing a better job of attacking Britain than they could ever muster.

On 5 May 1940, two parachutes opened in the skies over County Meath. One carried a radio set while the other carried a German spy clad in Luftwaffe uniform. His name was Hermann Görtz.[10] Görtz believed that by wearing this outfit (he had been a pilot in World War I) he could claim prisoner of war status if arrested and thus avoid execution as a spy.[11] In fact, he was to remain at large for the next eighteen months. A nervous farmer saw the parachute drop and was even more startled when Görtz pulled a pistol on him. The German asked if he had landed in

THE ROAD TO INTERNMENT

Northern Ireland, to which the farmer reputedly answered: 'Would you happen to know Ballivor?' Thus ended the brief encounter between a bewildered Meath farmer and the so-called master spy.[12]

The German airman then set out on a long hike, taking forty-eight hours to travel by night – he hid during the day – from Ballivor to the only safe address he knew in Ireland: Laragh Castle, the south Wicklow home of Francis Stuart's estranged wife Iseult. The Irish writer had met Görtz in Berlin and gave him the address. Reflecting on the incident fifty years later, Stuart told this author: 'I gave him my own address as a safe house to use as a last resort, but he went there first.' Unwittingly or otherwise, Stuart had placed his wife in danger. She was arrested on 24 May, along with an IRA contact, Stephen Held, who had secretly visited Germany in April 1940. Held's mission was to deliver Plan Kathleen, the IRA's outline for the invasion of Northern Ireland.[13] Iseult then spent five weeks in prison before being cleared of all charges through lack of evidence.[14] When Görtz first arrived at Laragh, Iseult wasted no time in phoning Jim O'Donovan, who came by car to collect the German agent. The spy's arrival was no surprise to the IRA man, who had been in nightly contact with the Abwehr via his secret transmitter.[15]

According to O'Donovan's son Donal, when the spy turned up on Mrs Stuart's doorstep

> ... she was terrified because she didn't want a raid by the special branch. She rang my father and told him that this man had turned up – a weird-looking tall man in a Luftwaffe uniform, if you don't mind, with a .32 automatic and a parachute knife of great beauty. I got a present of both of these afterwards, that's why I remember them so well. My father went down. He had a big 50-gallon tank of petrol buried in the garden and he was able to use that. You weren't otherwise encouraged to use your car. You could be asked where you were going. So he went down and

got Görtz and brought him back to my bed for the night. I was at school and my bed was vacant, so he put him in that for the first night. Then they devised a way of keeping him in the stable at night and under a eucalyptus tree in the orchard by day. My mother would bring his meals out to him. All this was going on and we'd no idea. We did not even see the man.[16]

In his coded diary, Görtz recalled that in the days immediately after his arrival 'Mrs [Iseult] Stuart, Miss Helena Maloney and [Jim] O'Donovan had saved me'. He also revealed that O'Donovan was driving him around to various safe houses in Dublin.[17] The existence of a completed Görtz diary is due to the ingenuity of Dr Richard Hayes, the director of the National Library of Ireland, who worked for Irish military intelligence, G2, as a code-breaker during the war. Following Görtz's arrest in November 1941, he was eventually locked up in Athlone barracks. Having broken a sample of Görtz's code, Dr Hayes and G2 linguistic expert Joe Healy (on secondment from University College Cork) hatched a plot to dupe the spy into believing he was getting covert messages from Berlin. Görtz agreed to provide a detailed account of his Irish adventures for the Abwehr, under the impression that his messages would be smuggled out by a sympathetic guard. After a plausible interval, 'Berlin' would reply to Görtz seeking more information, and so it continued until G2 knew pretty much everything about Görtz's failed mission.

There is reason to believe that the Irish authorities knew quite a lot before they decoded Görtz's fresh diary entries. This is because the papers of Colonel Éamon de Buitléar (deputy head of G2) contain a list of questions for Görtz's 1941 interrogation, which covers only the period up to his arrival at Iseult Stuart's home, Laragh Castle in County Wicklow. This suggests that for the following eighteen months, while appearing to evade capture, Görtz's movements and contacts were being closely monitored (including two botched escape attempts – in August and

THE ROAD TO INTERNMENT

September 1941 – using a small boat at Brittas Bay, in which Jim O'Donovan lent a hand at the behest of IRA chief of staff Stephen Hayes). Earlier that year, Görtz had planned to return to Germany from Donegal or from Fenit in Kerry, but both those attempts failed also. In the latter escape plan, from Inishduff island, Görtz was aided and abetted by Bernard O'Donnell who, like O'Donovan, was an ESB employee.[18]

Two weeks before Dr Görtz's arrival, Seán Russell had been smuggled aboard a liner from New York to Genoa. He was met on the quayside in the Italian port on 1 May 1940 by Professor Fromme, who drove the IRA leader to Berlin where he would soon meet Hitler's foreign minister, Joachim von Ribbentrop. In addition, Russell was trained in the use of explosives and small arms.[19]

At around the same time, Berlin had pressurised Franco to release IRA man Frank Ryan from prison in Burgos, northern Spain. Ryan had been on death row since his capture during the Spanish civil war where he had been fighting for the International Brigades against Franco's forces. In early August 1940, Helmut Clissmann was waiting to greet Ryan at the Hendaye border crossing into France. Both men travelled to Paris and on to Berlin for a meeting with Seán Russell, as well as Ribbentrop's coup d'état specialist Dr Edmund Veesenmayer and his assistant Kurt Haller. Soon afterwards, Russell and Ryan set sail for Ireland aboard a German U-boat but Russell died of a perforated ulcer 100 miles west of Galway. The plan to land both IRA men on the Dingle peninsula was then abandoned, with Ryan returning to Germany, although the failure of the Russell-Ryan mission remained unknown to the IRA leadership in Dublin until November 1940.

In Berlin, Ryan regularly met with Francis Stuart and advised him on the content of his weekly radio broadcasts to Ireland, which began in July 1942 (although he did a few initial talks, starting on St Patrick's Day, 17 March 1942). But Stuart was taken aback on one occasion when Ryan told him, 'When Germany wins the war, I will be a minister in the Irish government.' The Irish writer recalled: 'I took this as some sort of threat to me to keep in with him. I took that very much amiss.'[20]

MI5 files released in 2000 reveal that the head of Abwehr II, Erwin von Lahousen, 'told Allied interrogators after the war that he believed Russell was poisoned by Ryan. He suggested the "very radical" Ryan had fallen out with his old associate, adding "internal political difficulties and political rivalries within the IRA probably played a part in this matter".' Lahousen added that the Abwehr chief Admiral Wilhelm Canaris 'was deeply sceptical of the Irish operation which was the brainchild of Foreign Minister Joachim von Ribbentrop'.[21]

Meanwhile, Hermann Görtz remained free and was building up a wide circle of contacts, including the German ambassador, Dr Eduard Hempel, Jim O'Donovan, and various other like-minded republicans who proved only too happy to help the newly arrived parachutist.[22]

Three months into his Irish tour, Görtz was in regular contact with O'Donovan via letters delivered by trusted couriers. In one such letter, the spy advises the ESB man to monitor radio messages from Germany on the 38.25–40m band. For good measure, he added a list of 'terms', which resemble a suggested negotiating strategy between the IRA and de Valera's government, as follows: '1. to cease all activities of an armed body in the 26 counties; 2. to instruct police to suspend all activities – to suspend all sentences – gradually release; 3. Conference exploring possibilities of active co-operation towards Republic; 4. Truce for three month [sic]'.[23]

Görtz soon found out, however, that the IRA's command structure was in turmoil and its personnel in disarray. The picture he compiled was in stark contrast to that painted by Jim O'Donovan at his final face-to-face meeting with Abwehr agents in Berlin in August 1939. In fact, by 1941, the IRA was heading for a serious split which would be disastrous for the secret army. The Northern IRA leadership, under the command of Seán McCaughey, felt that Russell's successor as chief of staff, Stephen

THE ROAD TO INTERNMENT

Hayes, was a traitor feeding secrets to de Valera's government in Dublin. On 30 June 1941, just eight days after Hitler invaded the Soviet Union, Hayes was arrested and interrogated by his own IRA associates. To buy time, Hayes wrote page after page of a so-called confession – which later ran to over fifty closely typed pages – before escaping his captors after some weeks and seeking protection in a Dublin police station. Enraged by his perceived duplicity, the IRA circulated edited copies of the Hayes confession, claiming the document proved the former leader's guilt. The unedited confession document named many names and led to a wave of arrests by the Irish police. Among those named in the original confession – but not in the edited version – and subsequently arrested in a general round-up, was Jim O'Donovan who, until then, had been able to pose as a respectable senior employee of the state electricity board.

In his confession document, Hayes revealed that 'for a number of months [O']Donovan, Moss [Twomey], Dr [Andy] Cooney, and P[ete] Kearney were meeting pretty regularly to discuss ways and means of helping the Army'. Hayes added that Dr James Ryan, de Valera's minister for agriculture, 'could not figure out Donovan. He thought he might be working for Germany officially as one of their SS men. On account of his relationship to Kevin Barry's people and having a brother in the Irish diplomatic service, he felt he was too well placed for the government to arrest him unless they could have a definite charge to make against him. (He is married to Kevin Barry's sister and his brother was Irish representative in Berlin and Rome for a time. I do not know where he is now.) He also knew Donovan had a big pull with the Old IRA and the government did not want to lose any further support from that quarter, which was bound to happen if they arrested him without any charge.'[24]

Given the revelations it contained, O'Donovan could be forgiven for being alarmed when the Hayes confession was first circulated among top IRA members, including himself. Many years later, O'Donovan recalled: 'I got first copy of the Stephen Hayes "confession". I went to National Library and with the special help of James Carty, got photo-stat copied and had it delivered immediately to Cecil Lavery KC.' This note suggests that, just before his arrest, O'Donovan was taking legal precautions in case he was charged with an offence. In the event, however, he was interned without charge on 9 October 1941, having been initially arrested on 26 September 1941. This technicality enabled him to resume work at the ESB immediately following his release on 8 September 1943.[25]

Stephen Hayes was incarcerated in Dublin's Mountjoy prison where he provided a series of statements to the authorities from June to October 1941. In one statement, dated 30 June 1941, Hayes refers to Jim O'Donovan as having 'notified an agent in Holland or Belgium of the IRA's decision to send Seán Russell to Germany' (i.e. from the USA, in May 1940). The same statement refers to visits by Hayes to O'Donovan's home in Shankill, County Dublin.[26]

While the Stephen Hayes affair proved to be O'Donovan's undoing, his personal contacts with the German agents Weber-Drohl and Görtz may well have alerted the authorities to the fact that there was more to O'Donovan than met the eye. Given the nervousness provoked by the Hayes confession, the internal instability of the IRA, the backdrop of World War II and Ireland's fragile neutrality, the government acted swiftly to intern O'Donovan and hundreds of other republicans without charge, invoking special powers introduced two years earlier. According to historian Tim Pat Coogan, 'de Valera had a "now you see them, now you don't" relationship with the IRA'.[27]

A covert special branch photograph of O'Donovan – taken at Dublin's Bridewell police station just after his arrest – shows the IRA man looking anxious as he ponders his fate. It is one of the few photos of him to have survived this period of his life as a prisoner. Soon afterwards, he and many others were transported twenty-five miles from Dublin to the Curragh military internment camp where most would spend the remainder of the war. For O'Donovan it would prove to be a difficult and humiliating experience. Here was a senior republican who held an important state job being rounded up and imprisoned with others from around the country, at the behest of a man he detested, Éamon de Valera. O'Donovan would hold de Valera in contempt for the remainder of his life, considering him to have sold out to the British on the principle of a 32-county republic. For the next two years, O'Donovan would face long days of tedium and frustration as he found himself a captive of the state he had fought to establish.

11.

A GUEST OF THE NATION

Jim O'Donovan was having breakfast when the police raid began at 8 a.m. on 26 September 1941, effectively ending his role in the top echelons of the IRA. For the next two years he would be a prisoner of the state he had been instrumental in creating – from founding father to political internee in the space of twenty years. By any yardstick it was a remarkable trajectory. The special branch cars swept up the long gravel drive to 'Florenceville', O'Donovan's spacious riverside house. His son Donal recalls the events of that day vividly and was glad he didn't know the names of the varied visitors to his parents' home, who included 'Mr Saturday night, the radio operator'. (He later learned this was a Mr Conway, who sent coded IRA messages to Germany and got Abwehr replies in return).

> Thank God I didn't know names like that because when the special branch did swoop, they swooped in numbers and interrogated everybody. We obviously gave the right answers because otherwise he would have been tried and convicted. He would have lost his

job [but] the ESB couldn't sack him because he was only interned ... luckily, the maid was trotting out names like Michael Tierney [a Fine Gael UCD professor] and Todd Andrews [a founder member of Fianna Fáil]. All the right names.[1]

The file on the raid, held at the Military Archives in Dublin, reveals that in a small room off the dining room of O'Donovan's spacious house, gardaí found a 'diagram of a petrol bottle bomb', as well as instructions on incendiary operations and Davis guns. They also found an assortment of IRA pamphlets, including an anti-de Valera script in pencil entitled 'He hopes to have it both ways', a script for an IRA broadcast, a printed circular on the execution of Barnes and McCormick (7 February 1940), and a pamphlet dealing with the Irish government and events of 1914 to 1941. Outside the house they discovered 'leads and aerials which may have belonged to a receiving or transmitting set'.[2]

The raid also revealed documents naming Dr Andy Cooney (who had been IRA chief of staff 1925–26) and Maisie O'Mahony, who worked for Cooney and also acted as driver for German spy Hermann Görtz. Her mother's guesthouse, in Dublin's Gardiner Place, was used as an IRA safe-house from time to time during this period.[3]

Following the raid on his home, O'Donovan was driven to the Bridewell garda station in central Dublin for interrogation. He was formally detained under section 30 of the Offences Against the State Act, the emergency powers that de Valera had introduced on 2 September 1939. He was asked if two months earlier, in July 1941, he 'had visited a person known as "the Doc"[Dr Hermann Görtz] at the address of Miss Mary Coffey, 1 Charlemont Avenue, Dun Leary. "The Doc" resided there during 1941 as Mr Robinson.' O'Donovan declined to answer these questions, thus avoiding a charge of aiding and abetting espionage. In addition, he denied that the IRA texts were in his handwriting and said they had been sent to him. In his report of the interrogation, Superintendent Michael

O'Reilly noted: 'It was not my place to preach to him or to talk politics' but he told O'Donovan that he 'ought to consider the government's difficulties in preserving neutrality and consider whether he ought not to assist me.' But the IRA man would not play ball with the garda superintendent who noted that O'Donovan

> ... adopted an attitude of bitter resentment against the government who he suggested were only out to safeguard themselves. He appeared to think that his detention was a piece of personal spite against him. I told him his detention resulted from normal police enquiries which had led us to him and that the government were not even aware of his detention.

When O'Donovan was asked about newspaper clippings he had of army appointments, including a photograph of the chief of staff, Major-General Dan McKenna, and his aide-de-camp, he replied: 'I do not wish to say anything about it.'[4]

Thanks to the Stephen Hayes confession document, the special branch knew that O'Donovan had been a regular visitor to the Dún Laoghaire safe-house where Hermann Görtz 'the missing parachutist ... had been lodging under the name of Henry Robinson ... from August 1940 to the end of July 1941'. But during two days of questioning at the Bridewell garda station, the ESB man had skilfully avoided incriminating himself. The authorities did not have enough hard evidence to charge O'Donovan, but his fate was sealed on foot of an emergency powers order signed (on the advice of the garda commissioner) on 2 October by the minister for justice, Gerald Boland, 'in the interests of the public safety'. While the two men had shared a cell in Mountjoy prison almost twenty years earlier, they were now on opposite sides of the fence. As Jim O'Donovan was transferred to the Curragh camp to begin his period of internment – on 9 October 1941, following two weeks of imprisonment – his family were faced with the loss of a breadwinner. Five days after being incarcerated, O'Donovan wrote to the camp governor, Commandant James Guiney, seeking release 'for a period of seven to ten days ... to put my financial and general affairs in order' and 'handing over the loose threads' to his ESB successor. The IRA man was also considering selling his home since his salary had been stopped. O'Donovan listed a number of reasons for seeking parole, but item no. 7 must have caused some concern to the camp authorities. It read:

> To resume negotiations with Chief State Chemist's Department as to possible manufacture of explosives in this country. I had been approached on behalf of the Government by the assistant Chief State Chemist about three to four weeks ago in this connection. The particular explosives upon which I had been consulted were all of my own invention or adaptation as used here from 1918 onwards.[5]

But the newly arrived internee did himself no favours by citing such reasons for his release and, unsurprisingly, his request for parole was turned down on 27 October. He had to be content with penning letters to his solicitors and the ESB chairman, explaining his predicament.

Meanwhile, Monty O'Donovan was able to visit her husband once a month, the first such visit taking place at 3 p.m. on 18 October. The authorities noted that she brought the following items: four apples, three pears, four tomatoes, butter, lettuce and celery. She was generally accompanied on those visits by Eddie Toner, an old family friend, or by her brother-in-law, Richard O'Rahilly, son of the 1916 veteran Michael O'Rahilly.[6]

Jim O'Donovan had been less than a month in the Curragh camp when he penned a letter to 'Dear Gerry Boland', reminding de Valera's cabinet colleague that they had been locked up together in Mountjoy prison 'nearly twenty years ago' (i.e. in late 1923, after the civil war). O'Donovan's tone was one of indignation:

> The advisability of interning a person of my standing – the only surviving Republican [i.e. anti-treaty] member of the Tan-time GHQ Staff, not to speak of 25 years of selfless devotion to my country – must from time to time engage your serious consideration if only from the standpoint of pure expediency.... Whatever about the justice or injustice of my detention (and needless to say my view, before God, is that you and the rest of your Government should with greater justice occupy my present position) I submit that vindictiveness aside, or any intention to widen the punishment so that my children also must suffer – the possibility of which I cannot entertain – then there can be no just cause for withholding the granting of this brief period on parole to fix up my affairs which are now in a fairly desperate condition.[7]

As with the earlier parole request to the camp governor, O'Donovan's lack of subtlety proved to be his undoing. The justice minister was hardly likely to grant parole to someone who made no secret of his belief that the entire Cabinet should be locked up in the Curragh. And so it was that parole was duly refused on 26 November.

By February 1942 O'Donovan's letters home were beginning to cause concern. An officer of the Curragh command staff wrote to G2's chief staff officer about a request to Mrs O'Donovan to find a copy of a scientific chemical journal referring to explosive compounds her husband had invented

> ... when I was doing research for Nobel's Explosives Company, together with an indication of Japanese interest in one of my new compounds. Is it not interesting at the present time to think that perhaps deriving from the explosive stabiliser I had made, their torpedoes are more effective than those of other belligerents? Professor Ryan had said at the time (it

was only a chance, of course) that my compounds happened to be the only ones which proved to be of commercial value. Thank goodness it is all so long ago that I shall hardly be arraigned on a charge of being in receipt of Japanese gold.[8]

It is hard to fathom why O'Donovan would draw attention to himself by writing such a letter about explosives, right under the noses of his captors. In any case, the memo was marked 'no action' by G2. But whatever about O'Donovan's wish to re-read his explosive formulae from twenty years earlier, both the special branch and G2 were scrutinising the names on their prisoner's 'tea-time visiting list' at 'Florenceville'. They included: Eddie Toner, a native of the Six Counties, described as 'odd, arty and connected with Irish Film Society'; an 'Irish-Iberian' linked to a firm in Dame Street 'run by left-wingers Martin and Sasieta ... connected with H.E. Irish minister to Spain, Kearney'; Raymond Kennedy, a UCC chemistry lecturer, described as 'very IRA, spent some time in gaol ... suspected of having manufactured explosives for IRA at chemistry dept. UCC.'[9]

Meanwhile, back at the Curragh, the camp authorities were keeping G2 up to date on O'Donovan's regular correspondence with the outside world, which included a letter to his bank manager about maintaining his overdraft, similar letters to keep insurance policies active, and an application for help to the Electrical Industries Benevolent Association in London. Commandant Mackey told G2 that O'Donovan's 1941 ESB salary was £580 per year, plus an army pension of £110 and a disability pension of £75, adding the following jaundiced view: 'His brainwaves keep his wife busy on the manufacture of cheese, jam, the growing of fruit, onions, tomatoes, etc. – none of which is ever a success, judging from the correspondence and from which I deduce him to be one of Ireland's greatest "chancers".'[10]

As the summer of 1942 began, Jim O'Donovan busied himself by putting pen to paper and writing a 25-page essay entitled

'Germany and Small Racial Groups'. The extensive manuscript, filling a school exercise book, was composed in June and July, midway through his period of internment. In his classic IRA polemicist style, O'Donovan lashes into the 'USA and England' which he sees as 'centres of Freemasonry, international financial control and Jewry'. He then examines German policy towards various areas where certain groups are striving for national independence – including Ireland, the Ukraine, the Basque country, Flanders, Brittany and Macedonia – concluding that 'only after the peace will the jig-saw sort itself out and the pattern of post-war Europe emerge'. O'Donovan bases his arguments on 'the hypothesis of her [England's] defeat' and assumes Germany 'to be dominant in Europe'. He predicts an armistice by the end of 1942, with England 'to be semi-quarantined and excluded from trade with Europe'. Pressing for closer ties with Germany, O'Donovan says it would be 'madness' for Ireland 'to lie quiescent in the quarantined area and give up the rich contact with Europe'.[11]

When it came to his choice of reading material, Jim O'Donovan seemed most at home with anything that took a swipe at the British empire. One such book that survived his period of detention in the early 1940s was entitled *The Vanishing Empire* by Indian nationalist author Chaman Lal. The book, published in 1937, contained chapters on England's 'Broken pledges', 'Two centuries of plunder', 'Britain exposed' and 'Bayonets and bullets'. Chaman Lal dedicated his book to 'the American people … whose own struggle for independence against India's oppressors, the British, has been a perpetual inspiration to the millions of oppressed and liberty-less Indians'. O'Donovan signed the book in Irish: Séamus Ó Donnabháin, Currach, 1942.[12]

O'Donovan's political writings, reading material and letters to his family paled into insignificance, however, in light of an incident discovered by the camp authorities in mid-1942. Just after 5 p.m. on 23 June, two camp guards, Sergeant William Callaghan and Corporal P. O'Connor, discovered O'Donovan giving a bomb-making class to three other inmates in hut C6. They were: Thomas Costello from Tralee, County Kerry; Timothy Collins from Currans, County Kerry; and Frank Quinn from Greencastle, County Tyrone. In a report to the camp governor, Sergeant Callaghan described how he found O'Donovan and the others playing cards but 'the game didn't appear to be genuine. I observed internee J. L. O'Donovan sitting on a copy-book'. When O'Donovan 'reluctantly' handed over the book, the army guard found that it 'dealt with explosives'.[13]

Jim O'Donovan's seven copy-book pages containing his bomb lecture notes constitute one of the most unusual documents among his voluminous papers which today are to be found in the Military Archives, the UCD Archives, the National Archives and the National Library. At first glance the book appears full of notes in Irish, presumably written by O'Donovan when attending classes given by Mullingar teacher Gearóid Mitchell. The script includes vocabulary and annotations, dated 18 June 1942, from a well-known eighteenth-century poem 'Domhnall Óg'. Other pages also contain poetry references and translations of various Irish terms and phrases. But, whether due to a shortage of paper or an attempt to deceive the camp guards, some pages contain a mixture of Irish poetry and grammar, along with explosive formulae, fuse and detonation techniques, and advice on how to get best results from gelignite. O'Donovan must have known he was taking a risk by carrying around such notes, which included the following information on blowing up bridges: 'charges … must be detonated simultaneously'. (Several bridges in England – including London's Hammersmith Bridge – had been targeted during the S-plan campaign three years earlier.) Elsewhere, the copy-book is liberally sprinkled with references to low and high explosives and the sensitivity of detonators. In the lecture notes, O'Donovan exhorts his students to test each item in the bomb-making process 'systematically as you go along, because otherwise if left till the end, the location of a fault would become an impossible job'. In addition, he advises that a detonation 'cable must be long enough to protect firing party'. His notes contain precise instructions on how much gelignite to use and how far apart individual charges must be placed at a target, such as a bridge. He stresses that 'each detonator should be tested' and prefers 'many small charges' to a single large one.[14]

One page of O'Donovan's copy-book, dealing neither with explosives nor Irish, contains a flow chart similar to that in part IV of his S-plan (see Appendix 1, p. 257), targeting a wide range of public services in England. In this version, however, he favours the destruction of scarce food supplies: 'wheat granaries' and 'harvesting of crops' — targets that did not appear in the original S-plan. It is hard to ascertain from these notes whether O'Donovan was using his 1939 plan purely as a theoretical model, or if he envisaged a resumption of the S-plan campaign at some stage. The inclusion of food stores as a target suggests this version of the 1942 plan was designed to hit Britain at war, given that strict food rationing was in place. Although it had petered out in March 1940, the S-plan was not formally called off until March 1945.

Despite the implications of O'Donovan being discovered passing on explosives expertise to fellow inmates, the reaction of the camp authorities appears in retrospect to be unusually lacking in urgency. There is no record of Commandant Guiney tipping off his counterparts in military intelligence (G2). Instead, he wrote to the army's provost marshal, Colonel F. J. Henry, to discuss whether or not the troublesome internee could be charged with an offence on foot of his bomb-making lecture. On 6 July 1942, two weeks after the incident in hut C6, the provost marshal informed Guiney that

> ... the question of proving a charge in this case is very doubtful as you yourself agree. O'Donovan was known as 'Director of Engineering' at the time of his arrest and notes similar to those in the notebook were found in his possession. It is very necessary at all times to observe the movements or activity of such internees

and patrols should be constantly reminded to report anything unusual during their tour of duty.[15]

Just how much damage was actually caused by the authorities' decision to intern O'Donovan with other republican activists (rather than holding him elsewhere or in solitary confinement) remains unknown. After a moribund period in the 1940s and 1950s, the IRA did recommence an armed campaign – the so-called Border campaign – which ran from 1956 to 1962. It was the forerunner of the Provisional IRA's 1970–94 campaign.

Jim O'Donovan was granted seven days parole from 28 October 1942 in order to attend the funeral of his sister, Marguerite, at Dean's Grange cemetery in south County Dublin. She was the mother superior of a French order of nuns that ran an orphanage on Tivoli Road, Dún Laoghaire. Her nephew Donal remembers that, after the funeral, his father called to see him and his brother Gerry at Blackrock College: 'Our hopes were raised and then dashed again. We thought we were going to get out of prison'.[16]

Donal O'Donovan also recalls trying to find his father, in vain, during the school holidays: 'I remember cycling from Athy, where I used to go on holidays, to look at the No. 1 internment camp, to try and find it and see if I could see him. But, of course, I could never find it.' Whatever about Ireland's domestic political situation and the wider war outside, O'Donovan's 14-year-old elder son was feeling the effects of his father's incarceration and the absence of a family life: 'I wanted him home. I wrote to him, he wrote to me. I wrote silly things. I remember once I put something silly under the stamp when I was sticking it on, like "I'll see you soon" or "V-day *sub rosa*. Look under the stamp" – silly things like that.'[17]

Jim O'Donovan returned to the Curragh on 3 November 1942, facing the bleak prospect of further detention without charge or trial for an indeterminate period. There was little he could do apart from writing essays, reading innumerable books, attending Irish language classes, translating foreign texts, and engaging in political debate with fellow prisoners. He also created a crucifix made from matchsticks, while the figure of Christ was moulded from a metal toothpaste tube (O'Donovan's daughter Sheila still had the crucifix sixty years later). These were some of the methods devised by internees to stave off their feelings of boredom and utter helplessness. But, for O'Donovan, passing on his explosives expertise would now prove to be more difficult with the authorities keeping a closer eye on him, although no attempt appears to have been made to isolate him from other prisoners.

On 19 May 1943 (eleven months after the discovery of the bomb-making class in hut C6 and twenty months after O'Donovan's arrival in the Curragh) Colonel Dan Bryan, the head of military intelligence, wrote to the Curragh command, as follows:

> I should be glad if you would let me know to what extent the above-named internee [O'Donovan] is taking part in the normal life of the camp; also, as far as you can ascertain, the parties with whom he appears to be most intimate and if, in your opinion, he is making use of his knowledge of explosives to impart knowledge of same by way of lectures to his fellow internees.[18]

It is not clear why Colonel Bryan and his colleagues in G2 did not investigate this possibility earlier, particularly given O'Donovan's October 1941 letter to the camp commandant regarding explosives, his February 1942 letter to his wife seeking details of explosive compounds, and the discovery of his bomb-making class four months later, on 23 June 1942. Nonetheless, on 21 May 1943, Bryan's missive was duly passed on by his Curragh operative, Commandant D. Mackey, to James Guiney, the camp commandant. Despite the sensitivity of the inquiry, Guiney seemed in no hurry to reply, eventually putting pen to paper on 27 May, affirming that O'Donovan

> ... does not associate with prisoners or internees in the internment camp with the exception of internees

Diarmuid Fitzpatrick and James Cleary. He occupies most of his time reading and studying Irish. He is under constant observation and in my opinion is not making use of his knowledge of explosives to any other prisoners or internees.[19]

Despite Guiney's assurances to G2, he makes no mention of O'Donovan's bomb-making class the previous year. It seems, therefore, that Colonel Dan Bryan remained ignorant of the fact that O'Donovan was imparting his explosives expertise to other Curragh inmates. Perhaps because Bryan was unwilling to accept Guiney's word on face value, he instructed his Curragh representative, Commandant Mackey, to seek all 'incoming and outgoing correspondence' for O'Donovan to be forwarded to G2.[20] From the standpoint of military intelligence, however, this precaution was too little, too late, particularly since O'Donovan would be freed just two months later.

For his part, O'Donovan whiled away the days by compiling his own alphabetical collection of press clippings, mainly of high society figures in the Dublin social and political scene. His entries under the letter B include the Anglo-Irish writer Elizabeth Bowen (1899–1973) and British diplomat John Betjeman (1906–84) who became poet laureate in 1972. Whatever the credentials needed for inclusion in O'Donovan's bizarre version of *Who's Who*,[21] it is hardly a coincidence that both Bowen and Betjeman were British agents in wartime Ireland. Bowen's work in gathering intelligence for London has been well documented.[22] Although officially a press attaché at the British representation in Dublin, Betjeman had other roles too. Bowen's secret reports for the British ministry of information were read by Betjeman before being forwarded to London. In addition, in 1942, when MI5 discovered that one of the broadcasters on Berlin Radio's Irish service (Mrs Susan Hilton) had a brother (Edward Sweney) living in Oldcastle, County Meath, Betjeman was dispatched to check him out.[23]

But the dull moments in the camp's life were contrasted with tougher ones. For example, in the bitter winter of 1942, O'Donovan was hosed down with icy water as the prisoners staged a protest in the camp over conditions. His son Donal believes that this incident and the general deprivations of camp life led to his father's ill health in later years.

As well as teaching German classes, bomb-making techniques and writing political essays, O'Donovan also attended lectures by other inmates. These included Irish classes for learners, which were given by Gearóid Mitchell of Mullingar. More advanced classes were taught by Seán Óg Ó Tuama of Cork and Tommy Lynch from Beaufort, County Kerry, while the most advanced lectures were given by the writer Máirtín Ó Cadhain of Galway. (In the post-war years, Ó Cadhain retired from active IRA membership and in the 1960s became Professor of Irish at Trinity College, Dublin. He died in 1970.) O'Donovan seems to have enjoyed learning Irish and even managed to produce a greeting card *as Gaeilge*. The card was adorned with his coloured drawing of a twin-sailed boat making its way across the water from darkness to light. Below the drawing are the words of an old Irish blessing: 'If I were back amongst my own people, age would vanish from me and I'd be young again.' The card may well have summed up his feelings at the time, with the onset of middle age. He was forty-six.

In addition to studying Irish grammar and literature, O'Donovan began work on an Irish-English dictionary (basically an attempt to update an earlier work by Fr Patrick Dineen SJ, first published in 1904 and revised in 1927) some 75 foolscap pages of which survive among O'Donovan's papers in the National Library of Ireland. His collaborator on this project was Joe Deegan, who had been IRA commander in Liverpool at the start of the S-plan campaign in 1939. (In the post-war years, Deegan worked for Conradh na Gaeilge, the Gaelic League, before joining de Valera's *Irish Press* newspaper as Irish language editor.) In the summer of 1943, not long before his release, O'Donovan was in correspondence about the dictionary project with Seósamh Ó Néill, the secretary of the department of education, as well as the Government Publications Office, and Liam Gogan, a noted Irish-language poet who worked in the National Museum.[24]

During her husband's internment, Monty O'Donovan was forced to survive without his considerable ESB salary of £580 per annum, by using her cookery skills and taking in paying guests. She manufactured cream cheese, which she sold to Findlater's and Sewell's shops, to bring in much-needed cash. By monitoring mail destined for the O'Donovans' home, G2 discovered that Mrs O'Donovan had obtained a £100 bank loan in July 1942, which demonstrated her reduced circumstances.[25]

The family's financial burden was eased, however, by the fact that O'Donovan's two sons were taken in as boarders at Blackrock College secondary school in Dublin. No fees were ever sought for the boys' education in that period. The college was run by the Holy Ghost Fathers, originally a French order of priests, who did missionary work in Africa and had come to Ireland in the 1850s. At the same time, O'Donovan's two daughters, Aedine and Sheila, were taken in (one as a boarder) by the Loreto nuns in Bray, County Wicklow. No fees were ever sought for their education during this period. The kindly gesture had the imprimatur of the then Catholic archbishop of Dublin, Dr John Charles McQuaid, who had taken up the top job the previous year, in 1940. Before his elevation to this influential church post, McQuaid had been the president of Blackrock College, the school de Valera himself had attended as a young man. The instigator of this plan was Jim O'Donovan's younger brother Dan, who knew Dr McQuaid well (they played cards together) and had also been a pupil at Blackrock College, in the 1915/16 academic year, after the family returned from Glasgow. This unholy alliance of church and state worked on a 'nod and a wink' basis to ensure that, though technically an enemy of the state, O'Donovan did not fall on overly hard times during his incarceration. Perhaps, in his own way, de Valera was cognisant of the fact that O'Donovan had done the state some service, albeit in another era, twenty years before. Donal O'Donovan remembers that his Uncle Dan

> ... got in touch with John Charles McQuaid and got Gerry and myself into Blackrock. John Charles had just left Blackrock six months beforehand to become archbishop and Dan was able to swing free education for the two of us. Right through my school days, I assumed that Dan was paying for us and he didn't mind letting that be assumed either. But it was actually John Charles who gave the nod to Blackrock. I must say for the [Holy Ghost] fathers in Blackrock that there was absolutely no discrimination – never the slightest hint that we were 'orphans' or in any way disadvantaged except that, because we lived so near, they let us go home every weekend, which other boys [i.e. boarders] could not do.[26]

Sixty years after the wartime events in the Curragh, old republicans remembered Jim O'Donovan's time there. After being deported from Liverpool in 1939, Tom Byrne joined the IRA's third battalion in Dublin but he, too, was destined for internment:

> It was May [1940] before the first thing we were sent out on. It was this stupid thing out in the Featherbeds. Seven of us went out on bicycles. I pinched the bicycle from my Auntie Florrie's husband. They never saw the bike after that. Up we went to the Featherbeds. We must have been daft really. I said to one of them – Uinseann [Vincent] MacEoin or one of the other guys – 'There's an aeroplane there'. It was sort of circling around the top of the mountain. It was one of the Air Corps observation planes. We should have known. This was in the daytime. If it had been at night time we might

have had some chance. Vincent MacEoin was in charge. A brilliant strategist. I am saying it sarcastically ... we were sent up the mountain just to make a big show of it. I mean, what good could you do? What was the good of training in May 1940 – the Germans were at the gates – with a bloody stick in your hand? Were we going to wave the sticks at the Germans when they came, or would they throw their guns to you? Ah Jesus, I mean, that's daft.... There were seven of us just sitting there with branches of trees in the heather. The next minute, around comes a whole load of Special Branch with machine guns. The others were all from Dublin, and there was one fellow from Bray, Seán Hoey.... I ran like buggery and the next thing, someone shoots over my head, so I thought it was about time to stop. There were seven able-bodied men arrested just like that, all fit enough to do anything. They were locked up for six years, from 1940 to 1945. I was twenty when I went in and twenty-six when I came out. My life was really wasted completely.[27]

Byrne spent nine months in Arbour Hill prison before being interned in the Curragh camp in February 1941. He recalls meeting Jim O'Donovan in the camp later that year:

All I can say about O'Donovan is that he was a gentleman.... I talked to him but not about much because I wasn't the same age or anything. He was looked up to as one of the men who had fought the Black and Tans. There was no mention of Jim O'Donovan being pro-German that I remember. Tony Magan and he were friendly.... Magan was adjutant-general at one time; not in the camp, outside. He was from County Meath ... he used to teach German in the camp.[28] I heard about Görtz from somebody else, but I never heard about Görtz in reference to O'Donovan. He must have kept very quiet about it. He was a quiet man, by the way – a very, very quiet man. He was, as far as I recollect, very cultured, very quiet and a true gentleman. And that is saying something coming from me [*laughs*]. He wasn't anything like you'd think a revolutionary would be like; he didn't spout all the time like some of them. He was probably the better of them for that.

In the early 1940s, Belfast republican Eddie Keenan managed to escape from Crumlin Road prison, but in March 1942 he was arrested in the south and found himself in Mountjoy prison with Brendan Behan, Hermann Görtz, the German spy whom O'Donovan had sheltered two years before, and a Spanish refugee from the International Brigades: 'Every time Görtz saw the Spaniard he'd say "Viva fascista", and the Spaniard would say "No pasarán, los fascistas" – a whole lot of curses; it was a bit of a laugh.' After four weeks, Keenan was transferred to the Curragh: 'There was a hunger strike on at the time. The conditions were very bad. The fellows were walking around, some of them with baldy heads, some with beards. You'd think they were like a lot of rag men with old clothes.' According to Keenan, the hunger strike was not against the camp authorities but in protest at the IRA-run camp council. He recalls that 'just about a month before I went into the Curragh, the camp split in half. I went into the Gaelic hut then and Jim O'Donovan was in the hut. Though I didn't know him very well, he started teaching me a couple of songs. He taught me a German folk song [starts singing] "In einem kleinen Grüntal, mein liebchen ist…". And he taught me a couple of Nazi songs.' For a while, Keenan is lost in his memories, searching for the words of the old Wehrmacht song 'We're marching against England'. Then they come, in German with a Belfast accent:

A GUEST OF THE NATION

Gib' mir Deine Hand, Deine weisse Hand,
Leb' wohl, mein Schatz, leb' wohl!
Denn wir fahren, denn wir fahren gegen Engeland.[29]

Keenan remembers that

> O'Donovan wasn't like the other prisoners, he was a loner. You'd mostly see him walking about on his own. He was a very dapper wee man with a small brownish, grey moustache. His hair was always nice, clean and tidy. He always wore a collar and tie. He always wore his own clothes, while most of the prisoners just wore prison issue stuff. But O'Donovan was always tidy with a collar and tie. He reminded me of somebody – a fellow you used to see coming in in the English pictures saying 'Anyone for tennis?' [laughs] ... He always wore the best clothes in the camp. I think sometimes he wore Irish tweeds and other times he had a sports jacket and flannels. That's how I picture him ... he always had two or three types of clothes to wear ... sometimes he'd have a wee cravat. He was always walking about like a gentleman. He was distinguished from the other prisoners.

The Gaelic hut where 'you had to speak Irish, you weren't allowed to speak English', contained a motley crew of republicans. Keenan recalls that O'Donovan

> ... was a very quiet man in the hut. He was sleeping very near Neil Goold [Verschoyle], who was a Russian agent and a very sincere communist. He came from the landed gentry in Ireland. That was the funny thing about the hut we were in – there was Johnny Power, he was a commandant with the international brigades in the Spanish civil war and there were three or four other communists in the hut. The great friend of Jim O'Donovan was Dermot Fitzpatrick. He used

to have a bookshop in Cathedral Street in Dublin. Dermot was an advocate of a state something like Salazar had in Portugal. I don't know what Jim's political opinions were. I never talked to him about it but he had a great admiration for what the Germans did in Germany after the First World War, how they recovered. He had a great admiration for their cleanliness and the roads they built, the autobahns, and how they had done away with unemployment.... He wasn't a Nazi but he was very anti-British of course. He was an Irish republican and I suppose he looked on it that he was helping the republican movement by doing such things. He was the main man for the German spy connection.... O'Donovan went back and forth to Germany, he knew Germany pretty well. That is where he learned the songs. He had a good knowledge of German.... I was only a wee lad of twenty, as were a lot of my mates. We looked on him as an intellectual. The communists were inclined to look on him as pro-fascist.

Keenan recalls that no one in the camp looked up to Jim O'Donovan, despite his leadership role in the war of independence and the 1938–41 period:

He was just a prisoner like the rest of us. The only thing different with Jim O'Donovan was that he wasn't a mixer, he wouldn't mix around. I never saw him playing football for instance. I never saw him doing anything. I don't ever remember him even giving a lecture about anything. Fellows who were experts in things used to give lectures and talks. Maybe he did, but I don't remember him doing anything like that, or making himself anyway noticeable … he always had a book under his arm, but he wasn't a mixer.

Keenan also recalls that O'Donovan did not receive any special treatment in the camp:

> No, he didn't get anything more; he had to eat the same as what we got, he got the same lunch and everything. He didn't get treated any differently in the hut with the men. He was mostly reading all the time and studying. But he was very interesting to talk to. He wasn't stand-offish. If you went up to him and had a yarn with him, he would tell you anything you wanted to know, or talk to you about things. But you didn't ask people their business. You didn't go in and say, 'Well, what did you do about the S-plan?' You would never ask any questions like that, you'd never talk to him about things like that. You wouldn't.

Looking back on events in the Curragh sixty years before, Keenan summed up O'Donovan as follows:

> He didn't sound like a bitter man, but I don't think anybody was too pleased about being locked up. He had lost a big position and I don't know whether he ever got it back afterwards.... I believe Jim O'Donovan was a staunch republican until the day he died. He had an admiration for the Germans all right, and an admiration for the way they recovered after the 1914–18 war. He had an admiration for the way the Germans had built up the roads and the economy of the country. But, as I was told by the people who knew him, he thought the Germans were very arrogant. I know he had great admiration for Germany but I don't think he was a Nazi. He was a humane man. I don't think he would have been a man who believed for one minute that what was happening to the Jews in the concentration camps ... that he would have contemplated or encouraged anything like that. He'd

be dead enough against that. He was a republican. He was anti-British; most republicans were at that time. They weren't pro-German, they were anti-British.[30]

Another Belfast internee, Billy Joe McCorry – who as camp adjutant was second in command to the O/C Liam Leddy from west Cork – remembers Jim O'Donovan:

> He was very quiet, very intelligent. He kept very much to himself. He didn't ignore the others but he didn't mix a great deal at all with the ordinary prisoners. They may have been much younger and not of his time. I think that would probably be the reason … I had never met him before and very few in the camp had ever met him. The only conversation that strikes me was that he told me about going to Germany with the wife on a visit, a vacation, or whatever. And the customs stopped him because of some cigarettes his wife had, and made some disparaging remarks, which he very much resented. He was going to return home immediately [*laughs*]. What became of it, I don't know…. We were discussing Germany and he gave me the impression that, while he may not have been anti-German, that incident had a marked effect on him … he didn't appear very happy about that particular incident…. I never attended any lectures that he gave. He attended an Irish class with me. I think it was Gearóid Mitchell from Mullingar who gave that class. It was just a learners' class. He was much in the same class as myself with the Gaelic then. I was not a fluent Irish speaker and neither was he. He may have spoken German but he never held any classes in German. Neil Goold held classes in Russian.[31]

McCorry recalls that O'Donovan 'had no special privileges at all. He had to check in with the rest of us'. In addition, O'Donovan was not involved in an escape attempt in 1942; according to McCorry, O'Donovan's 'was not one of the huts involved. He wouldn't have known anything about that.' And despite being involved in the S-plan himself, McCorry did not know of O'Donovan's role in it until the ESB man arrived in the Curragh: 'I don't know if everyone would have known but, for instance, I didn't know until he came into the camp and I had been active quite a time. I was told that he was a personal friend of Russell, but outside of that I'd never met him.' In the few conversations he had with O'Donovan, McCorry got the impression that he admired Germany:

> Yes, I'd say he was very much in favour of Germany but that could be because of his pro-Irish activities, not so much that he was a Nazi or anything.... No, I wouldn't say he was a Nazi by any means, not to my thinking anyway. [Internees in the Curragh] were pro-German because they were beating the British, just like Neil Goold was pro-Russian, but outside of that I don't think they were really Nazi or red – Neil was red, of course, he made no bones about it.

McCorry never met Jim O'Donovan after the Curragh camp:

> He was out long before me. He must have had a bit of pull. I always had the impression that all those old ones would have known quite a few of the government party, and even the Fine Gael party. If there was any possibility of anyone getting out, it would be them. I always had that idea; I practically knew that. You didn't have to be a genius to deduce all that. It certainly helped because their friends on the outside would have been pushing for them.[32]

Another internee, Jim Savage from Cork, left the IRA in the mid-1940s to join first the Labour Party and then the Communist Party of Ireland. He vividly remembers Jim O'Donovan in the Curragh because they shared the same hut:

On the right-hand side of his bed he had lots of cardboard shoe boxes and he had a lot of books with him – he was a terror for Penguin books and he had them all at the side of his bed. If you asked him for one he'd give it to you. He would be reading most of the time. He wasn't very talkative but he talked to me all right. The thing about him was, I suppose, he was bitter too about his hand and what he went through … you couldn't blame him really. He lost a lot when he lost his hand. It looked awful with the old glove on it … I was only a young fellow, only eighteen, so it was all right for me to be critical of him but he went through his own share. But he did kind of – of course, most of them there did – take the German side. They were pro-German, the country fellows mostly, but I thought that if the Germans came in they'd shoot the blooming lot of us because they'd consider us an inferior race. But Jim O'Donovan didn't think that; he was so anti-British, he was very pro-German. I would say he would have been in favour of Hitler's Germany. He said to me that he [Hitler] solved the unemployment problem there. I said Hitler couldn't have proceeded with that without the invasion of the Low Countries and expansion, that he had to bring about a war. He wouldn't listen to that at all … he had no answer to that. He knew I did not have the same outlook as himself. He did not go near the left-wing people. He just carried on in his own old way … a lot of the men would have been pro-German because they'd be anti-British anyway. I was part of the left-wing group so I was not pro-German … the left-wingers in the camp were very small [in number]. There was myself and Mick O'Riordan, John Joe Haughey, Dinny McSweeney and Tommy McSweeney. There would have been about twenty in all. There was also Mick Conroy, he was known as Ger Tag, from Enniscorthy.[33]

According to Savage, Jim O'Donovan spoke openly about Nazi Germany and 'was pro-German to the core'. He avoided the left-wing group, which included O'Riordan and Paddy Smith – both veterans of the international brigades in Spain – and Johnny Power from Waterford.

Mick O'Riordan confirms that O'Donovan did not mix much with the left-wing internees: 'We were in the Curragh at the same time but not together there. There were 300 to 400 people there, and we spoke to each other. I knew of his background – one of the last of the IRA's headquarters staff from the war of independence. He nearly blew himself up on one occasion. He was reticent and did not talk much. In the Curragh I was in the communist or Connolly group and we produced a hand-written, clandestine prison magazine. O'Donovan never talked politics. I knew he had been the owner or publisher of *Ireland To-Day*, a very good magazine which during the Spanish war was pro-republican. At least it was not pro-Franco and anyone who was not pro-Franco was pro-republican. O'Donovan never propagandised in the magazine.... O'Donovan never proselytised or took sides in the Curragh. He had his own private opinions which he did not publicise. I did not know about his pro-German views. When later I read Enno Stephan's book *Spies in Ireland* I realised what his real views were. Most of the people in the Curragh were pro-German.'[34]

Meanwhile, Jim Savage also recalls discussing the Stephen Hayes confession with O'Donovan, who said it was 'rubbish'. Savage adds that O'Donovan was

> ... distant in his own way. He didn't talk to you unless you talked to him. And then he could cut you off quick, too, with one word like 'rubbish'. He always dressed very well. He never wore the old clothes ... the Curragh was a very cold place in the winter. I

> mean, in fairness, I was young but people like Jim O'Donovan, Mick Conroy, George Plunkett and Jack Plunkett, they'd have felt the cold more.... He [O'Donovan] was not allowed out but if he had visitors he'd be taken outside the gate and into a hut. They'd listen in to the conversation. The PAs [póiliní airm or military police] were bastards, they were degrading.... I never saw O'Donovan attending mass but he could have.

Savage remembers life as an internee in detail:

> When you're in jail you get very cranky. I suppose it's the boredom and that, it would make you kind of irritable. We did things to keep ourselves occupied. We made crosses and rings, and things like that. We had Irish classes and there were a lot of teachers there. Seán Ó Tuama was there.[35] There were a good few Irish teachers, including Máirtín Ó Cadhain. I attended classes run by a chap by the name of Tommy Lynch. He was fluent. He was an attendant in the mental hospital in Killarney, but I didn't go to Máirtín Ó Cadhain's class at all.... I was in the bunk next to Jim O'Donovan. We were sleeping on the ground on trestles. They were old timber trestles, a board and a thin old mattress and one old blanket, just up from the floor. And you'd get an old pillow. It would be the same pillow you'd have all the time and the same blanket. They were never washed or anything. There was an awful lot of lice there. A lot of fellows had to be fumigated. O'Donovan wasn't fumigated ... he was treated by the PAs as just another prisoner. They didn't care who he was. He was very bitter. I suppose you wouldn't blame him. He was director of chemicals in the war of independence. I think he was

> more bitter than anyone else. He was a very proud man. He was so pro-German. He argued that Hitler solved the unemployment in Germany – this kind of small talk, you know, but he wasn't a very talkative fellow. Of course, he was a very clean man and clean-spoken. He was an educated man. He didn't give lessons himself. He didn't actually do anything. He just kept to himself. He wasn't close to anybody in the camp. I suppose he was talking to me because I was sleeping next to him. Joe O'Connor from Kerry was on the other side of him. Remember him? He was tried with George Plant. He was acquitted and George was sentenced to death … Joe attended the left-wing classes in the Curragh. There'd be about forty men in the hut. We were very close together there. It was very boring.

Savage also recalls the poor diet in the Curragh internment camp:

> It was only a bit of bread. It would be about the size of your fist, and jam and margarine. Guiney, who was commandant of the camp, used to buy the meat. One time he bought meat and they must have been old knackers because everyone got sick. Jeepers, there was a smell in the camp. They must have been old dead cattle, so we were nearly poisoned. O'Donovan was sick as well.

Savage noted that O'Donovan 'was a bit friendly with Harry White [another internee, from Belfast]. I saw him talking to Harry White once and I think he told White where to go to get money when he got out – from Jim O'Donovan's people, I suppose.'

John Murphy from Hacketstown, County Carlow, joined the army at the age of eighteen in 1940 'because of the Emergency' and became a military policeman in the Curragh. He recalls:

I volunteered to go into the internment camp. The reason I did so was that £2 danger money was paid. My wages were 30 shillings and the extra £2 brought me up to £3/10s. My mother was in very poor circumstances at home and I used to send home £2 every week. The danger money was justified. There was a fire in the internment camp in 1940 when ten huts were burned to the ground. There was a dispute between themselves [IRA prisoners] in the camp and that is how the camp authorities discovered the tunnels through which a terrible lot of them could have escaped, but the army discovered them. When I was there they [the prisoners] used to be teaching Irish and playing football matches. They made rings and leather purses. They walked around the camp. That is how I remember Mr O'Donovan. I remember him distinctly because of his three [missing] fingers. We all knew the prominent people and we were told he was a brother-in-law of Kevin Barry. We all knew him by sight but we would never be talking to him unless you wanted him for some reason. I remember he used to teach Irish over in a hut called D11. He was a leader inside – he was one of the leaders. He was treated with respect … Jim O'Donovan was looked up to by the others. He was better dressed than the others. As far as I remember, he wore a trench coat a lot. The other prisoners wore their own clothes, there were no prison uniforms, but O'Donovan seemed to be better dressed than the others … he may have been let out for health reasons.

Murphy recalls that in 1944, the year after O'Donovan left the camp, 'they built another tunnel under hut D11' – the same hut in which O'Donovan had given Irish lessons:

> I remember going in one day to D11 and they were doing Irish dancing. If I had stopped there for three hours they would never have stopped dancing. I can still see the sweat dropping down off those big fellows. The reason was that they were working underneath and if they stopped dancing I would probably have heard the noise going on. They had tunnelled out under the wire but their mistake that time was that they wanted to go to another hut. They broke into the old tunnel and started putting clay in it. We had a small policeman who used to go through this tunnel like a rabbit. When he came that night he could go no further because of the fresh clay. So the next day they surrounded hut D11 and a Sergeant Dunne discovered the new tunnel. If they had not broken into the old tunnel, however, ninety-five of them could have escaped.

Murphy adds: 'I remember that many of the letters for prisoners were in Irish and we had an Irish-speaking military policeman who would translate them. They would be censored. All the letters were censored, coming in or going out.'[36]

Ruairí Brugha – the son of Cathal Brugha, a contemporary of Jim O'Donovan's who died in the civil war – was also interned in the Curragh but not at the same time as O'Donovan. Brugha, who later became a Fianna Fáil TD, recalled a friend bringing him around the camp:

> He was pointing out, 'That camp over there', he said, 'That's the German internment camp. And there's another one on the far side that you can't see, that's the British internment camp.' And what I couldn't say was that if there's a British internment camp and a German internment camp, what side am I on? It suddenly struck me, but of course that's a part of Irish history isn't it?[37]

On 3 May 1943, Monty O'Donovan notified her husband by letter that his war of independence service medal had arrived at 'Florenceville' and asked if she should send it on to him at the Curragh camp.[38] Donal O'Donovan recalls that the medal was eventually delivered to the camp: 'I remember being appalled at the idea that the medal should be addressed to James L. O'Donovan, No. 1 internment camp. You know, being jailed by the people that he fought with.'[39]

The government had decided to issue service medals to survivors of the war of independence who were in receipt of military service pensions. As a leading member of the IRA headquarters staff from December 1920 to July 1921, O'Donovan had played a key role in those events and, as such, was entitled to the medal. The Service (1917–21) Medal was created on 24 January 1941. The 27-month delay in giving it to O'Donovan is most probably explained by his arrest and internment in autumn 1941. In the event, the authorities ignored the fact that O'Donovan had been interned as an enemy of the state and issued the medal to his home address. Thus, prisoners received the war medals, along with pillars of the establishment including Cabinet ministers, and some on the opposition benches in the Dáil including Dick Mulcahy, O'Donovan's civil war nemesis.

Whatever his innermost thoughts at this time in his life, O'Donovan must have wondered what had prompted de Valera to issue such medals to friend and foe alike. The wartime Taoiseach may have been attempting to curry favour among old republicans, particularly since such medals had not been issued before. In addition, the medals coincided with the 25th anniversary of the 1916 Rising which was marked by a major army display at the GPO in Dublin. While honouring the 1916 heroes, Dev may have wanted to ensure that those involved in the subsequent *cogadh na saoirse* (war of independence) did not feel left out. At any rate, the Taoiseach was applying the same strictly-by-the-book approach which, in May 1945, would see him paying condolences to the

German ambassador Dr Eduard Hempel on the death of Hitler. At an official level, there had been a certain reluctance up to then to celebrate the war of independence, given the internecine bloodbath of the civil war that followed. De Valera and his inner circle – most of whom had seen action in both conflicts – must have felt that, after a generation, the time was right to honour those who had fought in the pivotal 1919–21 period. They included a small number of people who, like Jim O'Donovan, had steadfastly refused to embrace mainstream politics, opting instead to continue the armed struggle to establish a 32-county republic. They remained on the fringes – or, as in O'Donovan's case, locked up – but they still got their war medals from Dev. It was a very convoluted Irish story.[40]

Towards the end of his sojourn in the Curragh, Jim O'Donovan was becoming increasingly concerned about his health. On 18 May 1943, he wrote to Commandant Guiney seeking a 'further electro-cardiographic examination' following representations by his heart consultant, Dr R. V. Murphy of Jervis Street Hospital. But the camp medical officer, Captain C. A. O'Neill, showed little sympathy for O'Donovan's condition. Captain O'Neill told Guiney that while an electro-cardiograph of that internee 'showed a certain amount of involvement of the myocardium … rest is the chief treatment of his particular disease and he has ample opportunity for this in his present surroundings.'[41] Nonetheless, on 2 June O'Donovan was escorted to St Bricin's military hospital in Dublin for an examination. On 11 August 1943, O'Donovan wrote to Guiney demanding the 'immediate granting of [medical] treatment' or 'my immediate release' to avoid being 'permanently incapacitated'. By now the camp doctor's patience with O'Donovan was wearing thin, and he told Guiney:

> Since his internment about two years ago he has been complaining of numerous ailments, including rheumatism, neuritis, sciatica, pain in cardiac region, dental cyst. He has been treated for all these on

different occasions with varying results…. In my opinion this man is of the hypochondriac type.⁴²

Military intelligence officers appear to have been taking O'Donovan's condition more seriously, however, because on 8 September 1943 – coincidentally or otherwise the same date on which the ESB official was finally released – Lieutenant Fleming, the senior G2 officer at Curragh command, wrote to the camp governor asking whether O'Donovan has

> … been known to suffer from melancholia; or is his general demeanour one which would suggest to a non-medical observer to be out of the ordinary? Is it considered that continued internment would eventually bring about a mental collapse? The considered opinion of the camp MO [medical officer] is also required immediately on his return off leave.⁴³

Whether for health reasons, lobbying by his well-placed contacts outside, or Colonel Bryan's fear that he would continue to pass on bomb-making expertise to a new generation of IRA men, Jim O'Donovan was eventually released on 8 September 1943, almost two years after his initial arrest. Given all that had unfolded during those twenty-three months of internment, it seems clear that the authorities considered he would pose less of a threat outside the camp than inside it. Donal O'Donovan is convinced that his father's release was secured through lobbying, not least by the internee's own brother Dan, who was commissioner for County Dublin during the war. According to his nephew, Dan O'Donovan 'drove around with a revolver in the glove compartment of his car, to resist the Germans should they invade'. Donal also recalls that 'Uncle Dan's weekly whiskey associates included de Valera's minister Seán T. O'Kelly'.⁴⁴

O'Donovan's final release from the Curragh was not without incident, as a row erupted when he was searched by a camp guard. The guard, Sergeant Thomas Byrne, reported that 'when I told him to remove his boots and trousers he became hostile and called me a "fucking bad bastard". I proceeded and searched him without further incident.'[45]

Six weeks after O'Donovan's release, the head of military intelligence, Colonel Dan Bryan, sought a profile of the ESB man from Commandant James Guiney, who pulled no punches in his reply, stating that his former prisoner

> ... cannot be trusted. He is a very intelligent man and has a perfect knowledge of explosives. It was with difficulty we kept him from imparting his knowledge to the other internees; this was during the earlier portion of his internment, latterly he became very indifferent principally due to the fact that he lost caste with the internees generally.[46]

Guiney's revelation that 'it was with difficulty we kept him from imparting his knowledge [of explosives] to the other internees ... during the earlier portion of his internment' suggests that O'Donovan was endeavouring to give bomb-making classes in the Curragh for the first eight months of his time there – i.e. up to the discovery of his 'card game' in hut C6 on 23 June 1942. The subsequent decision of the camp authorities to keep him 'under constant observation' (according to Guiney's report to G2 on 27 May 1943) appears to have hampered O'Donovan's efforts in this respect.

A fortnight later, Colonel Bryan was back in touch with his trusted Curragh officer, Commandant Mackey, inquiring if at any time during his internment O'Donovan 'wrote a letter apparently to his wife saying that in the event of his non-release he had determined to commit suicide apparently by cutting his throat'.[47] But Mackey assured the G2 chief that 'all who had had occasion to handle or censor O'Donovan's correspondence are unified in the opinion that no such threat was ever made by him'.[48]

As 1943 drew to a close, O'Donovan would have to adjust to the new realities of life on the outside, as a family man with a nine-to-five job. He would have to rebuild ruptured relations within the family circle and re-establish his standing at work. And, with almost two decades to go to retirement, O'Donovan was faced with having to leave his covert, double life behind in favour of a more mundane role as an operations technical assistant at the ESB. The high-ranking, high-flying IRA activist who had designed the 1939–40 bombing campaign in England – and acted as the secret army's chief liaison officer with Nazi Germany – had finally fallen to earth.

12.

A TIME FOR REFLECTION

The years of internment took their toll on O'Donovan, who emerged from captivity on 8 September 1943 to find his elder son, then aged fifteen, somewhat estranged from him. Donal O'Donovan recalls that he and his father 'went for a walk up Katie Gallagher [a hill] in south County Dublin and he tried to teach me the facts of life and started to tell me the story. And I told him that he was far too late, that I'd been to school.'[1] The coolness between father and son was destined to last for their respective lifetimes. It worsened when, as a mature adult in the 1960s, Donal sought, and received, a meeting with de Valera at the presidential residence, Áras an Uachtaráin, in Dublin's Phoenix Park. O'Donovan senior remained implacably opposed to de Valera and everything the Fianna Fáil leader stood for. His son, however, saw no point in continuing a fight that was not of his making and so resolved to bury the hatchet. But the visit to Dev deepened the rift between father and son, with neither exchanging a word for years afterwards. Donal O'Donovan subsequently joined Fianna Fáil and by 1979 had become the party's director of elections for the Wicklow constituency.

In the first flush of freedom back in 1943, Jim O'Donovan realised that his war was over and that, at the age of forty-seven, he would never serve the IRA in an active capacity again. In any case, his closest colleague in the organisation, Seán Russell, had died in 1940 and the IRA was now in the hands of a new generation of leaders. His son Donal recalls that, following his release, his father 'came home to my [maternal] grandmother's house in Fleet Street. That's where we met him and he took us for a bottle of stout over in the local pub, and that was the first time he'd ever done that.'[2]

Historian Michael MacEvilly notes that the former IRA chief of staff, Dr Andy Cooney, marked Jim O'Donovan's release from internment by dispatching a group of men from the TB hospital where he was working, to dig the garden for Monty O'Donovan.[3]

O'Donovan resumed his work at the Electricity Supply Board without much difficulty. (Shortly afterwards, he finally got round to joining the company's pension scheme, too, perhaps beginning to think of his family's future stability for the first time.) He could resume his old job because, as an internee, he had not been charged with any offence and thus, from a legal standpoint, had a 'clean sheet'. But just how close O'Donovan had come to losing his livelihood is clear from a Garda Síochána memo to the department of justice in 1941. Shortly after O'Donovan's two days of questioning in the Bridewell Garda station (on 29/30 September 1941), a Deputy Garda Commissioner wrote to the secretary of the department of justice as follows:

> Mr O'Donovan's period of detention expires at 9.15 a.m. on Sunday, 6 October 1941. The Commissioner recommends that he should be interned pending consideration as to whether he should be charged on the documents found [i.e. copies of IRA broadcasts and an appeal for IRA recruits in O'Donovan's handwriting].... This man is drawing a salary of £580

a year from a semi-Government institution and enjoys a [war of independence] pension of £110 per annum. He should be shown that he cannot have it both ways.

Luckily for O'Donovan, the authorities never pressed charges, opting to give him the benefit of the doubt on the IRA documents found at his home, as the Deputy Garda Commissioner explained:

> The copies of IRA broadcasts would no doubt serve as grounds for charges under sections 12 and 21 of the Offences Against the State Act, 1939, but in fairness to O'Donovan it is reasonably probable that these broadcasting documents were, as he states, handed to him for safe keeping.[4]

The ESB management did not quibble with O'Donovan's demand for reinstatement, probably guessing that if they did not give him his job back, they would be forced to do so by the courts. More sensitive was the question of the IRA man's loss of service from 1941–43 for pension purposes. And O'Donovan wasted no time in taking his case to the ESB's staff council, which found in his favour; thus, his pension records show no loss of service for the two years spent as an internee. In addition, retired ESB man John O'Brien recalls that O'Donovan 'fought his case for recompense for being interned quite strongly'. While the IRA man did not get anything like a full refund of his lost two years' salary, according to O'Brien (who in the post-war years worked in the ESB secretariat with O'Donovan), 'Years after he had come back [from the Curragh camp] he applied to our conciliation tribunal for compensation for his internment. He got a nominal amount. It wasn't a lot but there was a nominal amount conceded all right, on what grounds I have not the slightest idea because I certainly could not see any at the time.' O'Brien considers that O'Donovan was lucky to get his job back, given that the ESB had 'a blacklist published by the government of people who weren't to be employed ... as a semi-state body, we used to get the circulars that these people weren't to be employed. But in his case he came back after internment. I just don't know how he got his job back.'⁵

Tomás MacGiolla was another ESB republican of a later generation. He joined the semi-state company in 1947 and recalls:

> There was a blacklist because I was dismissed myself in 1956. There was a blacklist all right, from the 1940s, but it [being rehired] was a question of whether you had ceased to be involved or not. I don't know whether he [Jim O'Donovan] was or had ceased to be involved at that stage or not, but certainly after getting involved in 1951 myself, I never heard anybody refer to him as being active, so I would say he wasn't involved any more.

MacGiolla adds that, although an 'element of secrecy' prevailed, 'the ESB management knew about' O'Donovan's IRA involvement. He recalls that the blacklist system against IRA members affected his career in the state electricity company: 'It definitely did affect my career. I mean, I never got any place in the ESB.' He also recalls other IRA men in the company in the 1950s: 'Joe Christle's brother Colm was an active republican. I would not say he was on the blacklist as well; he was there all the time. You see, he wasn't that involved. Joe Christle would have been involved. Colm was involved in the cycling federation.' In addition, MacGiolla believes that Seán MacBride was able to help people avoid the blacklist when he was foreign minister in the inter-party government of 1948 to 1951:

> MacBride would have been in a powerful position in government, and would have been in a position to have people assisted or helped in overcoming blacklists or anything like that. He had been [IRA] chief of staff in the 1930s, so he would be close enough to people in the IRA and to people who were involved in the 1940s … he would have been very

sympathetic at that time, even in the 1951 period when I joined [the IRA]. I would say that MacBride was helping people at that stage.[6]

Former ESB employee Jack Wyley recalls that when O'Donovan's involvement in the 1939–40 S-plan bombing campaign in England became known, 'It came as a bombshell to many people in the ESB, who thought he was out of such activity. He was a very dapper man. One would not think he was involved in the IRA.'[7]

Pádraig Ó Conaill's ESB service also overlapped with O'Donovan's; he recalls that in the 1940s, in dealing with staff who had served sentences for IRA activities, ESB management

> ... took the view that they had served their punishment and it was not up to the ESB to apply a second punishment. In later stages, in the 1970s, there was specific legislation that compelled the ESB not to re-employ people who had been found guilty of offences against the state. As regards people who had been involved in the [IRA in the] 1950s, like Tom Gill [Tomás MacGiolla] and Joe Christle, I don't think there was any specific legislation at that time [barring their re-employment].[8]

Over the next eighteen months, from the comfort of his south Dublin home, O'Donovan could contemplate the slow and steady defeat of Nazi Germany at the hands of the Allies. His hopes of a united Ireland brought about by a German victory were to be dashed. Dr Hermann Görtz, the German spy he had sheltered at his house in Shankill, was incarcerated in Athlone army barracks. By that time, the war had taken its toll on Görtz, who spent his days writing coded messages for his bosses in Berlin, carving a headstone for his grave and practising simulated suicide techniques to prepare for an Allied invasion. Jan van Loon, a pro-Nazi Dutch deserter who was incarcerated with Görtz in Athlone, recalls that the German regularly plunged his arms into a bucket of icy water in preparation for slashing his wrists should the Allies invade and try to seize him.[9] Görtz had no intention of being captured alive by the Americans or the British. While a prisoner in Athlone, Görtz was under the impression that his coded messages were being successfully smuggled out by an Irish soldier he had paid to act as a courier. Unknown to Görtz, however, the soldier handed all these messages to the canny operators in Irish military intelligence. They included the expert cryptologist Dr Richard Hayes, who was director of the National Library in Dublin. Dr Hayes's team simply decoded Görtz's messages and, after a plausible interval, got the soldier/courier to deliver bogus replies 'from Berlin' back to the German spy's cell. The ruse worked so well that at one stage Görtz believed he had been promoted to the rank of major by his Nazi spy masters. Dr Hayes had the last laugh at the expense of Görtz, who reportedly wept with joy on learning of his 'promotion'. Görtz's final resting place in the German military cemetery at Glencree, County Wicklow, is adorned by a headstone bearing the fake rank of 'major'.[10] Douglas Gageby (1918–2004) was a member of the army's 'German' team which reported to G2 chief Colonel Dan Bryan. He recalled:

> Bryan would have meetings in his office with me, Joe Healy, Éamon de Buitléar and Richard Hayes. I sometimes translated material from English to German which Hayes then encrypted and it was fed to Görtz when he was in Athlone and they were trying to get stuff out of him ... messages were passed to Görtz as if they came from the legation or via another spy.[11]

Meanwhile, Jim O'Donovan was back in the bosom of his family but his long absence from home had ruptured relations within the family circle. His son, Donal, recalls that in the late 1940s his father

> ... summoned a kind of family conference because some of them recognised that they were breaking apart – that they were not relating to each other as they should be. My Uncle Colman brought a Webster Chicago wire-recorder (before tapes) to the party. They taped each other and they had great fun with that. And much jar was consumed as far as I remember.[12]

Jim O'Donovan's siblings were, for the most part, solid establishment figures. His brother Dan also had an IRA background in the war of independence, having worked in Michael Collins's office. Later on he joined Fianna Fáil and, when that party took power in 1932, he worked as private secretary to Seán T. O'Kelly. He subsequently became chairman of the national health insurance society and in 1946 was appointed secretary of the department of social welfare, a top civil service post. In 1951 he was fired from that job by Taoiseach John A. Costello for 'refusing to reinstate a civil servant who had used public time to work for the Labour Party. William Norton, the party's leader, was Tánaiste and minister for social welfare'.[13] But when Fianna Fáil returned to office later that year, Dan O'Donovan was reinstated as an advisor to the minister for social welfare. Dan later became secretary to President Seán T. O'Kelly and, in 1959, President de Valera. Dan O'Donovan was married to Dorothy Browne from Sligo, whose brother Fraser Browne was a Fianna Fáil TD 1933–37. Dan died in 1967.

Another brother, Colman (1893–1975), had been an intelligence officer in the IRA's Dublin brigade from June 1920 to July 1921. He later worked in the department of industry and commerce and from 1930 in the department of external affairs. He was appointed as Ireland's first diplomatic representative to Portugal in February 1942 (until May 1945). According to Donal O'Donovan, 'the story was that the secretary of the department, Joe Walshe, didn't want Colman O'Donovan in Dublin any more, so he sent him packing to Lisbon.' He also served as a diplomat in Washington (1930–33), Berlin (1933–35), London (1935–38) and the Vatican (1938–42). He married his first cousin Moll Brennan, a niece of Joe Brennan, former governor of the Central Bank.[14]

Peter O'Donovan rivalled Jim for the title of black sheep of the O'Donovan clan. Like his father before him, he worked for the customs and excise service. 'He carried an attaché case adapted to hold four bottles of spirits. His best friend was Maurice Walshe, author of *The Quiet Man*, and also an excise man. He was a fan of G. K. Chesterton and was married to Ethel Boucher-Hayes, the daughter of a family from Charleville, County Cork, that ran a well-known medical firm.'[15]

Jim O'Donovan had three sisters. Marguerite O'Donovan was mother superior of St Joseph's orphanage in Dún Laoghaire, County Dublin. Nuns in that order did not wear habits since the order had been formed during the French Revolution of 1789 when the religious were barred from schools and prohibited from wearing clerical clothing. She died in 1943.

Mary 'Minnie' O'Donovan worked as a senior staff sister at Dublin's Richmond Hospital. According to her nephew Donal, 'She used to buy expensive clothes – on one occasion spending four guineas on a hat in Switzer's, which in the mid-1940s was a senior journalist's weekly wage. My mother was appalled.'

Eileen O'Donovan was committed to St Ita's psychiatric hospital, Portrane, County Dublin, in 1932, aged 29. She died there on 14 April 1996. Donal O'Donovan remembers: 'The children never knew she was there. Nurse Farrell in St Ita's said "Up to three years ago [i.e. 1993] that woman was as sane as you or I". On a bus trip to Dublin, when passing by Nelson's Pillar, Eileen recalled that she had a brother in Dún Laoghaire. According to St Ita's records, Eileen had been admitted in 1932 due to religious mania.' Donal's sister, Mrs Sheila Hanna, recalls that her Aunt Eileen 'spent years locked up in Portrane. Daddy never admitted her existence at all. I think he was ashamed of it.' Mrs Hanna said her aunt was committed to the mental hospital following the death of her parents, whom she had been looking after.[16]

A TIME FOR REFLECTION

As well as trying to repair a ruptured family circle, O'Donovan would also have to rebuild his standing at work. With almost two decades to go to retirement, he was now faced with the reality of having to leave behind his covert, double life in favour of a more mundane role at the ESB.

By the time Jim O'Donovan walked free from the Curragh in September 1943, the world outside had changed. The IRA was in a moribund state and, with most of its personnel under lock and key, would not re-emerge as a force to be reckoned with until the border campaign of 1956 to 1962. The horse that O'Donovan and Russell had backed to win the war, Nazi Germany, looked increasingly unlikely to be first past the post. Germany had suffered heavy losses at Stalingrad in January 1943 and things went downhill for Hitler's armies after that. In Berlin, Francis Stuart – who had acted as O'Donovan's courier to Berlin in January 1940 – continued to toe the Goebbels' propaganda line. In a radio broadcast to Ireland, Stuart portrayed the end at Stalingrad – one of the biggest defeats in military history – as 'a triumph of flesh and blood', adding 'If I were a German, I would be proud to belong to a nation which could produce such men. As it is, I am glad to be among them.'[17]

O'Donovan was now back working for a state whose legitimacy he did not recognise. And while he had no difficulty in resuming his career at the ESB, he would remain a middle manager, with no prospects of further promotion. Soon after his release from the Curragh camp, O'Donovan was sent to Dublin's Pigeon House power station to do a report on it. He held the post of operations technical assistant at the time.

In February 1945, with the war in Europe entering its final months, O'Donovan wrote to the Catholic Truth Society (CTS) in London with a draft proposal for 'a prayer book specifically designed for prisoners and internees entitled *The Prisoner's Companion.*' He told John Boland of the CTS that the 'idea occurred to me about two or three years ago and I felt that in the absence of any such publication already, as far as I know, there would be a tremendous outlet for it.' The CTS undertook to raise the proposal at its March 1945 committee meeting, but there is no record of what happened subsequently. O'Donovan did not mention that when the idea occurred to him he was an internee himself. The CTS reply of 19 February 1945 was opened by the postal censor in Dublin, which suggests that since his release from the Curragh in September 1943, O'Donovan's mail was being routinely checked.[18]

In December 1946, O'Donovan wrote an anonymous article asking de Valera's government to spare the life of Belfast IRA man Harry White, who was due to be hanged in Dublin for the murder of Garda Detective Mordaunt. He criticised the state for never having 'given due consideration to the case for the abolition of capital punishment'. Characteristically, O'Donovan couldn't resist using the article to embarrass the Taoiseach and, in passing, the Catholic hierarchy:

> Violence has always been an unpleasant background to our struggle. When Mr de Valera was collecting money in America for the Army and Government of the Republic, and Dr Fogarty, the Bishop of Killaloe, acted as Trustee for the funds so raised, many deeds of violence were thereby made possible that neither personage would like to be intimately confronted with.[19]

In the immediate post-war period, Dr Hermann Görtz (who had been released from Athlone barracks) and Jim O'Donovan worked together in the Save the German Children organisation, which found foster and adoptive parents in Ireland for German orphans. One of O'Donovan's brothers, Peter, fostered one such child.[20]

On 23 May 1947, Hermann Görtz – terrified at the idea of being sent back to Germany, where he was convinced he faced interrogation and torture – killed himself in the Aliens Office in

A TIME FOR REFLECTION

Palace Street beside Dublin Castle. It was never explained how he got hold of the cyanide tablet, but like many other German spies, he may simply have hidden it in a tooth cavity. The following day's newspapers were full of the Görtz story. Even the normally staid and sober *Irish Times* coverage veered towards a tabloid style with a headline that shrieked: 'Görtz aimed at a quisling government in Ireland'. Other minor headlines told of a 'rising and invasion plan', and that 'Görtz planned to start rebellion'.[21]

If, indeed, Görtz had planned to instal a 'quisling' Taoiseach in Dublin, it is tempting to speculate on the possible candidates. The IRA men Seán Russell and Frank Ryan come to mind since both were alive when Görtz began his mission to Ireland on 5 May 1940. The same month, Russell arrived in Berlin from America for sabotage training and even met German foreign minister Ribbentrop. Ryan arrived in Berlin that August, having been freed from death row in Burgos prison, Spain, through the efforts of Dr Veesenmayer, Helmut Clissmann and the Irish ambassador to Madrid, Leopold Kerney.[22]

In mid-August 1940, Russell and Ryan were dispatched to Ireland aboard a U-boat on the orders of Dr Edmund Veesenmayer, Ribbentrop's coup d'état specialist. But the voyage was aborted following Russell's death, from a perforated ulcer, aboard the U-boat. The former IRA chief of staff was buried at sea. After Ryan's death in Dresden in June 1944, eligible Irish quislings were few and far between. As the main agent of German military intelligence in wartime Ireland, Jim O'Donovan may well have been considered for such a position in the event of a German invasion. Another candidate could have been the IRA's chief of staff at the time of a German invasion (from 1939 to 1941 these were: Stephen Hayes, Seán McCaughey, Pearse Kelly and Seán Harrington). One other possible 'quisling' candidate was the pre-war head of the Nazi party branch in Dublin, Dr Adolf Mahr. The Austrian-born archaeologist lived in Ireland from 1927 to 1939 and was director of the National Museum in Dublin from 1934 to 1939.[23]

Dr Hempel – who, by 1947, was the ambassador of a country that no longer existed (the new German Federal Republic would not emerge until 1949) – was advised by the department of external affairs not to attend Görtz's funeral at Dean's Grange cemetery on 26 May 1947.[24] Jim O'Donovan, however, felt under no such restrictions and made it his business to attend the obsequies, during which people were reported to have raised their arms in the Nazi salute. The following day, *The Irish Times* published a photograph showing O'Donovan in the crowd who were paying their last respects to the dead spy whose coffin was draped in the swastika flag. It was to be one of the last public displays of Nazi insignia in post-war Ireland.

Behind the scenes, however, the Görtz funeral was causing some disquiet in official circles. When a picture of the funeral – complete with swastika-draped coffin – appeared in the Italian newspaper *Buonsenso*, on 1 June 1947, it prompted a missive from the Irish ambassador to Rome, Michael MacWhite, to his boss Freddy Boland in Dublin:

> From the annexed photo one can figure the amount of publicity the Görtz affair has got in the European press. It gives the impression that Dublin is a Nazi stronghold and the only country outside perhaps of Spain where the Nazi emblem is publicly displayed and honoured. People who had persistently refused to believe Anglo-American war propaganda about Ireland's pro-German sentiments are somewhat perplexed by incidents such as this.[25]

A month later, Boland tried to allay his Rome ambassador's fears: 'The event attracted nothing like the same amount of attention here.' He describes European press coverage of the Görtz funeral as 'ridiculous', adding:

> The numbers present were much smaller than reported in the papers and the mourners consisted of

IRA sympathisers whom Görtz had met during his period of liberty, rather than of Görtz's own compatriots in this country. In fact, the whole German colony – including the former German minister [Hempel] – were conspicuous by their absence.[26]

Rather disingenuously, Boland omits from his letter to MacWhite the fact that Dr Hempel wanted to attend the funeral – others had sought a military funeral – but that Boland himself advised the German diplomat that it would be unwise to go.

There appeared to be a voracious appetite for Görtz stories and it was one which the newspapers were only too willing to satisfy if it meant additional sales. *The Irish Times* outdid the competition with an eight-part series on Görtz, which ran from August to September 1947. The series was unusual in that the spy's story was written in the first person singular under the by-line of Dr Hermann Görtz himself, notwithstanding the fact that he had been dead for three months! The articles purported to be based on the spy's secret diaries, but the originals (which were translated by Irish army intelligence officers) are not written in the same style. According to one historian, the articles were, in fact, rewritten from the original material by Joe Charleton, a Dublin tax accountant.[27] Jim O'Donovan collected the voluminous newspaper accounts of Görtz's peregrinations around Ireland, from 5 May 1940 up to his arrest on 27 November 1941. He was no doubt relieved that his name did not appear once, although he had played a key role in assisting the spy.

A 1947 application by O'Donovan for promotion within the ESB, to the post of senior administrator, ended in failure. O'Donovan's four-page curriculum vitae for this job application is revealing in its detail. Then aged fifty-one, it would be his last stab at getting promotion in the semi-state company. But his appearance at Görtz's funeral that year would not have gone unnoticed – particularly since he had been photographed in *The Irish Times* standing not far from the spy's swastika-draped coffin – and probably led a cautious ESB management to deny him preferment. The CV laid out the details of O'Donovan's Jesuit education in Scotland, his UCD degrees and his brief teaching career at Clongowes Wood College from 1919 to 1921. The CV deliberately glosses over his IRA explosives work at UCD and makes no mention of his imprisonment during and after the civil war. He is listed as director of chemicals on the GHQ staff 1920–23, with the additional post of acting director of munitions during the civil war. Naturally, there is no mention of the bankruptcy of his City Chemical and Colour Company in the late 1920s, and the Curragh internment period is described blandly as 'Absent with allowance of continuous service'. For the 1931–41 period (i.e. up to his internment), O'Donovan lists no less than seven different roles in the ESB, including work undertaken for the company's secretary/chief accountant, Friedrich Weckler, who was a member of the German Nazi party and died prematurely in Dublin in 1943. Following his release from internment, O'Donovan worked in the ESB's generation division from 1943 to 1948.

In any case, O'Donovan's bid for promotion in the ESB was to no avail and he was destined to remain at middle management level for the next 15 years, until his retirement in 1962. Former ESB employees John O'Brien and Pádraig Ó Conaill, who worked for a period in the same department as O'Donovan, note that other old republicans in the company did not get promoted to higher positions either. O'Brien remembers that 'John Broy was in the ESB also, and he was one of Collins's right-hand men. He didn't do any better than O'Donovan, you know, and possibly took as many – certainly as many – risks'. Ó Conaill adds: 'Seán Ryan, Joe Guilfoyle – there were quite a number of them there who had been active in the war of independence, and they certainly didn't end up in top management, or anything like top management'.[28]

According to the ESB archives, O'Donovan ultimately worked in the electricity supply company's 'Secretary's Organisation specialising in legislative issues and their impact on the ESB'. His salary in 1960, shortly before his retirement, was a lucrative £2,000 per annum.[29]

Some members of O'Donovan's family believed that he had been offered the job of state chemist by de Valera at around this time, and had turned it down. In fact, there is no record of any such offer to O'Donovan but, coincidentally, his one-time UCD professor, Hugh Ryan (1873–1931), was the first person to hold the post of state chemist, from the inception of the state laboratory in 1924 until his death seven years later. Professor Ryan was, of course, the man who had conveniently turned a blind eye to O'Donovan's explosive experiments in the UCD laboratory thirty years earlier.[30]

While O'Donovan was content to work for the Electricity Supply Board, he had nothing but contempt for the central organs of the state, including the army. Thus, in 1947, when his son Donal joined the Pearse Battalion of the FCA (army reserve), while a student at UCD, his father thought 'this was treachery of the highest order'. Nonetheless, as a proud father, O'Donovan senior grabbed a camera to photograph his son in uniform as he departed for Gormanstown camp in County Meath.[31]

As the 1940s drew to a close, O'Donovan was sought out by writers anxious to pick his brains with a view to writing histories of the various conflicts in which he had been involved. One such was his ex-IRA comrade Florence O'Donoghue who had been the IRA's director of intelligence in Munster during the war of independence. (O'Donoghue's book *No Other Law* was published in 1954.)[32] Another former comrade who contacted O'Donovan was Joe Deegan, the ex-IRA commander in Liverpool. Both men had been incarcerated in the Curragh camp in the early 1940s. Before becoming Irish language editor of the *Irish Press*, Deegan had worked in Dublin for Conradh na Gaeilge (the Gaelic League) which promoted Irish language interests. In 1962, his memoirs were published in Irish under the title *Ag Scaoileadh Sceoil*. O'Donovan was also interviewed by Tim Pat Coogan (editor of the *Irish Press*, 1968–87) and American historian J. Bowyer Bell (in January 1967), both of whom were writing histories of the IRA.

O'Donovan's surviving letters disclose a wide variety of correspondents on both sides of the Irish Sea. For example, in late 1947, he helped Dublin businessman Patrick Russell to compile details of his late brother Seán's career in the IRA. When he began research for his own (unpublished) memoirs in 1962, O'Donovan wrote to Lord Birkenhead, son of the signatory to the December 1921 Anglo-Irish treaty, to ask if Lord Halifax (British foreign secretary, to whom O'Donovan's IRA ultimatum had been sent in January 1939) had ever received a papal award. He also wanted to know about an IRA document from the time of the treaty. Birkenhead replied from his Belgravia home to say he had no information on either query, but he would make further inquiries. Birkenhead added that just before he died, the Belgian Cardinal Mercier had given 'his Episcopal ring to Lord Halifax's father, and, after he inherited it, Lord Halifax had it set above the base of a chalice and presented it to York Minister.'[33]

As the 1950s dawned, Jim O'Donovan was to be presented with a glorious opportunity to lay out his anti-partitionist stall to a public audience, and with the tacit approval of his employers. The occasion was a historic north-south agreement on the Erne hydro-electric scheme – a major ESB project which involved a quid pro quo for drainage north of the border, to which O'Donovan's company paid £750,000 (an enormous sum in 1950). O'Donovan seized the chance to write an article entitled 'Significance of the Erne Agreement' for the Jesuit magazine *Studies*. Dazzling his readers by citing international declarations and conventions, O'Donovan covered waterways from the Thames to the Rhine and the Nile. But his real purpose was to lambaste the neglect of Irish infrastructure since the Act of Union in 1801 and what he saw as the negative effects of partition since 1922. He noted that Ireland's parliament was 'independent of and co-equal in stature with Westminster ... but it has not yet overcome the loss of the partitioned smaller area which, until re-integration of the full territory of Ireland, will continue to retard and truncate its development'. O'Donovan hailed the Erne agreement as an 'achievement ... of great practical value', concluding that in this case of cross-border co-operation 'mutual self-limitation of pristine rights has been not merely imperatively imposed by the necessities of every order, but has become acceptable as the threshold of voluntary and amicable agreement.'[34]

O'Donovan's clear message was that things would work much better in a united Ireland since the effect of 'this complication [i.e. partition] has been to defeat for a period of thirty years any effort at co-operation'. His admission that 'The evolution of the greater legislature [i.e. the Dáil] has conferred world importance, a high degree of complete independence and all the external manifestations of independent statehood' was presumably a sop to his employers – the ESB was a wholly state-owned company. The seemingly conciliatory article belied the fact that only twelve years previously its author had devised the IRA's bombing campaign in England. In addition, O'Donovan would continue to agree with the principle of armed struggle, including the IRA's border campaign (1956–62), but not the subsequent Provisional IRA campaign (1970–94).[35]

13.

BELATED THANKS FROM THE THIRD REICH

During the 1950s, O'Donovan successfully managed to rebuild his life following the years of internment and, despite being refused promotion in the ESB, things were not looking that bad. Just as importantly, he had managed to avoid being publicly linked to the S-plan bombing campaign, German spies and all his other IRA activities in the 1938–41 period, including his four visits to meet German agents on the continent. Perhaps predictably, though, he could not hope forever to escape being unmasked as the Abwehr's top agent in wartime Ireland. And these touchy subjects were to become increasingly awkward for him as the 1950s drew to a close. The first salvo came in the form of a series of newspaper stories entitled 'German Spies in Ireland', which ran in *The Irish Times* from 3 to 7 June 1958. Essentially, the articles were extracts from the Irish chapter of a new book called *They Spied on England*.[1] Uncomfortably for the ESB man, the following sentence appeared in the first newspaper article: 'To strengthen that link [Abwehr-IRA] an Abwehr agent known ... by the name of

O'Donovan had been recruited...'. Luckily for O'Donovan, however, only the surname appeared, being liberally sprinkled throughout the series of articles. He was no doubt relieved that there was no mention of a first name and, thus, nothing to link him directly to the agent named in the series.

But while Jim O'Donovan wisely kept silent about the *Irish Times*' coverage, others did not. No sooner had the articles finished than a leading German businessman in Dublin, Helmut Clissmann, wrote to the newspaper complaining about 'inaccuracies' that malign 'the character of genuine Irish and German idealists, and thereby deeply hurt the feelings of their relatives and friends'.[2] Clissmann did not mention in the letter that he had worked for the Abwehr during the war. A few days later the well-known Donegal republican, Peadar O'Donnell, wrote to the same paper to protest that Frank Ryan was described as a 'gangster' in the newspaper's 'German Spies in Ireland' series.

In July 1958, the *Evening Press* picked up the *Irish Times*' idea and decided to run a review of the same book, *They Spied on England*. The anonymous reviewer, described as 'an authority on wartime spying in this country' was most probably the paper's then editor, Douglas Gageby. He knew more than most about the subject, having worked for Irish military intelligence, G2, during the war as a German-language expert specialising in translating German documents. Gageby would have known about O'Donovan's wartime activities from Colonel Dan Bryan, the head of G2, but he chose not to reveal the ESB man's full identity, referring only to an Irish courier (presumably Francis Stuart) having reached Germany, who 'was obviously the envoy of O'Donovan mentioned by the authors of this book...'. O'Donovan could still breathe easily, since his cover had not yet been blown.[3]

It seemed, however, as if the ghosts of Hitler's Germany were somehow destined to pursue O'Donovan and, as 1958 progressed, he was to come face to face with a figure from the Nazi past. Kurt Haller had been one of foreign minister Ribbentrop's top aides. He had worked alongside Edmund Veesenmayer who, as Ribbentrop's coup d'état specialist, had organised the failed Russell-Ryan U-boat landing plan in August 1940. A year later, in 1941, Haller (by then working with Erwin von Lahousen of German military intelligence) had been involved in recruiting Irish POWs for 'an invasion of England via Ireland'. At least four volunteered for the plan and were transferred from Friesack Camp to Berlin where 'they came in contact with Dr Haller, Helmut Clissmann, Dr Schreiber and were introduced to a Frank Richards aka Mr Maloney (Frank Ryan)'. The POWs were then sent to a demolition school near Potsdam for 'radio work and sabotage' training.[4]

Haller's first visit to Dublin in 1958 (he returned the following year) appears linked to his friend Enno Stephan's plans to write an account of the Third Reich's spies sent to neutral Ireland from 1939 to 1943. In a series of notes written in the early 1960s, O'Donovan reveals that 'Haller, on his previous visit [in 1958], had more or less formally thanked me for my work during the war on behalf of the former Germany'. O'Donovan does not record his reply to Haller's formal thanks on behalf of Hitler's regime, but it is noteworthy that he thought it merited documenting among his many unpublished records, which date approximately from his retirement in 1962. In fact, O'Donovan was not the only Irish recipient of thanks, although somewhat belated, from the Third Reich. The writer Francis Stuart – who broadcast Nazi propaganda from Berlin during the war – was also on Kurt Haller's visiting list. Stuart told an American researcher that Haller 'came over here afterwards to Ireland to visit me. He was a charming person ... I knew him very well and liked him.'[5]

O'Donovan had been tipped off about Stephan's research on the wartime links between the IRA and Germany by an ESB colleague, Paddy Corr. He recalled that:

> Paddy (P. J.) Corr had shown me letters from a German friend of his – skiing in Austria a couple of years running – who was writing up Görtz. He had

asked Paddy about *The Jackboot in Ireland* by Seán O'Callaghan [published in 1958 by Allan Wingate, London] and I had supplied all the relevant information. This was Enno Stephan, a journalist in Deutsche Presse, who proposed to write a proper historical book on the Germans (particularly Abwehr) in other countries, and as he had met Pfaus, Marwede etc. in Hamburg, he was able to show that he knew all about my work and my German visits. As it was felt that references to me [in Stephan's proposed book] might be harmful, this formed the subject of discussion at Clissmann's. Haller agreed that nothing would be published without my consent and he undertook to see that Stephan wrote nothing that would embarrass me.[6]

It is clear from this account that O'Donovan had misgivings about Enno Stephan's planned book, particularly because he still had three or four years to go until retirement. It appears as if Stephan sent Haller as an emissary to reassure O'Donovan. The nervousness about the book project is reflected in the fact that O'Donovan, Haller and Helmut Clissmann met in 1958 and 1959 at Clissmann's Dublin home, in Dartmouth Square, to discuss the matter. O'Donovan remembered that, in 1959, Haller

> ... said I must come to Hamburg as their guest. (He has some post like head of legal section of the grain board) and they have a kind of guest-house for entertaining visitors. Colonel Bill Donovan of the US secret service had been their guest, also Seán MacBride.[7]

In between the visits from Germany, O'Donovan still found time for writing. In January 1959 he wrote a letter to *The Irish Times* praising the train service from Dublin to Cork which he had recently used. He told the newspaper's readers that he had 'resolved to become more CIE-minded' and said the non-stop journey 'knocked off 164 miles in three hours exactly'. O'Donovan did not mention, however, that the new CIE chairman, Todd Andrews, was an old anti-treaty IRA colleague and a regular visitor to O'Donovan's home. Perhaps the CIE boss had asked his friend to write the letter to counter negative publicity arising from his closure of the celebrated Harcourt Street line from Bray to Dublin in 1958. (Todd Andrews was CIE chairman from September 1958 to October 1966.)

Mick O'Riordan recalls meeting O'Donovan at the RDS Spring Show in Dublin. O'Riordan, who was then general secretary of the Communist Party of Ireland, added:

> It was a day out for the kids. I saw him passing by with his RDS membership badge. I said, 'Jesus, that fellow's gone over', but he had probably always been a member. By caste or status he would qualify for RDS membership, but I thought it was incongruous given that we had been in the Curragh.[8]

Ex-IRA man Jim Savage met O'Donovan on a bus to Bandon at around that time. The two men had been interned together in the Curragh about fifteen years earlier. Savage recalled that O'Donovan

> … was quite friendly when I met him on the bus going out to Bandon.… I sat down beside him and did not pretend anything. He was talking about every old thing. He was talking about the Curragh and the dirt of the place. I think he told me he was going down to the Brennans, some relation by marriage [his mother's family]. He was happy to see me. Mind you, he was a changed man. He was grumpy when he was in the Curragh. I suppose you wouldn't blame him. He went through a lot. He was happier when he was out. He'd take a short temper and that kind of thing. You'd have to make

conversation with him in the Curragh, but going out on the bus he'd talk a rat to death.[9]

In a busy year, O'Donovan still found time to write a detailed 7-page broadcast for Radio Éireann on his brother-in-law, the republican martyr Kevin Barry. The talk went out on 8 November 1959. O'Donovan had planned to write a biography of his illustrious relation but never completed it. Some thirty years later, his son Donal did write the story of his famous uncle, using the material amassed by his father, as well as additional data.[10]

Two months later, in January 1960, O'Donovan finally got to meet Enno Stephan in Dublin. The ESB man had little hesitation in helping Stephan with his research, taking him around Ireland to meet various Old IRA men, including Stephen Hayes, the former chief of staff then living in retirement in his native Wexford. During his Irish trip, Stephan asked Helmut Clissmann to make copies of the relevant extracts from the Abwehr war diary, and gave his own copy to O'Donovan as a souvenir. O'Donovan recalled:

> Enno Stephan then came over and I had several meetings with him and got a lot of Görtz, Drohl, Margareta, Stephen Hayes and other documents photostatted for him. On his leaving, he posted me a photograph of himself at Görtz's grave with the following inscription on back of photo: 'Für Jim O'Donovan mit herzlichem Dank für die hilfreiche Unterstützung bei meinem Dubliner Aufenthalt und für die gastfreundliche Aufnahme'.[11]

Despite Stephan's apparently sincere thanks, and Haller's earlier assurances that nothing would be published without his consent, O'Donovan would have reason to regret co-operating so closely with the German journalist. Apart from the fact that the book named names, including O'Donovan's, this was also because the original German-language version of Stephan's work appeared six months before O'Donovan's retirement from the ESB, thus causing some red faces at the company. In addition, Stephan included in his book details of Mrs O'Donovan's strip-search incident on arriving at Hamburg in August 1939. Donal O'Donovan recalls that

> Enno Stephan, the famous man who wrote *Spies in Ireland*, wrote the story of her in Hamburg being searched on the docks. She was very cross with him because it was in conversation; she had not meant it as an interview or ever to be mentioned. It embarrassed her.[12]

The appearance of *Geheimauftrag Irland* (Secret Mission: Ireland) in 1961 caused consternation in the O'Donovan household in Rathgar. (The family had moved from 'Florenceville', Shankill, County Dublin, to 114 Rathgar Road, Dublin, in 1947.) The cat was now out of the bag since the book linked O'Donovan directly to the S-plan, as well as detailing his pre-war trips to Germany for meetings with Abwehr agents in Hamburg and Berlin. O'Donovan was due to retire from the ESB in 1961 but had opted to work an extra year, so the publication of Stephan's book, albeit in German, had the potential to cause him difficulties at work. To make matters worse, O'Donovan's photograph appeared in the book with the caption: 'Jim O'Donovan (above) made return visits to Germany on behalf of the IRA. Described by Abwehr as their "Chief Agent" in Ireland'.

O'Donovan's predicament worsened when, on 26 October 1961, he received a letter from Douglas Gageby, by then joint managing director of *The Irish Times*, explaining that the *Sunday Review* was about to publish extracts from Stephan's book. Gageby was acting for his close friend John Healy, then editor of the *Sunday Review*. Fluent in German, Gageby recognised the news value of Stephan's book and sought an appointment with O'Donovan. The newspaperman called to 114 Rathgar Road on Friday 27 October at 3.30 p.m. staying for half an hour. O'Donovan recalled that they discussed matters in a 'general way'. The former IRA man told

Gageby he 'would take exception to misstatements – reference to my wife, etc.' Gageby then gave O'Donovan a proof of the forthcoming instalment concerning Stephan's book in the *Sunday Review*, asking him to mark with an asterisk anything he objected to. O'Donovan takes up the story: 'I made three marks: 1) Whole story of my wife and customs, or even accompanying me [to Germany in 1939]; 2) ref. to occupying high post in Electricity Supply Board; and 3) address of party [i.e. Breton courier Paul Moyse] in Brussels'. When Gageby called back at 9 p.m. that night, O'Donovan noticed he was disappointed the ESB man wanted all references to his wife dropped from the story 'as he thought it an interesting sidelight'. Handing back the proofs, O'Donovan remembered that 'no guarantees [were] given' by Gageby, whom, he felt, 'was a little disingenuous re Clissmann now being very pleased at what really is a vindication of his honourable part in war as a soldier'.[13]

Helmut Clissmann called to see O'Donovan at noon on 29 October, when both men were able to peruse that day's *Sunday Review*. The ESB man was relieved that 'the issue contained no reference to my wife – nearly a column deleted. The other two references [ESB and Brussels contact] had also been omitted.' O'Donovan's opinion of Gageby deteriorated, however, when Clissmann showed him a copy of the previous week's *Sunday Review*, which featured an enlarged photograph of O'Donovan taken from Stephan's book alongside the banner headline 'Hitler's Irish Spies'. When he saw this embarrassing coverage of his wartime exploits, O'Donovan felt that Gageby had been 'much more than disingenuous'. Clissmann then told O'Donovan that on foot of the first book extract in the *Sunday Review* on 22 October, he had issued a writ against the newspaper on 26 October. However, despite discussing the matter with Clissmann, Jim O'Donovan decided not to take legal action against the newspaper.

O'Donovan's handwritten notes on the affair record that, 'Most of the offence – both against him and against me (which he pointed out) – was in the blurb part for which editor John Healy was apparently responsible … all through the implication is that we were working for Hitler (or Germany) and that the then events in England [i.e. the 1939–40 IRA bombing campaign] were inspired and/or undertaken on Germany's behalf.'

O'Donovan's notes also record that Helmut Clissmann's 'Counsel, Seán MacBride, and also J. Costello, both regard the whole set-up as extremely libellous and of malicious intent.' MacBride drafted a seven-page statement and an apology, which the *Sunday Review* was to publish. O'Donovan noted that Clissmann's action was based on three grounds: 1. suffering in profession or trade by loss and prejudice; 2. misstatement as to training IRA; and 3. misstatement as to his status and work during the relevant period. But Helmut Clissmann's widow, Mrs Elizabeth Clissmann, recalls that the action was not pursued:

> The newspaper had a headline saying 'Spies in Ballsbridge'. It said 'Helmut Clissmann had a spy school'. It was all sensational but there was nothing in it. Helmut thought of taking an action but Costello's advice was to do nothing because otherwise the paper would have publicity. Whatever steps we had begun, we dropped them. It was a joke in the family for years afterwards.[14]

The *Sunday Review* episode, exposing O'Donovan's links to German military intelligence, had the potential to cause severe problems for him at the ESB. And the newspaper stories were the talk of the town, as O'Donovan found out when his brother-in-law Jim Moloney visited him on 7 November 1961. Moloney (who was married to Kathy Barry, the elder sister of Monty O'Donovan) had had lunch a day or two earlier with Lieutenant-General Michael J. Costello, managing director of the Irish Sugar Company, where Jim Moloney worked. In an aside, Costello said: 'I see your brother-in-law is hitting the headlines these days. His boss won't like that very much.' According to O'Donovan, Jim

Moloney then 'proceeded to explain about my retirement, etc.' Since O'Donovan had only another six months to go until he retired on full pension from the ESB, it appears that the company's management chose to bite their corporate lower lip and take no action against their errant employee lest it would attract further unwanted publicity.

When Enno Stephan's *Spies in Ireland* was published in 1963, O'Donovan was comfortably retired in the leafy Dublin suburb of Rathgar – his pension no longer under threat. The book was reviewed in *The Irish Times* by none other than his son Donal, an assistant editor with the paper. Natually enough, the review made no mention of his father's role in the events covered by the book. But those in the know would appreciate the subtlety of the piece when it stated that Enno Stephan

> ... does not find it as necessary as must a reviewer to tread softly over names and incidents. Many, indeed most, of the protagonists are alive and, while one feels certain that some of them would act differently if events took the same course again, it is equally sure that they would even now resent the broad glare of daylight shed by Mr Stephan on some of their cloak and dagger performances.[15]

While airbrushing his father's key role from the review, Donal O'Donovan praised the book as 'a major contribution to modern Irish history', containing 'an account of the courage displayed by Mr de Valera in maintaining his [neutrality] policy'.

Jim O'Donovan's misgivings about *Spies in Ireland* appear in his unpublished notes written in early retirement:

> In a book like Stephan's, facts are given without association of motive, aims, etc. This hardly gives them their place in history ... in many such accounts (as Stephan's e.g.) that purport to be factual, no consideration seems to be given to motive or plan.

Thus separated from any ostensible aim or purpose or explanation, certain actions seem meaningless and for that reason carry the stigma of being pure foolishness ... but only proper historical analysis would put such action in its proper perspective.

O'Donovan felt the IRA's

> ... linking in any way with G[ermany] might now seem remote, foolish and in some vague way treacherous ... but in essence it was not a crazy scheme. Germany, if and when engaged in war with England, had only a near miss (as Eisenhower and others have admitted). Had success possibly preceded America's joining [the war] and had the insane mistake of the 2nd front not been made by them, Germany, with victory, would have been very generous indeed towards a small weak state on its periphery.

O'Donovan's feelings about the war, prompted by Enno Stephan's book, are revealing. Less than twenty years after the conflict that destroyed large parts of Europe and cost tens of millions of lives, he still appears to regret the defeat of Germany and believes that Ireland would have done better from a 'very generous' Hitler had the Allies lost. In addition, he defends the IRA's decision to collaborate with the Nazi regime on the basis of hoping 'for improvement nationally by co-operation with Germany and to expect something from a German victory....'[16]

In 1966, Patrick O'Donovan, a columnist with *The Observer* in London, prompted a letter from Jim O'Donovan (no relation), having written about de Valera's small margin of victory (10,000 votes) in that year's presidential election. He told *The Observer* writer:

> Make no real historical mistake about this: we were 'neutral' on England's side, and the poor Germans caught or grounded or interned got a very raw deal

compared with the RAF who were helped to a quick and safe get-away any time they landed in trouble. Actually, there was a fairly complete liaison between the Americans, the English and the puny Irish forces.[17]

However, in his letter to *The Observer* the ex-ESB man did not spell out his own wartime role as the IRA's main liaison officer with Nazi Germany, or his work as the architect of the S-plan.

O'Donovan's retirement left him with more time to ponder his own life and the hand of cards that fate had dealt him. He collected voluminous material on Irish history, and historical accounts of the crucial treaty ratification period, in January 1922, would always trigger a reaction. One such example occurred in 1969 when journalist and historian Seán Cronin penned a long-running series for *The Irish Times* entitled 'The Fenian Tradition'. O'Donovan, naturally, collected all the instalments, most heavily underlining the one which included the following commentary:

> Elections for the parliament of Southern Ireland were set for June 16th [1922]; the Second Dáil (which by accepting the Treaty had put an end to the Republic of which it was the National Assembly) adjourned on June 8th with the intention of meeting again on June 30th to transfer its powers to the new assembly, and dissolve. Much was made later of the fact that it did not reconvene; but the issue is academic: even if it had met again what purpose could it serve since a majority of the members in effect had voted to abolish the Republic anyway?[18]

Though obviously unaware of it, Cronin had hit a sensitive nerve from O'Donovan's viewpoint. The Old IRA man's heavy underscoring of this particular paragraph served to emphasise his lifelong concern that power had not been properly transferred from the Second to the Third Dáil. For him, therefore, the 32-county republic still existed. And nearly half a century after the pivotal events of 1922, O'Donovan still felt as strongly that he had been duped, first by Richard Mulcahy and later by Éamon de Valera.

In 1970, O'Donovan made his first, and only, television appearance in a programme to mark the 50th anniversary of the execution of his wife's brother Kevin Barry – the 18-year-old medical student hanged by the British on 1 November 1920 for his part in a fatal IRA ambush on 20 September that year. The RTÉ interviewer, Cathal O'Shannon, remembers that O'Donovan 'was confined to a wheelchair and so wasn't in the best of form, but his recollections of events were clear and lucid. He was not a man to show an ounce of self-pity, but neither was he one who ever questioned what he had done in the past.' Off camera, though, O'Shannon recalls:

> Jim said that he had much rougher treatment from Free State soldiers than Barry ever did from the British, but that his real heroism was his stoicism during the three nights which he had to undergo as a man, or boy, under sentence of death.[19]

In the RTÉ documentary 'Kevin Barry', O'Donovan explained why, despite a number of plans (a proposal to blow up the wall of Mountjoy was considered too dangerous for passing civilians, while an attempt to send in an IRA snatch squad posing as prison visitors failed to work out as planned), the IRA was unable to free Barry:

> We were being arrested day after day. He wasn't alone in Mountjoy and he wasn't alone in all the jails of Ireland. They were picking them up every day and there were ambushes every day.... Collins, McKee, Seán Ó hUadhaigh and Myles Keogh decided that so little time was left that almost nothing could be done. That would account for what Piaras Béaslaí in his book talked about – Michael Collins spending the night practically in tears and frustration, the fact

Jim O'Donovan holding his daughter Sheila, with (foreground) sons Donal and Gerry, Dublin, early 1930s. *Photo courtesy of Aedine Sànta*

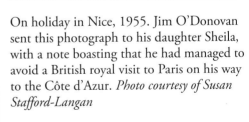

On holiday in Nice, 1955. Jim O'Donovan sent this photograph to his daughter Sheila, with a note boasting that he had managed to avoid a British royal visit to Paris on his way to the Côte d'Azur. *Photo courtesy of Susan Stafford-Langan*

Plinth of IRA chief of staff Seán Russell's statue in Dublin's Fairview Park, daubed with swastikas in 2009. *Photo courtesy of www.shanetobin.com*

Stone statue of Seán Russell (IRA chief of staff, 1938–1939) in Fairview Park, Dublin. The statue was decapitated by anti-fascist protestors in 2004 and replaced by a bronze statue in 2009. The new statue has a tracking device in the head to deter theft. *Photo: author*

Colman O'Donovan, Jim's brother, served as a senior diplomat in Rome and Lisbon during World War II.
Photo courtesy of Diarmuid O'Donovan

Ambulance driver Ted Cross helped to ferry the wounded to hospital after the IRA bombing of Coventry on 25 August 1939.
Photo: author

Paddy Fleming from Killarney, County Kerry, signed the IRA's declaration of war on England in January 1939. He gave the British four days to withdraw from Northern Ireland. Fleming was IRA chief of staff from 1945 to 1947 and later worked as chief steward of the Irish greyhound racing board. *Photo courtesy of Colm Connolly*

Billy Joe McCorry from Belfast was interned in the Curragh camp with Jim O'Donovan in the early 1940s. *Photo: author*

John Murphy from County Carlow worked in the Curragh internment camp as a military policeman. *Photo: author*

Eddie Keenan from Turf Lodge, Belfast, met Jim O'Donovan in the Curragh and described him as a 'dapper' man who was always well dressed. *Photo: author*

IRA man Tom Byrne carried out bombings in Liverpool during the S-plan campaign. He was deported to Ireland in 1939. *Photo: author*

Clockwise from top:
Jim Savage from Cork city proudly holds his Communist Party of Ireland membership card. He slept in the bunk next to Jim O'Donovan's in the Curragh camp. *Photo: author*

German agent Oscar Pfaus's wife Eda pictured with Jim O'Donovan in Hamburg, 1939. This is the only known photograph of O'Donovan in Nazi Germany.
Photo courtesy of Enno Stephan

Friedrich Weckler (1892–1943) was a friend and colleague of Jim O'Donovan's at the ESB. He was appointed chief accountant of the ESB in 1930, having worked previously on the Shannon hydro-electric scheme for the German engineering company Siemens. Weckler joined the German Nazi party in June 1934.
Photo courtesy of Bundesarchiv, Berlin

Crowds gather at the scene of the IRA bombing in Broadgate – Coventry's main shopping street – on 25 August 1939.
Photo: UK National Archives

that he could do nothing and that he realised he could do nothing.[20]

O'Shannon adds:

> I always felt that Jim was a cold sort of man who had no conscience about bombing civilians in England. I always felt that his attitude was not too far removed from support of Nazism. But he did have a lot of charm and was very much a man of his time.... While I admired his work during the Anglo-Irish war, I always found his association with the Nazis unpleasant. It is one thing being anti-British or English; another altogether embracing the German-Nazi ideals of the Thirties and Forties.[21]

Their failing health in the early 1970s led Jim and Monty O'Donovan to be admitted to a nursing home, Our Lady's Manor, overlooking the sea at Dalkey, County Dublin. Their visitors included the historian John Duggan. A retired lieutenant-colonel from Kilmallock, County Limerick, Duggan recalled:

> I became quite a regular visitor to the nursing home that he was in. It seemed to be too good an opportunity to lose. I couldn't believe that I had this living piece of history ... the two things that I can remember about him is being enraged and caged. He was enraged with everyone that I mentioned. There was never a light moment with him at all, he was railing against life. He said, 'Look at me now. Look what fate has dealt me in life. Look at what they've done to me.' I can remember that phrase well. He was disgruntled at his disability and although I had the impression of a man of great ability and character, I never met such a poisonous man in all my life ... what he was really simmering about was a volcanic annoyance with IRA inefficiency. He despised their inefficiency and he had nearly the same

sort of contempt for the much-vaunted German efficiency. He said the Germans were the greatest crowd of bunglers. My abiding impression of Jim O'Donovan is disenchantment with everybody and disenchantment with life, which I can understand now that I have got old.[22]

O'Donovan's son Donal remembers the stress of visiting his father, from whom he had become estranged over the years:

I found it very hard. I did go but it was always a struggle for me because I was jarred or half-jarred, and bringing him a bottle of whiskey as a kind of compensation. And having to bear the criticism for not having been for so long – maybe six weeks or whatever it was – you would have to take that every time you went. You'd put it off then.[23]

Dental surgeon Joe Briscoe, a leading member of Dublin's Jewish community (whose father Robert had been a member of the Four Courts garrison with O'Donovan in 1922 and, four years later, a founder member of Fianna Fáil) recalls Jim O'Donovan:

I met him originally when he was employed by the ESB and he came to me as a patient. Before very long we became good friends and he told me much about his IRA activities. However, he never mentioned his contacts with Nazi Germany and I still believe that he was not ideologically a supporter of Nazism. He was a fervent Irish nationalist and looked upon England as an enemy of Ireland. He told me that he was, up to 1932, a loyal supporter and admirer of Éamon de Valera. He was a poet and used to send Dev poems whilst Dev was in gaol. However, when Dev and FF took the oath in order to enter the Dáil [in 1927] all this loyalty and admiration ceased…. Eventually, he became too unwell to visit my surgery in Fitzwilliam

BELATED THANKS FROM THE THIRD REICH

Street and I used to go to him in Our Lady's Manor in Dalkey. He was a very unhappy man and I used to visit him socially on Saturdays, as I felt that he could talk and tell me about his activities. He was distraught when his wife had a stroke [in 1972] and could not communicate with him. I remember on at least one occasion when he said the following, he was actually crying: This, he said, was 'God punishing him' (I assume for the loss of life in England). I should like to imagine also that he regretted his contacts with the Nazis when their evilness became apparent – especially their 'Final Solution'. He never mentioned this but I still have that strong feeling. I also seem to remember that he was very opposed to the bombing that was then taking place in the North. He told me that, in some way, he felt responsible for this 'renewed' bombing campaign. This is not an assumption on my part, he actually said this. I have to repeat again that he felt that his poor health and pain, plus his wife's stroke, was a punishment from God. On many occasions he told me that he wished he would die. Needless to say this was most upsetting for me and I tried to alter these thoughts, but without avail.... I was, of course, well aware of the IRA's pre-war links with Germany. I think everybody knew that the IRA ideology then was 'England's enemy was Ireland's friend'. Many Irish people wanted to see England whacked. After the Holocaust and other evilness were revealed, many realised their mistake. I think that James was one of these. Perhaps he may even have been rationalising when he chose to become a patient of a Jewish dentist. However, I doubt this. Needless to say, this is an assumption on my part, as my Jewish heritage was never once discussed.[24]

THE DEVIL'S DEAL

Towards the end of his life, O'Donovan received an unexpected visit from the son of his old comrade, and later adversary, General Richard Mulcahy. Mulcahy had passed away in 1971, but his son Professor Risteárd Mulcahy, a leading heart surgeon, recalls:

> It was purely a chance remark I heard from somebody – it may have been a nurse. I heard that he was the last of the thirteen GHQ men, so I thought surely that my father would be very pleased if I went out to see him. So I went out and I think he was so surprised, so moved that he began to weep, actually. It is interesting. Of course, they had such a high regard for each other before the split. It was a desperate thing … the climax of it was when he began to weep when he met me. There was something climactic about that. He held my hand and found it hard to speak. But he did say complimentary things about my father. That's all I know. I found it a little emotional myself, particularly after leaving him and saying to myself how delighted my father would have been if he knew I'd done that. I went back to see him again when he was more or less in the last stages. The second time I saw him there wasn't the same tension or the same emotion. He was obviously very ill as I recall it. It was the first meeting that is much more vivid in my mind.[25]

So it seemed as if the self-professed 'heart of stone' could produce some tears after all. In his final years, O'Donovan spent many hours in conversation with Father Jordan, a chaplain at Our Lady's Manor nursing home – it might have been his way of finding some peace of mind before time ran out. O'Donovan was admitted to the home on 28 January 1971. His wife, Monty, joined him there following a stroke the following year, on 27 April 1972.[26]

But if sorrow was the emotion felt by Jim O'Donovan, his elder son was experiencing anger as his father's life ebbed away. Donal adds:

I did get angry. That anger came later when I realised that he had really been irresponsible in rejoining a movement that he had served twice and had no real reason to serve again ... especially to do it unsuccessfully. I did get angry. I was fortunate that I stopped drinking two years before he died and I had some time with him. But he was very miserable, in pain, in a nursing home. My wife and myself were the only people in the bedroom when he finally expired, so that was some kind of reconciliation ... I still have trouble grieving him. That may come but it hasn't yet.[27]

POSTSCRIPT

Jim O'Donovan's long and eventful life ended in Dublin's Meath Hospital on 4 June 1979. He had been rushed there from Our Lady's Manor nursing home in Dalkey, County Dublin, suffering from kidney failure. He was eighty-two years old. An obituary in *The Irish Times*, signed 'O'R' (O'Donovan's brother-in-law, Richard O'Rahilly), described him as 'a man of honour and of courage. He was unpopular, as he did not suffer fools gladly or at all. His endurance was outstanding.'[1] But Risteárd Mulcahy had the last word with a letter to *The Irish Times* a week later, correcting numerous mistakes in the obituary, including the erroneous claim that the IRA's GHQ staff had split seven-five for the treaty. Professor Mulcahy pointed out that the GHQ comprised thirteen men, not twelve, and that it had voted nine-four in favour of the treaty.[2] Even in death, it seemed that Jim O'Donovan still had the capacity to stir controversy.

POSTSCRIPT

By any standards, James Laurence O'Donovan had led an extraordinary life. Few Irish people could claim to have fought in a revolutionary war that created a new state, and still be fighting for what he perceived to be the same cause almost twenty-five years later. There was more than a little irony in the fact that, in 1941, O'Donovan ended up as a prisoner of the state he had helped to create, albeit not quite the one he had in mind when he began his struggle in December 1917. His dream, of course, was for a 32-county republic free of British influence – something he was never destined to witness. In a long lifetime he had known many setbacks, including his venture into private enterprise which ended in bankruptcy – some might say that his political and military aims, post-1921, ended the same way – and his dalliance with the Nazi regime. There was also an element of irony in the fact that it was the state payroll that kept the O'Donovan family ship afloat – through his middle management job with the ESB. This prompts the question as to just how much de Valera knew about his errant citizen in the crucial 1938–41 period when O'Donovan resumed active service. We may never know the precise answer to that question, but it seems likely that O'Donovan's close links to Hermann Görtz proved to be his undoing, while the Stephen Hayes affair was the final nail in the coffin of his IRA career. Luckily for him, he had the day job to fall back on.

And what of the extreme republicans' *danse macabre* around the Nazi flame in the 1933–45 period? On balance, it appears that the attraction of Britain's defeat at the hands of Germany proved too great for O'Donovan and others to resist. Some might say that there is a difference between seeking Germany's help to weaken or destroy Britain with a view to reuniting Ireland, and espousing Nazism. But O'Donovan's four 1939 trips to meet German agents on the continent, his willingness to help Abwehr agents on Irish soil, his apparent enthusiasm for teaching Nazi songs to Curragh internees, his lack of concern about being photographed near Görtz's Swastika-draped coffin, his apparent willingness to accept Kurt

Haller's post-war thanks for having helped the Third Reich, and his contention that a victorious Nazi Germany 'would have been very generous' to Ireland, all tell a different story – if not of a direct or fully fledged support of the Nazi ethos, then surely of a desire to do a deal, at any price, with any power that could defeat Britain. It just so happened that in the late 1930s that power was Hitler's Germany, whose infamy predated the discovery of the concentration camps in the spring of 1945.

As World War II got underway, Seán Russell and Jim O'Donovan shared the same delusion as other extreme nationalists in places as far apart as Croatia, India, Brittany, Belgium (the Flemish and Walloons), Wales and Scotland: that a German victory would bring independence, self-determination and, in Ireland's case, a reunited country. At best this high-risk gamble was a recipe for living under the Nazi jackboot in a satellite of the Third Reich. Helmut Clissmann, the Abwehr agent who had assisted Russell, O'Donovan, Frank Ryan and others, put it best when he told British author Robert Fisk in 1979:

> Hitler would have sold the Irish down the river. I would have told the Irish that their freedom was coming. I would have been a Lawrence of Arabia. It happened to several friends of mine, with the Bretons and the Walloons. Their freedom was promised but then, when the Germans had what they wanted, the separatist groups were abandoned.[3]

Did it ever occur to Jim O'Donovan that Ireland could suffer the same fate as befell Brittany or Walloonia in 1940, when the Germans made no attempt to grant these regions any form of autonomy? Did he care? While taking great risks, not least with de Valera's fragile neutrality policy, there is no evidence that he did. In O'Donovan's mind, a united Ireland came first and foremost, while the ultimate cost – and the fraught question of who would have to pay the price – remained issues for another day.

POSTSCRIPT

Jim O'Donovan's story is a complex and multi-faceted one. From his perspective, it also has its fair share of tragedy – some would say self-inflicted – in that after 1921 practically nothing went his way. With the luxury of hindsight, it would be too facile to say that he should have chosen an alternative path for, if nothing else, Jim O'Donovan was not for turning. He nailed his colours to the mast early on and remained steadfast in his dream for a lifetime. Some might put this down to stubbornness and an inability to grasp what was on offer, rather than lose everything. O'Donovan himself, however, would no doubt put it down to loyalty to a republic that remained forever beyond his reach.

APPENDIX 1

AUTHOR'S NOTE: Jim O'Donovan's S-plan ('S' for sabotage) – the IRA blueprint for the bombing campaign in England – was discovered when British police raided houses around London in early February 1939. Twelve suspected IRA members subsequently appeared at Bow Street magistrate's court in London on 6 February 1939, charged with conspiracy to cause explosions. The court also heard that police had seized gelignite, weapons and ammunition as a result of the raids and arrests.

The S-plan, which is reproduced here in full, seems to have been dictated from an original document, since lost, and was presented as exhibit 82 in the subsequent trial of the twelve IRA suspects. It contains a number of typographical errors, which are left uncorrected here, as they appear in the prosecution document (*source*: UK National Archives file CRIM 1/1086).

S-PLAN.

I. TIME.

(a) In order to exercise maximum world effect, the diversion must be carried out at a time when no major war or world crisis is on.

(b) If it is carried out at a time when trouble is anticipated, the jumpiness and nervous expectation of the government, as well as the potential panic of the people, can be exploited to the full.

If it is carried out at a time of recovery from crisis or relief after a serious war-scare, a certain amount of demoralisation and general relaxation of vigilance and precautionary measures can be relied upon. This will assist operations.

APPENDIX 1

(c) Since for ordinary guerrilla, winter conditions and darkness are advantageous, zero hour should be about the beginning of winter. Since further for reasons which will be discussed later, the campaign should open with the more major operations and these will both be facilitated by darkness and at the same time cause greater havoc or disorganisation by being carried out when hours of darkness follow, the campaign should begin at a moonless period.

(d) All the indications point to either October 20th or November 18th.

II. PROCLAMATION

(a) Republic to be re-proclaimed and the allegiance of all Irish subjects demanded, special reliance being placed on the response of the young, virile element of the nation and also those who, however subsequently divided by the rivalries and chicanery of leaders, showed that they had the true interests of Ireland at heart by fighting the enemy at a time when that enemy was unequivocally defined, i.e. when the struggle was a straight, direct issue (for this purpose 1,000 facsimile reproductions of the original Proclamation should be in readiness).

(b) Ultimatum to be issued to England demanding her complete evacuation of all Irish territory and territorial waters, demanding her absolute and registered renunciation of all claim to suzerainty over the whole territory of

Ireland as bounded by the seas and channels, demanding her complete withholding of all subsidy or financial influence from subordinate legislature or agents within the territory of Ireland who might be partial to the continuance of English interference in Irish affairs, abrogating unilaterally all and any pacts or agreements entered into by usurping legislatures; imposing time limits for the fulfilment of these demands and declaring that failure to express immediate willingness to negotiate under Four-Power guarantee of safety to negotiators will be followed by effort on our part when opportunity arises and by every means at our disposal, to ensure that the repeatedly expressed national will of Ireland to own absolutely her own soil and to control it independent of any outside influence shall be supreme.

(c) Copies of the Ultimatum, together with the Proclamation, shall be sent, <u>so as to arrive</u> simultaneously, to the British Premier, the Prime Minister of Northern Ireland, the Prime Minister of Southern Ireland, the Vatican, the French President, the American President, the Ambassadors of Germany, Italy, etc., for transmission to Chancellor Hitler, il Duce Mussolini, etc.

(d) Copies shall also be transmitted to the following with the intimation that originals have been sent to the British Government:

APPENDIX 1

> Scottish Nationalist Party
> Welsh Nationalist Party
> British Labour Party
> Independent Labour Party
> (English) Council of Civil Liberties
> (American)   "   "   "   "
> (Belfast)   "   "   "   " etc.

(i) The Scottish and Welsh Nationalist Parties will be assured of the sympathetic interest of Ireland in their aspirations and of the abiding affection of the Irish people for them as kindred of a common race. Assurance will be given also that there can be no enmity between these peoples and ours and that no conflict of opinion or loyalty can eventuate unless in these countries their own best national interests are subordinated to alien imperialistic interests. (The above and the 'every means at our disposal' at the end of par. II (b) are as far as hint can be given of the nature of the measures contemplated.)

(ii) The two Labour Parties will be assured of the sympathy of the democratic Irish people with their efforts for the betterment of the conditions of the English people, with whom the people of Ireland have no quarrel except in so far as acquiescence in the actions of their government, they assume admittedly wholly undesired a degree of responsibility for its conduct. They are in a position of great strength to demand immediately a cessation of interference in Irish affairs and a complete withdrawal and evacuation, which can be the only possible prelude to the much desired and lasting amity of two neighbours, whose propinquity places each in a position of interdependence. The Labour Parties must, however, bring every pressure to bear to secure the instant concession of the whole and historic demand. Their failure to do so will indicate that they are prepared to subordinate morality and justice to their superficial material interests and thus that they are content to share equally with the imperialist and undemocratic oligarchy in control, the responsibility for the continued repression of Ireland.

III. THE GENERAL PLAN

The main plan divides into two Departments: Propaganda and Action. It is difficult to say which is the more urgent and important — the release of the Propaganda campaign or the pushing ahead of the preparations, military and otherwise, for Action.

It is vitally necessary that a start be made immediately on the wide diffusion of the case for Ireland and the justification of the adoption of any and every means at our disposal to subjugate the obdurate will of our inveterate and powerful opponent to the still indomitable but weakly effective will of Ireland. It must be shown that this is the time to strike, that

APPENDIX 1

England has never been in so critical a condition, barred as she is by political tradition from adopting the only measures that would ensure her strength, namely totalitarian methods. The efforts of the principal organisers may be over-exclusively concentrated on the Action side of the conflict; hence it is essential immediately to take into at least partial confidence as many of the reliable active workers and sympathisers as can be of assistance in the neglected Propaganda department. It holds there even more than in the case of the military preparations that the job cannot be done overnight. It is already much too late to be making an organised start in this direction — every day from now will count vitally. Numbers of energetic workers must be pressed and recruited into this service <u>immediately</u>. The misinterpretation, the ridicule, the false propaganda or counter-propaganda that will be broadcast a <u>thousandfold</u> more effectively than we can possibly aspire to, may have a shattering effect on otherwise moderately effective military action. It may make all the difference between sympathy and hostility at home. The need for instant concentration on this side, with plenty of expenditure on printed matter, booklets, maps, leaflets etc., is again stressed. It will be reverted to again. (Germany's insistent success is due to the people's comprehension of their aims through radio and the printed word. People will think — and on right lines — if they get enough reading matter etc.)

The general plan, already described as consisting of two departments, Propaganda and Action, can be further developed as roughly shown in the following schematic diagram.

IV. PROPAGANDA

APPENDIX 1

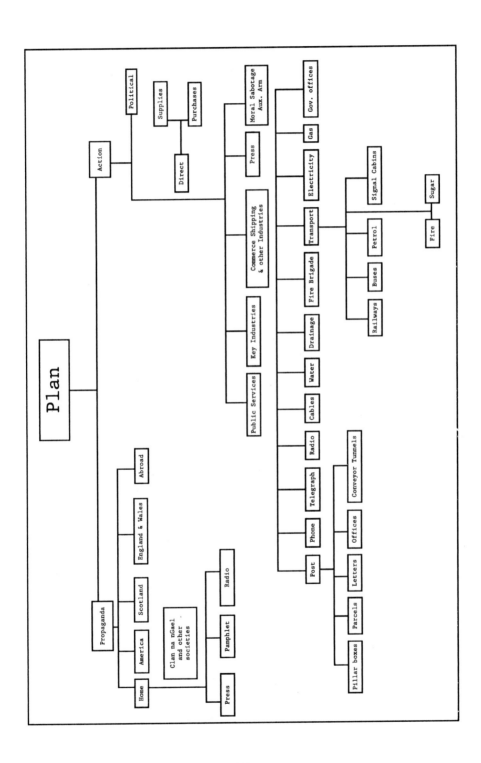

V. ACTION

As shown in III above, Action is divided into two main branches: Direct and Political. No attempt is made at this stage to sub-divide Direct Action into Tactical or Strategical considerations. The Political Division will be dealt with later (See V.b below).

A. DIRECT ACTION

<u>1.</u> This may concern itself with Military Air or Naval Opposition or movements, should these arms be called actively into service in suppressing our sabotage and other activities. Our weakness would reduce this form of action to a minimum.

<u>2.</u> The second legitimate but probably very inaccessible aim could be the destruction or sabotaging of aeroplane factories and stores, munition factories and stores etc. These would probably be so well guarded that success would be chancy.

<u>3.</u> The third target, and this will probably be the most important, because the most effective, the most unequivocal and the most justifiable, is the Public Services.

<u>4.</u> The fourth group could be such key industries as were at all accessible.

<u>5.</u> The fifth group could be commerce, banking and shipping; ordinary industries; cotton mills etc.; grain, tobacco and spirit stores; motor tyre stores; timber yards; etc etc.

These would constitute the second most

APPENDIX 1

important group, but the reactions and political implications might be such as to render its adoption inexpedient and more difficult of justification than the public services.

<u>6.</u>   The last group to be considered might prove to be an important one, especially if adopted as punitive action for incitement to repressive violence against our campaign or merely for the spreading of injurious propaganda about the revolutionaries and Ireland generally. This is the large-circulation English Press.

We come now to the consideration of each of these groups in detail:

1. <u>PUBLIC SERVICES</u>

Most of the Public Services considered below will be found to offer two types of target, one where it is centralised or concentrated, the other where it is scattered or widespread; the latter will be referred to as diffused outposts.

(i) <u>The Postal Service.</u>

This lends itself to a wide range of destructive activity, which will be hard to localise or trace and easy to have repeated. In this case, the diffused outposts would be the pillar-boxes and smaller post offices.

(a) As a last stage operation, the dropping of incendiary material into letter-boxes and its ignition by the familiar methods could be fallen back on with virtual impunity.

(b) As an intermediate stage operation there could be the despatch at G.P.O.s of letter packages made up containing incendiary unit No. 1 (See Manual of Instructions) just in time for collection, so as to permit of their transit such distance as to make it possible that they would form part of a large bulk of similar packages.

(c) As an intermediate stage operation also, there could be the similar dispatch of the same Incendiary unit No. 1 made up into parcel post packages. This would have the great advantage of allowing very much more combustible and flame-spreading material to be included, but against this as compared with letters there probably would not be the same volume of parcels in sufficiently close proximity.

(d) There are special cases in which a major operation might be possible if Intelligence is capable of organising it. Such operation on the theory accepted in this Plan should be arranged for the earliest possible stages of activities, as otherwise, in the general alarm and precautionary atmosphere brought about by the commencement of the campaign, it would be too well guarded subsequently.

An example of the type meant would be an attack by incendiary, explosive, or mechanical blockage on the 6½ mile long postal tunnel between Paddington and Whitechapel. The

APPENDIX 1

assumption is that at various points along this unattended route, there would be manholes or access of some sort.

(ii) The Telephone System.

Most action here is suggested as later stage type.
(a) Tapping and other forms of interference.
(b) Destruction of instruments.
(c) Disconnection of police-boxes and any other important and clearly defined lines.
(d) Cutting of wires and cables in quantity.
(Note: In Britain the figures show Birmingham has fewest phones per population. The towns with the largest proportion of phones are London, Eastbourne, Bournemouth, Worthing, Southport, Brighton, Cambridge, Edinburgh, Chester, Blackpool and Oxford.)

(iii) The Telegraph System.

Similar throughout to (ii) a-d above

(iv) Radio and Broadcasting.

Since other stations can always carry on, this would be a doubtful type of operation.
(a) Interfering or sending conflicting and disturbing items.
(b) Destruction of instructions or stations.
(c) Demolition of aerials might in certain cases be possible.

(v) <u>Cables.</u>

These are usually clearly indicated and are often in very isolated places.

A delay-action land-mine might possibly be employed. The disorganisation would probably not be very great unless simultaneously planned at various points. The operation is essentially one that might be left to intermediate or later stage in programme.

(vi) <u>Water.</u>

As water is essential to life, any ideas such as pollution etc., must be rigorously ruled out and <u>this principle applies generally</u>. Apart altogether from ethical considerations, the Hague Convention representing civilised international opinion and agreement condemns all such actions and we would be doing Ireland and our cause infinite harm by adopting any such means.

(a) Scarcity and rationing would however prove a warrantable dislocation and often viaduct pipe-lines are exposed, not buried, and, in isolated districts, would lend themselves to delay-action landmine treatment, flooding being caused at the same time as shortage.

(b) The only exposed pipe-lines connected with a hydro-electric scheme are those serving the Galloway scheme. But this is in Scotland and therefore probably outside the Plan.

There are, however, subject to confirmation,

APPENDIX 1

exposed pipe-lines connected with a now no doubt very important aluminium factory in Scotland (Argyll) which is probably engaged on shadow aeroplane parts, etc. production.

(vii) <u>Drainage</u>.

This important service in large towns might be made the object of an early stage attack. The method would demand considerable self-possession and possibly (in the event of any questioning which however is unlikely) some resourcefulness. It is to hire or procure a lorry, load up one or two tons of quicksetting cement, also a manhole guard-rail and tarpaulin. Stop at a main sewage conduit manhole. Erect manhole guard-rail and cover over with tarpaulin, dump in bag the whole load. A 'Repair Work' street notice might heighten the illusion and help to render the activity unremarkable. The whole operation could be completed in 15-20 minutes at most with two men.

(viii) <u>Fire Brigade.</u>

No effort should be made to make a major operation out of this service (for humanitarian reasons).

(a) The methods adopted by the Black and Tans in Cork and elsewhere, however, should be borne in mind – they cut fire-hoses, which rendered them ineffective for the extinction of fires already caused and were not readily replaceable.

(b) as a late stage operation of diffused type, false alarms could be raised in many quarters simultaneously. Without active intervention this in large centres would be equivalent to setting fire to certain buildings, for a real fire that coincided with the false alarms would stand a smaller chance of timely aid (ix).

(ix) Electricity.
As a brief indication of the tremendous importance of this service, the following figures might be considered. It might first be said that apart altogether from dislocation of industry business and transport, the moral and panic effects of extensive black-outs, i.e. from the viewpoints of lighting only, can be very great.

There are 118 generating stations directly controlled from the Central Electricity Board's control rooms at Newcastle, Manchester, Leeds, Birmingham and London. (This is the largest number ever operated in parallel anywhere).

The length of the transmission in the 'Grid' is 4125 miles, of which 2898 miles are at 132,000 volts.

There are 300 switching and transformer stations. The total capital invested in overhead transmission lines is £9,700,000, in underground cables is £5,800,000 and in switching and transformer stations is over £14,000,000. (Note: supplementary details of a more practical nature will be found in the Manual of Instructions.)

APPENDIX 1

If destruction is contemplated it can be carried out at many points. Study of the 'Grid' map of its transmission lines would indicate towns which could be isolated by simultaneous attack on the two or more alternative feeds afforded by its position in the 'rings' or 'loops'. Also towns, to which only one major supply is available, thus confirming the necessity of attack to only one point.

The stations and numerous small sub-stations in towns and cities are all open to attack, but probably the remote isolated lines passing through open country are the easiest target.

In selecting these consideration should be given to the size of towns and the degree of dependence from industry on electricity. Of all towns, Coventry would seem to be the most dependent in relation to its population (but see Par.b below). It is not wholly dependent on the Grid as it has its own generating station.

Delay-action Land-mine attention is indicated, and should be simple to organise, but obviously must be practically the very first job, as, consequent upon the opening of the campaign, the defensive measures adopted would almost certainly include patrolling of the major transmission lines. Even if no operation of this nature were carried out, yet if as a precautionary measure, patrols were established, this would be a very successful result owing to the sense of insecurity created and the actual immobilisation of so many men (on patrol, guard, and watchman duties). This applies generally and must be borne in mind when gauging the effect of operations in other spheres.

(a) The numerous London generating stations are almost entirely, if not entirely, interconnected by very high voltage (oil-fitted) underground cables. As they will be inaccessible unless Intelligence has localized them carefully and shown attack to be practicable, London from this viewpoint must be overlooked.

(b) The second most important centre is that centred around Birmingham, within a fifty mile radius. Besides Birmingham itself, which is the second biggest city in England (greater in population than either Liverpool or Manchester), there are small towns and important industrial centres such as Coventry, Wolverhampton, Northampton, Rugby, Leicester, Warwick, etc. (see map in rough note). These all have their own generating stations, but it is legitimate to assume that forcible rupture of the 'Grid' feeds into any of them will either leave them inadequately supplied or deprive the 'Grid' of their surplus production on which the system would be partially dependent.

(c) The double-circuit line of towers (i.e. with six wires) running south out of Birmingham for some miles would obviously give _twice_ the return in dislocation for the same effort as compared with the more common single-circuit (with three

APPENDIX 1

wires) lines. This line also, in the event of simultaneous attack on the other alternative feeders out of Birmingham (two more only) and accompanied by possible disturbance in London, would have added importance, since <u>via</u> Warwick and it is one of the standby feeds into London.
(d) The third most important area which will repay examination is the Liverpool, Manchester, Leeds area. The same principles as previously indicated should hold here.

(x) <u>Gas.</u>
This does not lend itself to favourable condsideration for two reasons, first, damage could hardly be inflicted without loss of life, and second, the ever-present dangers of fire ensure that the maximum precautions against it have already been taken and success would be doubtful. The latter principle, as explained elsewhere, is generally applicable in all such cases, e.g. petrol stores, explosive factories etc., where there is a great and ever-present risk from fire and explosion.

(xi) <u>Government Offices.</u>
Under the circumstances these are legitimate targets. Where collusion is possible, i.e. where a sympathetic or active government employee is available, nothing could be simpler than the depositing in suitable form of Incendiary Unit No. 2 preferably or alternatively I.U. No.1 in

cupboards or such places prior to locking up or closing hour. Owing to the wide scattering of staffs, especially senior officers, on a Saturday afternoon, the dislocation would be probably be greater if the job were timed for 1 p.m. on Saturday rather than 5 p.m. or 6 p.m. on a weekday. Moreover, the likelihood of any other of the staff working late on a Saturday is very much less than on a weekday. This lessens the possibility of a too-early alarm being given. Again, flames or smoke would be much longer in attracting attention during daylight hours than at night-time.

(a) The only sub-divisions necessary at this stage are the central targets such as Admiralty, War Office, Foreign Office, etc. as contrasted with diffused outposts. The older buildings, although no doubt brought moderately up to date with automatic fire-extinguishing equipment, are probably a better mark than such new buildings (the example given, though not governmental, would no doubt otherwise be a fair mark) as the London County Council building.

An operation against any of the above would have to be one of the early jobs, depending on the facilities available to the particular member of the staff or person otherwise gaining legitimate entry, and the general tightening-up brought about by the opening of the campaign.

(b) Diffused outposts, e.g. post offices, inland revenue offices (Customs and Excise), Coastguard

APPENDIX 1

stations, etc., could be regarded as intermediate or late jobs.

(xii) <u>Transport.</u>

This section of the public services is probably the most important of all, because, even more than interference with electricity which is a comparatively small factor in industry and social life, serious dislocation would have a paralysing effect on every branch of industrial and commercial life. Even to produce partial or local dislocation simultaneously would have a completely unsettling effect on the country's economic life, because the sense of insecurity would slow down the whole stream of commerce and cause tremendous dissipation of energy by necessitating a policy of protection or watchfulness for every movement. (See also Va 2 on Key industries.)

(a) <u>Sea</u>

Stores in shipping sheds. Ships cargoes. I.U. No.2. Interference with navigational lights or warnings not to be considered.

(b) <u>Air</u>

Military aviation at all times a legitimate target. No delay-action to be contemplated which could happen during flight. Any operation which would have the effect of delaying the start of Air Mails etc. for the Continent would occasion world-wide comment and interest.

(c) <u>Rail</u>

This sub-divides into steam and electric, the latter including Tubes, etc. Both are highly accessible at sidings, junctions and in loCounty sheds and this forms a desirable, justifiable, and fairly easy objective – the electric being easier to put out of action. This form of attack is most desirable since it can inflict no personal injury. Trains, coaches and their laden cargoes should all be easy to arrange for.

As parts of ordinary cargo, I.U. 2 should be suitably arranged. Electric signal cabins as nerve centres of big lines would also be a target. It should first be established that wrecking would not involve wholesale collisions. This possibility is extremely unlikely as in that case an electrical black-out which is a normal contingency to be guarded against, could have the same effect. (In this connection, from a technical work, is taken the instance of an electric line falling on railway, telephone and signalling lines; a big North Sea storm caused the insulators on the 35kv. line to be covered with salt, resulting in almost constant flashing over. It had the effect of rendering the signalling instruments almost inoperative and this, in turn, had the effect of slowing down all the trains.)

Railway cloakrooms, luggage stores and merchandise sheds constitute a first class objective for the application of I.U.2. Since

APPENDIX 1

the certainty of grip of the initial flames would be largely conditioned by time, the success of such jobs depends on delay action arrangements prior to definite locking-up time.

(d) <u>Trams, Trolley-buses and buses</u> can all be tackled during garaging periods. It would be necessary to find out at what hour cleaners commenced their duties – probably midnight or 1 a.m. to 5 or 6 a.m. I.U.2 could here be employed or smallest possible units of I.U.1 dropped into many petrol tanks simultaneously.

A minor degree of dislocation could be secured at a late period in the campaign by the addition of sugar (molasses or golden syrup, etc., better if in suitable capsules with loose lid) to the petrol.

(e) <u>Private and commercial transport</u>

Open to attack at intermediate or late stages in ways similar to those described above, when major operations for any reason could not be safely carried out.

The above concludes what may be regarded as the system of Public Services.

Va Continued.

(ii) <u>Key Industries.</u>

These, especially in so far as armament or aeroplane factories, etc. are concerned, constitute a very important target, though naturally less diffused or widespread than the Public Services.

THE DEVIL'S DEAL

In fact, from the viewpoint of damaging the military strength of the nation, a well-organised or fortunately times and circumstances attack on a particular key industry might have a crippling effect on the country's re-armament programme.

Analysing various such industries, there could hardly be found one which would have a more crippling effect on the military aviation and mechanisation programmes than the destruction or dislocation of magneto factories. A glance through aeroplane or automobile magazine advertisements will show where these are mostly manufactured. Precision instruments of all kinds, including lathes etc., all form a similar target.

Generally it might be hazarded that heavy chemical industries are mostly in Glasgow or Lancashire, coal-mining etc. in Newcastle and northern areas and South Wales, cotton in Manchester etc. - all above a line north of the Birmingham area. South of the Birmingham area and in the London area, heavy chemical industries again and the lighter engineering and other industries. But in the Birmingham area itself, many vital key industries. This is largely a guess and should be confirmed.

3. <u>COMMERCE, SHIPPING, BANKING, other industries</u>.

There is no need to elaborate on this

APPENDIX 1

section, which is too wide in its scope to commit to detail. Generally, attack on any of these would come at intermediate or later stages of the campaign.

4. PRESS NEWSPAPERS.

This section also requires no explanation. If certain newspapers habitually behave in a hostile fashion towards Ireland or if in connection with this particular campaign they have incited to fiercest reprisals or have distorted the obvious aims and suppressed the truth as furnished to them by our Propaganda Bureau, then they have let themselves in for legitimate punitive action. The time and weapon employed are of our own choosing. Here, it is unlikely that incendiary methods would avail, although if the most delicate and vital parts of the huge machines can be located and if suitable access can be had at the idle hours, this also might be possible. Sledgehammer methods would serve but would almost certainly be impracticable. What is desired therefore, is to ascertain the number and types of the machines, study these in an up-to-date text book or Printing machinery catalogue or get experts' information and devise some type of sand or spanner in the works which will have the effect of permitting the usual trial run through of the machines but will ensure their progressively increasing gumming up or disintegration (e.g.

crown wheel in motor-car can be 'chewed up' very rapidly once one chip off a cog is present).

5. <u>MORAL SABOTAGE. AUXILIARY ARM.</u>

(a) The most essential preparation for this from the viewpoint of DIRECT ACTION is to secure from every possible source, clean stocks of stationery (i.e. letterheads and official envelopes, rubber stamps, etc.) from Government and other Departments.

Such a store of notepaper etc. laid in previously to the opening of our campaign, in the possession of our Intelligence or Headquarters, would be an invaluable asset. Instructions and documents of all kinds could be successfully counterfeited as emanating from Admiralty, War Office, Air Ministry, Foreign Office, Dominions Office, Department of Education etc. and also the various Railways, Shipping Companies, Electricity Commissioners etc.

These could be availed of in thousands of ways as the imagination dictates and could be used to play into or co-operate with direct attack on certain objectives.

Numerous letters could be despatched at the same time causing simultaneous action, perhaps of a secret nature, such as troop or A.R.P. mobilisations etc., using some such safe and express method of delivery as the District Messenger Service.

APPENDIX 1

(b) For two reasons it might be desirable to have our men join various of the precautionary units such as A.R.P. Given men well suited to 'carry this off', they should join at once or on the wave of the first popular organising appeal that may be made. First, it would give them an insight into the kind of precautions that are being actually taken against outbreaks of fire. Secondly it would make them 'respectable' in the eyes of neighbours and might serve to cloak various activities of theirs e.g. carrying packages which might ultimately arouse suspicions. Further, if equipped with badge, armlet or gas mask, etc., and being able to produce their certificate as to unit and rank, etc., it might come in useful when in a tight corner by nearly being caught in the act or in the neighbourhood just after a job.

(c) A National Register of England will probably soon be decided on. She cannot organise efficiently for War without it. The prevention of its being taken should be easy by burning depots where returns go to etc.

This concludes the details of Section A of ACTION as distinct from PROPAGANDA. It might be well to add certain general principles that emerge from consideration of Section A (i.e. DIRECT ACTION).

ADDENDUM TO SECTION A:
GENERAL PRINCIPLES

1. For every man we have the enemy has ten thousand men. Operations must therefore be so

fool proof and so certain in action as to afford a 10,000:1 margin of safety, i.e. freedom from detection or capture.

2. Included in the very first series of operations should be those major operations at centres where the favourable population available is very small and where at a later date, such major operations would be difficult. This would incidentally put off the scent for those whose duty it would be to try to locate the headquarters of the organisers of the campaign.

3. The most major and 'centralised' operations should come first. This, because at the first spot of bother, all precautionary measures, special patrolling corps, watch guards, etc. will be put on a war time basis. These will probably be sufficient to render operations of this type impossible or much more chancy at a subsequent date.

4. The discovery of one dud Incendiary Unit or Delay-Action mine would give away the focal points of action, the probable scope of activities, and, still more vital, the materials on which our weapons are based. The procuring of even the most innocent of these materials at a subsequent date might conceivably arouse dangerous suspicions. Supplies (adequate to the campaign) of _all_ materials down to the last item, must therefore be laid in and suitably divided into at least three dumps in each area,

APPENDIX 1

so that the capture of one would inflict only a 33 1/3 % blow at that area's organisation.

<u>5.</u> Since the avoidance of the discovery of a dud is important, two units should be incorporated in every case where feasible instead of only one.

NOTES

1. Origins of a Revolutionary

[1] The author is grateful to Senator Terry Leyden for details of the O'Donovan family in Roscommon in the 1890s. Mr Richie Farrell, Roscommon county librarian, Ms Caitlín Browne, senior library assistant, and Ms Mary Skelly, Roscommon Heritage and Genealogy Company, Strokestown, were also of assistance.

[2] The author is grateful to Mr John McCabe, alumni director of St Aloysius' College, Glasgow, for details about O'Donovan's early education in Scotland.

[3] Author's interview with Gerry O'Donovan, 25 August 1999. According to Donal O'Donovan, his father had 'applied for a purser's position with the navy but did not win a place. The ship he was due to join sank a few months later' (author's interview with Donal O'Donovan). The irony is that had Churchill approved O'Donovan's application to join the royal navy, the IRA's top explosives expert would have ended up serving the British crown instead.

[4] Author's interview with Mrs Aedine Sànta, 31 May 1999. Mrs Sànta adds: 'Father's school motto was *Ad Majora Natus Sum* (I was born for greater things) – that was the Jesuit school motto and he always acted like that'; the archivist of St Aloysius', John McCabe, notes that '*Ad Majora Natus Sum* is the college motto and now appears on the school blazer. *Ad Majorem Dei Gloriam* [For the greater glory of God] is the motto

NOTES

with which James L. O'Donovan would have been familiar, and it would have been written at the beginning of every written piece of work or exam' (McCabe to author, 20 October 2009).

[5] The UCD archives contain no second-year results for James Laurence O'Donovan because 'second-year exams are not regarded as university exams, but as college tests… he did take the M.Sc. in autumn 1919'. The author is grateful to UCD archivist, Seamus Helferty, for his help in clarifying O'Donovan's academic record for the years 1914-19.

[6] NLI file MS 21/987, Bliss to O'Donovan, 30 December 1916. According to the St Aloysius' College archives, Fr Bliss taught English and history while on the staff there from 1911 to 1920. He taught Jim O'Donovan English literature in the 1912/13 academic year. The Jesuit eventually left the school in 1920 to become editor of *The Sacred Heart Messenger* (McCabe to author, 2 March 2009).

[7] Dillon appears to have been the initial formative IRA influence on the young O'Donovan, not only recruiting him into active service but also training him in the formulation and use of explosives. In 1962, Dillon told an American academic: 'Through my fiancée, Geraldine Plunkett, I got to know her brother, Joseph Plunkett, who was one of the leaders of the Volunteers and who later was one of the signatories of the Proclamation of the Irish Republic in 1916, and was executed by the British. Through Joseph Plunkett I became adviser to the Volunteers on the production of simple explosives and hand grenades. To carry on this work, I was sworn into the IRA.' (See Joseph A. Schufle, 'Thomas Dillon: Chemist & Revolutionary', in *Chemistry*, the journal of the American Chemical Society, vol. 43, April 1970, pp. 18–21). The treasurer of the UCD chemical society was Margaret 'Pearl' Egan. In 1928, she married Michael Flannery (1902–94) in New York. He founded the Provisional IRA's American fundraising arm Noraid in 1969 (author's interview with Donal O'Donovan, 12 February 1999).

[8] Author's interview with Mrs Sheila Hanna, 27 March 2000.

[9] NLI, O'Donovan papers, file 21/155.

[10] MA (Military Archives, Dublin), file S.1536, O'Donovan's 1957 deposition to Bureau of Military History, pp. 3–5.

[11] MA, BMH deposition, p. 6.

[12] Seán MacBride briefly became IRA chief of staff in 1936 but soon afterwards opted for mainstream politics. As leader of the Clann na Poblachta party, he became minister for external affairs in the 1948–51 inter-party government, and in later years worked for the United Nations, overseeing Namibia's transition to independence. MacBride won the Nobel peace prize in 1974 and the Lenin peace prize in 1977; Richard Mulcahy began his medical studies at UCD in October 1917 and 'registered for his second year in 1918 but did not proceed because of his duties as chief of staff. He continued to use the department of physiology as one of his more frequented "joints" during the War of Independence'. The author is grateful to General Mulcahy's son, Professor Risteárd Mulcahy, for these details (Mulcahy to author, 25 February 2009).

[13] See Conor Foley, *Legion of the Rearguard* (London 1992), p. 196; also D. J. Hickey and J. E. Doherty, *A New Dictionary of Irish History from 1800* (Dublin 2003), p. 87.

Córas na Poblachta was founded on 21 February 1940. Many of its members, but not O'Donovan, later joined Seán MacBride's Clann na Poblachta, founded on 6 July 1946.

2. The Unfinished Portrait

[1] The official-sounding title meant, in effect, that O'Donovan was 'in charge of explosives', as he told the Bureau of Military History in his 1957 submission to that body.

[2] According to Professor Risteárd Mulcahy, it was his mother, Mrs Mary 'Min' Mulcahy, who suggested the idea of a group portrait: 'Shortly after the Truce [11 July 1921], Dad and my mother had afternoon tea in the Gresham Hotel. It was probably Dad's first appearance in public after being on the run. At the next table they recognised the painter Leo Whelan, who was with a priest. During the conversation with their two neighbours, my mother was inspired to suggest that Whelan should take the opportunity of painting the general headquarters staff while the truce lasted. Whelan apparently responded enthusiastically to the idea' (R. Mulcahy, *Richard Mulcahy (1886–1971): A Family Memoir* (Dublin 1999), p. 48).

[3] Collins sat for Whelan only twice, on 17 and 20 February 1922. See 'An Irishman's Diary', in *The Irish Times*, 27 September 1969.

[4] *Irish Independent*, 10 November 1945, p. 3. Whelan's individual portrait of Richard Mulcahy was purchased in 1962 by the general's son Professor Risteárd Mulcahy, and now hangs in the officers' mess in McKee barracks, Dublin, where a copy of the group portrait is also displayed. (Other copies of the GHQ group portrait are to be found in army barracks around the country, including Cathal Brugha barracks in Rathmines. The original painting hangs in the National Museum at Collins barracks, Dublin.) In 1952, Jim O'Donovan – perhaps wishing to preserve a pictorial record of his own place in Irish history – bought his individual portrait from Leo Whelan. It is now in the possession of the O'Donovan family. Full details of Leo Whelan's works are contained in *Michael Leo Whelan RHA (1892–1956)* by Geraldine A. Molloy, MA (Master's thesis, 2007, UCD).

[5] *Irish Independent*, 10 November 1945, p. 3.

[6] Seán Russell was similarly committed, but died aboard a German U-boat off the Irish coast in mid-August 1940. Russell had met the Nazi foreign minister, Joachim von Ribbentrop, in Berlin on 5 August 1940, two days before leaving from the occupied French port of Lorient.

[7] In compiling the above pen-pictures of the 13-member pre-treaty IRA GHQ staff, the author acknowledges the help of Commandant Victor Laing, Director of the Military Archives; Maedhbh McNamara, Oireachtas Library; Ruairí Ó Brádaigh, former president of Sinn Féin; Seán O'Mahony, historian; Pat Butler, RTÉ; James McGuire, editor of the *Dictionary of Irish Biography from the earliest times to the year 2002* (Cambridge 2009); John Chambers; and Seán Ó Briain. *The Oxford Companion of Irish History* and *A New Dictionary of Irish History from 1800* were used in completing the list.

[8] Author's interview with Donal O'Donovan, 12 February 1999.

NOTES

3. Active Service

[1] MA (Military Archives, Dublin) file S.1536, O'Donovan's deposition to Bureau of Military History, pp. 5, 12; American historian W. H. Kautt notes that 'O'Donovan spent several years working on various explosive concoctions at his apartment on Richmond Road in Dublin. As early as 1918, he and an unnamed professor [presumably Tom Dillon] were producing mercury fulminate and even more complex explosives …' (W. H. Kautt, *Ambushes and Armour* (Dublin 2010), p. 162).

[2] Sir William Mills (1856–1932) designed the Mills bomb, a hand grenade that was widely used by British troops in World War I. Some 70 million Mills bombs were used in that conflict. (See www.firstworldwar.com/bio/mills.)

[3] MA, O'Donovan deposition to Bureau of Military History (BMH), pp. 7–9; Dr Kautt adds that 'grenade cases' and 'all other bomb parts' were being cast in a clandestine foundry 'in the basement of the small Heron & Lawless bicycle shop at 198 Parnell Street, right in the centre of Dublin' (Kautt, p. 163).

[4] Author's interview with Seán Clancy (10 August 2006). In 1922, Clancy supported the treaty and chose to become a career officer in the new national army. During the civil war he was based in his native County Clare. He retired in 1959 with the rank of Lieutenant Colonel. Shortly before his death in 2006, aged 105, he granted the author an interview.

[5] The author is grateful to the director of the Military Archives, Commandant Victor Laing, for granting access to the relevant files. Further material on O'Donovan's two pension applications can be found in NLI file 22/300.

[6] These and subsequent details of O'Donovan's pension applications are contained in MA file G2/1590.

[7] Mulcahy's son, Professor Risteárd Mulcahy, notes that: 'It was a disagreement between a minister who was in his official capacity refusing a request from O'Donovan acting for the anti-treaty IRA executive, a request which was incompatible with the Provisional Government's commitment to a democratic constitution. And there was no transferring of executive power from the IRA to Dáil Éireann, for the pre-treaty IRA had no executive powers. As head of the army, my father always claimed that the army was the army of the Sinn Féin parliament [i.e. the First Dáil] and was there to serve parliament and the people. He also claimed that the war of independence was forced on the Volunteers by the increasing British harassment of the Sinn Féin leadership, a leadership which had been confirmed by the democratically elected parliament in 1919' (Mulcahy to author, 26 October 2007).

[8] Details of O'Donovan's May 1922 grenade injury are contained in his pension application file G2/1590 at the Military Archives, Dublin. The Kildare county infirmary, to which O'Donovan was taken for treatment, was located in Kildare town, six miles from Monasterevin. Today the building is the Derby House Hotel. (The author is grateful to Mario Corrigan of the County Kildare Library and Arts Service, for this information on the old county infirmary.)

[9] Author's interview with Donal O'Donovan, 16 March 2005.

[10] James Toner to Professor Mark Hull, 6 January 2003.

[11] Author's interview with a former ESB employee who wished to remain anonymous.

[12] Author's interview with Donal O'Donovan, 16 March 2005.

13 According to Professor Risteárd Mulcahy, 'O'Donovan and Béaslaí were appointed to the [GHQ] staff early in 1921'. Mulcahy adds that 'The original GHQ staff, appointed in March 1918, had the following members: Mulcahy, Collins, MacMahon, R. O'Connor, Dick McKee and Austin Stack (appointed but never acted)'. Mulcahy notes that Austin Stack's 25 November 1920 'nomination was not agreed by the GHQ staff' (Mulcahy, *My Father, The General: Richard Mulcahy and the Military History of the Revolution* (Dublin 2009), pp. 33–34).

14 MA, O'Donovan deposition to BMH, pp. 10–11.

15 Dr Hermann Kast (1869–1927) was a leading academic expert on explosives. See obituary of Dr Kast in *Nature*, vol. 121, p. 66, 14 January 1928.

16 Professor Risteárd Mulcahy comments: 'I do not believe that there were such titles as commandant-general in the pre-treaty army. For instance, Béaslaí called himself general after the treaty but to the best of my knowledge he never played a military role. His presence in the GHQ picture in the museum only confirms that even by the truce the army structure had not yet evolved fully along the lines of a professional army. Some of these titles were self-adopted. On one occasion when my father complained to Collins, who was chairman of the Provisional Government at the time, that a certain army colleague had claimed the title of general, Collins replied "Let the baby have his stripes".' (Mulcahy to author, 26 October 2007). In his most recent book, Professor Mulcahy describes Piaras Béaslaí as 'a nominal member of GHQ, his connection was almost entirely with Collins and the Vaughan's Hotel [IRB] group'. See Mulcahy, *My Father, The General*, p. 35.

17 According to Francis FitzGerald's nephew, the former Taoiseach Dr Garret FitzGerald, his uncle 'ran a chemical works at Stratford, near his home in West Ham'. See G. FitzGerald, *All In A Life: Garret FitzGerald, an Autobiography* (Dublin 1992), p. 4; Dr FitzGerald told this author: 'My uncle Francis was supplying explosives to Collins – this was after the truce – for use in Northern Ireland' (author's interview with Dr Garret FitzGerald, 21 May 2008). In January 1921, 'Michael Collins ordered his agents in Britain to purchase springs for bombs by the gross … by February, he increased his order to 1,000 springs per week' (Kautt, p. 163); Francis FitzGerald died in 1941 as the result of a Luftwaffe air-raid which caused a gas explosion at his London factory.

18 Jim O'Donovan's papers contain an undated nine-page typed letter from Colman O'Donovan to his brother Dan, detailing his war of independence incarceration in Hereford Prison and Bush Camp at Pembroke Dock, south-west Wales.

19 In his 1957 submission to the BMH, O'Donovan wrote, 'I was under a contract with employers at this time and they would not release me, so it was agreed with the director of organisation [O'Hegarty] that I should do the best I could part-time for the time being…. Mulcahy immediately approved of the suggestion by the director of organisation about taking me on to headquarters.' (MA, BMH submission, p. 12). For whatever reason, O'Donovan did not tell the BMH that his employers were the Jesuits at Clongowes Wood College where he worked as a senior science master from 1919 to 1921.

20 The army investigators appear to have got their dates mixed up here, confusing 11 July 1921 (the date of the Anglo-Irish truce) with 10 May 1922, the date of the

NOTES

explosion that maimed O'Donovan's right hand. In an earlier submission to the pensions board, O'Donovan cited 10 May 1922 as the date of the mishap. However, the location, Monasterevin, is the same in both cases.

[21] The army transcript refers to Tom Daly, but this is probably a transcription error. Tom Dillon was an assistant professor in UCD's chemistry department (1909–19) under Professor Hugh Ryan when Jim O'Donovan was a student there (1914–19). Dillon was later professor of chemistry at University College Galway (1919–54).

[22] Whelan's group portrait is officially designated as representing the pre-treaty IRA GHQ staff, not the pre-truce GHQ staff, as O'Donovan describes them.

[23] Professor Risteárd Mulcahy notes that, 'Much of what he [O'Donovan] describes corresponds to my father's accounts of these times. Of course, my father disagreed profoundly with the policies of O'Donovan, Russell and their active anti-treaty colleagues, but in his memoirs he praised all those who fought in the war of independence, irrespective of their subsequent views on the treaty. I believe he would have supported O'Donovan's claim for a pension by the 1930s when the anti-treatyites were included in the pension list for the first time' (Mulcahy to author, 26 October 2007).

[24] Professor Risteárd Mulcahy notes that his father, General Mulcahy, 'was a go-between for all the members of the [general headquarters] staff, but he never allowed them to meet as a group'. This was in order to avoid a mass arrest of all the leaders (author's interview with Risteárd Mulcahy, 2 April 2007).

[25] Professor Risteárd Mulcahy states that O'Donovan's stance 'only serves to confirm the intention of the anti-treaty IRA executive to establish a military-controlled state. I am afraid that a large number of military leaders were driven into the anti-treaty camp by their ignorance of the real ethos of the Volunteers which were established in 1913 to protect home rule, an ethos which fortunately prevailed among many others, even during the most turbulent times of the war of independence' (Mulcahy to author, 26 October 2007).

4. The Road to Civil War

[1] A leading Old IRA figure from Cork, O'Donoghue had been adjutant and intelligence officer of the First Cork Brigade, IRA, and later director of intelligence for the IRA's First Southern Division during the war of independence. In 1952, he was researching material for a book which appeared, in 1954, under the title *No Other Law*.

[2] O'Donovan to Florence O'Donoghue, 'Answers to Questionnaire', 1952, pp. 1–2 (part of O'Donovan's private papers); O'Donovan claims that Joe Vize was 'not really entitled to be present' at the meeting on 25 November 1921. But Vize had been director of purchases on the GHQ staff up to the reshuffle in late 1920 and may have been there as an observer. O'Donovan's antipathy towards Vize continued up to the latter's death in 1959. O'Donovan's papers include a cutting of Vize's obituary in *The Irish Times* ('Major-Gen. J. E. Vize', 5 January 1959) with the words 'was appointed director of purchases for the IRA' underlined. In the margin, O'Donovan wrote 'Not true. Liam Mellows was director of purchases'. In fact, both Vize and Mellows held

the same post at different periods. A 1916 veteran from Wexford, Joseph Vize joined the national army in 1922 and retired in 1929 with the rank of major-general. He subsequently worked for Irish Shipping as an engineer.

[3] O'Donovan to Florence O'Donoghue, pp. 2–4.

[4] Tom Garvin, *1922: The Birth of Irish Democracy* (Dublin 1996), p. 110.

[5] Professor Mulcahy to author, 25 November 2007. In one of a series of articles in *The Irish Times* in 1969, Seán Cronin pointed out that by accepting the treaty in January 1922, 'a majority of the members [of the Second Dáil] in effect had voted to abolish the Republic anyway' (*The Irish Times*, 24 April 1969, p. 12). Cronin, a Kerryman, was well qualified to write on republican matters having been IRA chief of staff twice, in 1957 and 1959 (Ruairí Ó Brádaigh was chief of staff in 1958); historian Dr Fearghal McGarry notes that 'negotiations with anti-treaty leaders (conducted by Collins, Mulcahy and O'Duffy, through IRB channels) continued in early 1922' (see Fearghal McGarry, *Eoin O'Duffy: A Self-Made Hero* (Oxford 2005), p. 96).

[6] T. P. Coogan, *De Valera: Long Fellow, Long Shadow* (Dublin 1993), p. 295.

[7] Author's interview with Ruairí Brugha, 9 March 2001.

[8] E. O'Malley, *The Singing Flame: A Memoir of the Civil War, 1922–24* (Dublin 1978), p. 51. The O'Donovan/Mulcahy correspondence forms part of the James L. O'Donovan papers at UCD's archives, Dublin.

[9] O'Connor *et al* to Mulcahy, 11 January 1922, in O'Donovan papers, UCD archives, Dublin.

[10] Mulcahy to O'Donovan *et al*, 13 January 1922, in O'Donovan papers, UCD.

[11] O'Malley, *The Singing Flame*, p. 53.

[12] Author's interview with Professor Risteárd Mulcahy, 2 April 2007.

[13] In subsequent years not everyone involved in the occupation of the Four Courts thought it was such a great idea. On his deathbed, in 1986, the Donegal republican Peadar O'Donnell told Ruairí Brugha that 'the Four Courts was wrong' (author's interview with Brugha, 9 March 2001); on 28 March 1922, two days after the anti-treaty IRA convention, O'Donovan received a letter from Joseph Dunne seeking to take over his job as GHQ director of chemicals. The new chief of staff, Eoin O'Duffy, presumably offered Dunne the job. In his letter to O'Donovan, Dunne wrote that he (Dunne) was 'absolutely devoid of any wish to sacrifice myself in any way whatsoever for this benighted country. I look upon the above matter [i.e. taking over O'Donovan's job] now simply in the light of a job…' (McGarry, p. 96). O'Donovan's reply is not recorded, but he considered himself to be the GHQ director of chemicals at least until his release from prison in 1924.

[14] C. O'Malley and A. Dolan, *'No Surrender Here!': The Civil War Papers of Ernie O'Malley 1922–24* (Dublin 2007), p. 45.

[15] MA, G2/1590, O'Donovan's army pension claim papers.

[16] *The Irish Times*, 17 March 1923, p. 7.

[17] O'Malley and Dolan, p. 80.

[18] ibid., p. 86.

[19] ibid., p. 100; Mary 'Minnie' O'Donovan was a nurse at Dublin's Richmond Hospital.

[20] O'Malley and Dolan, p. 104.

NOTES

[21] Dermot Keogh, *The Vatican, the Bishops and Irish Politics 1919–39* (Cambridge 1986), pp. 105–66; Tim Pat Coogan notes that the joint pastoral letter condemned the republicans' [i.e. the anti-treaty IRA] war effort as 'morally only a system of murder and assassination of the National forces' (T. P. Coogan, *The IRA* (London 1970), p. 54).

[22] O'Donovan to de Valera, 6 November 1922, de Valera papers, UCD. The author is grateful to UCD archivist, Séamus Helferty, for his help in locating this memorandum.

[23] Keogh, p. 114; another historian, Eoin Neeson, notes that when Luzio was asked in Rome 'if he had seen the Irish bishops, he replied: "No. But I saw 17 Irish Popes".' (Eoin Neeson, *The Civil War in Ireland 1922–1923* (Cork 1966), p. 330).

[24] Author's interviews with Donal O'Donovan and David Andrews; for more on the work of Thomas à Kempis and the extreme republican ethos, see Owen Dudley Edwards, 'Shaw and Christianity: towards 1916' in F. M. Larkin (ed.) *Librarians, Poets and Scholars* (Dublin, 2007), pp. 102–33; for a more detailed examination of the Irish Catholic Church's attitude to the anti-treaty IRA in the civil war period, see Keogh, pp. 101–21.

[25] Garvin, pp. 136, 143–44; In a subsequent book, Professor Garvin notes that Dan O'Donovan 'ended up in the anti-treaty ranks and tried to teach his comrades how to win in peacetime what they had lost in battle. He and other lecturers suggested that the victory of W. T. Cosgrave could actually be reversed by peaceful means under the rules of Free State democracy. Non-violent penetration of the local government representative apparatus, in particular, would, in the long term, deliver the country into their hands; capture the local councils and you will have the Dáil drop into your laps soon enough, was the message .... The true genesis of what became Fianna Fáil occurred in the Free State's prison camps, as young guerrillas learnt the ABC of democratic politics' (see Tom Garvin, *Judging Lemass: The Measure of the Man* (Dublin 2009), p. 91). Fianna Fáil eventually gained power in 1932, but Jim O'Donovan continued to choose militant republicanism over constitutional politics.

[26] O'Donovan's son Gerry recalls that the safe house was on Dublin's northside: 'He was always very welcome there but they had a dog who hated him. The house was raided and he ran out the back with another man. He dropped his glove which had wire fingers in it to fill out the missing fingers. The dog was yapping and when he dropped the glove the dog grabbed it and brought it into his kennel and bit it to death, which saved him' (author's interview with Gerry O'Donovan, 25 August 1999).

[27] According to one source, O'Donovan was 'opposed to the IRA's policy of executing pro-treaty TDs, which he believed was 'ineffectual and unnecessary, though not unjust' (Maguire and Quinn, *Dictionary of Irish Biography*, vol. 7, p. 417).

[28] Deasy to O'Donovan, 29 January 1923, O'Donovan papers, UCD.

[29] John P. Duggan, *A History of the Irish Army* (Dublin 1989), pp. 105, 336.

[30] Michael MacEvilly, Unpublished biography of Dr Andy Cooney. Cooney was IRA chief of staff 1925–26.

[31] Garvin, *1922: The Birth of Irish Democracy*, p. 137. In fact, Lynch's view of the general public wasn't much better. Professor Garvin notes that in early 1923 the

anti-treaty IRA chief of staff said the people 'were merely sheep to be driven anywhere at will' (Garvin, *1922*, p. 46).

[32] The author is grateful to Mr Gerry O'Donovan and Mrs Aedine Sànta for copies of their father's poems, including the one cited here.

[33] Hickey and Doherty, *A New Dictionary of Irish History* (Dublin 2003), pp. 67–68.

[34] John M. Regan, *The Irish Counter-Revolution 1922–1936: Treatyite Politics and Settlement in Independent Ireland* (Dublin 2001), pp. 374, 376.

[35] NLI file, LO 8678. The author is grateful to Harriet Wheelock of the National Library of Ireland for help in locating this file.

[36] The book was written by An Philibín, the pen-name of John Hackett Pollock (1887–1964). A poet, novelist and playwright, Pollock was also a founder member of Dublin's Gate Theatre.

[37] The author is grateful to the following for their help in completing this list of Jim O'Donovan's fellow prisoners: Michael MacEvilly, Seán O'Mahony, Martin Ferris TD, Colman Cassidy, Nicholas Sweetman, Barbara Sweetman-Fitzgerald, Alexis Fitzgerald, Ann Carville, Dr Rory O'Hanlon TD, Peadar Murnane and Maedhbh McNamara.

[38] MacEvilly, Unpublished biography of Dr Andy Cooney, pp. 142, 147–49.

5. Picking up the Pieces

[1] Author's interview with Donal O'Donovan. The claim to have 'outdone Christ' was, of course, a reference to the biblical account of Jesus fasting in the desert for 'forty days and forty nights'. O'Donovan may have intended it as a jibe against the Catholic bishops who had opposed the anti-treaty IRA.

[2] Donal O'Donovan, 'To Bray and Back', in *Old Bray Society Journal*, March 2006.

[3] *Irish Builder and Engineer*, 20 February 1926.

[4] MA file S.1536. O'Donovan's 1957 deposition to Bureau of Military History, pp. 11–12. In fact, Cotter was not the only anti-treaty IRA man whom O'Donovan helped out in straitened circumstances. A decade later, O'Donovan told an army pension inquiry that he undertook the enterprise (i.e. the City Chemical and Colour Company) 'in order to give employment to the ex-members of my former IRA department' (O'Donovan to army pension board, 29 November 1935, MA file G2/1590).

[5] NLI MS 21/987, Brennan to O'Donovan, 13 July 1925.

[6] Author's interviews with Gerry O'Donovan (25 August 1999), Donal O'Donovan (12 February 1999) and Mrs Sheila Hanna (27 March 2000).

[7] Author's interview with Donal O'Donovan, 16 March 2005. Commenting on the Kevin Barry connection, historian John Duggan notes: 'Of course, Monty was greener than he [Jim] was. It was a time of "wrap the green flag round me, boys". It was a time to worship the dead heroes and if you didn't you were regarded as an apostate. You don't see much of it now, but without them nothing would have happened – no 1916, nothing.' (Author's interview with Lt Col John P. Duggan, 6 June 2008).

[8] Kathy Barry's third daughter, Katherine Barry Moloney (1928–89) married the poet

NOTES

Patrick Kavanagh in 1966, a year before his death. The author is grateful to Professor Eunan O'Halpin of TCD for these details.

[9] O'Donovan's handwritten notes, dated 31 January 1929. The author is grateful to Gerry O'Donovan for supplying a copy of these notes.

[10] *The Irish Book Lover*, November/December 1929, pp. 127–28.

[11] O'Higgins was minister for justice in the Cumann na nGaedheal administration. His father, Dr T. F. O'Higgins, had been shot dead in front of his family on 13 February 1923; Éamon de Valera also lived on Cross Avenue, as did Oswald Müller-Dubrow, a director of German engineering group Siemens (which won the contract to build the Shannon hydroelectric scheme in the late 1920s). The German joined the Nazi party in October 1933 and was active in its Dublin branch, which was run by the Austrian-born director of the National Museum, Dr Adolf Mahr.

[12] Uinseann MacEoin, *Harry* (Dublin 1985), p. 106. MacEoin, an architect and republican historian, died on 21 December 2007, aged 87. He had been interned in the Curragh at the same time as Jim O'Donovan, in the early 1940s. See *The Irish Times* obituary, 29 December 2007, p. 16; in later years, George Gilmore (1898–1985) became a stern critic of O'Donovan. In a 1973 interview with Seán Cronin, Gilmore said that 'of the [IRA] leaders at the time [i.e. in 1939], Jim O'Donovan was the most Fascist-minded. We were in Mountjoy prison together in 1923 and he was anti-working class' (Seán Cronin, *Frank Ryan: The Search for the Republic* (Dublin 1980), p. 183).

[13] The author is grateful to Gerry O'Donovan for supplying a copy of his father's August 1929 memorandum. As adjutant-general, Gearóid O'Sullivan was a colleague of O'Donovan's on the pre-treaty IRA's GHQ staff. He accepted the treaty and served as a top army officer. After O'Higgins's assassination, O'Sullivan represented the slain minister's seat in Dáil Éireann from 1927 to 1937. O'Sullivan was prominent in the Blueshirt movement led by Eoin O'Duffy.

[14] The author is grateful to Gerry O'Donovan for supplying a copy of his father's memorandum of 19 February 1930.

[15] Author's interview with Professor Eunan O'Halpin, TCD. Professor O'Halpin is a grandson of Kathleen Barry-Moloney (a sister of Monty Barry, Jim O'Donovan's wife) whose papers are held in the UCD archives.

[16] Author's interview with Donal O'Donovan, 16 March 2005. In an earlier interview with the author, Donal O'Donovan said his father 'developed silver paint for the pylons for the new national grid'. Father and son 'travelled around the country to inspect paint on pylons' (author's interview with Donal O'Donovan, 12 February 1999).

[17] This note, dated 27 February 1932, and subsequent O'Donovan memoranda in this chapter, were supplied to the author by Gerry O'Donovan.

[18] Given the mood at Portobello barracks following his arrest, it appears that O'Donovan was lucky to survive. His son Gerry recalls: 'My father was sentenced to death at one stage during the civil war. He had to get everyone in the family to pull strings to get this commuted to imprisonment for life. That was at the time when the prisoners were hostages to the Free State government. They said, "If you do anything bold now, we'll shoot a half dozen of your men."' (Author's interview with Gerry O'Donovan, 25 August 1999.)

[19] The Sixth Dáil was dissolved on 29 January 1932 and the general election was held on 16 February. The Seventh Dáil first met on 9 March.

[20] Author's interview with Donal O'Donovan, 16 March 2005. Dr Joe Briscoe (whose father Robert was in the Four Courts with O'Donovan in April 1922) recalls that Jim O'Donovan was originally 'a loyal supporter and admirer of Éamon de Valera. He was a poet and used to send Dev poems whilst Dev was in gaol. However, when Dev and F.F. took the oath in order to enter the Dáil [in 1927] all this loyalty and admiration ceased' (Briscoe to author, 9 May 2007). Both recollections, putting the O'Donovan-de Valera split in 1927 or 1932, are not necessarily contradictory. O'Donovan may well have opposed Fianna Fáil's decision to enter the Dáil, an assembly whose legitimacy he did not recognise. However, on polling day, 16 February 1932, O'Donovan saw his chance to end ten years of Cumann na nGaedheal rule. In this context, he would have seen Dev as the lesser of two evils. But the Fianna Fáil leader's sporting of a top hat (a symbol of the English ruling class) on his way to Geneva proved to be the last straw.

[21] NLI, MS 21/987, Barton to O'Donovan, 4 October 1932.

[22] O'Donovan to Minister for Finance, 24 October 1933. Copy of letter provided to author by Gerry O'Donovan.

[23] O'Donovan memo of 22 September 1934, supplied to author by Gerry O'Donovan.

[24] Frank Shovlin, *The Irish Literary Periodical 1923–1958* (Oxford 2003), p. 71.

[25] When interviewed by Donal O'Donovan in 1985, Ó'Faoláin denied ever having been associated with *Ireland To-Day*, despite the fact that he was on the payroll as literary editor from June to October 1936. Ó'Faoláin went on to found *The Bell* magazine, which ran from 1940 to 1954.

[26] NLI, MS 21/987, Andrews to O'Donovan, 8 December 1936. Despite this clash and other disagreements, the two men remained close friends. O'Donovan's daughter Aedine recalls that they often discussed the war of independence at social gatherings in the O'Donovan family home: 'It was always very much alive because Moss Twomey, Todd Andrews and Eddie Toner, who had all been there with him, talked openly and it was just as if it was happening at the time. They sat in the house and reminisced' (author's interview with Mrs Aedine Sànta, 31 May 1999).

[27] Author's interview with Donal O'Donovan, 16 March 2005.

[28] Peter Denman, 'Ireland's Little Magazines', in *Three Hundred Years of Irish Periodicals* (Dublin 1987), p. 132.

[29] NLI, MS 21/987, EAJ8 to *Ireland To-Day*, December 1936. Gerry O'Donovan notes that his father's magazine 'began as very left-wing but the church killed it with their reaction. He was pro the proper, socialist government of Spain in the Spanish civil war and, of course, that was anathema to the church, to be against Franco'. Gerry O'Donovan adds that his father went to Spain in 1935 and later owned a book about 'Basque freedom fighters' which was signed by twenty Basque nationalists (author's interview with Gerry O'Donovan, 25 August 1999); a year after O'Donovan's trip to Spain, in October 1936, a measure of autonomy was granted to the Basque country by the republican government in Madrid. But the region's newly found freedom did not survive Franco's victory in the civil war.

NOTES

30 Shovlin, *Irish Literary Periodical*, p. 83.

31 ibid., p. 73. Shovlin includes businessman Joe McGrath, who ran the lucrative Hospital Sweepstakes, as one of the magazine's benefactors. In 1932, O'Donovan had privately criticised McGrath as a government 'crony' and linked him to civil war 'murders' (O'Donovan memo, 27 February 1932). Yet, six years later, the publisher of *Ireland To-Day* had no qualms about accepting money from him for the ailing publication.

32 NLI, MS 21/987, Bender to O'Donovan, 29 April 1938.

33 For more on the Bender-Mahr relationship, see Gerry Mullins, *Dublin Nazi No.1: The Life of Adolf Mahr* (Dublin 2007), p. 30 passim.

34 Shovlin, p. 85.

35 William Tierney, 'Irish Writers and the Spanish Civil War', in *Eire – Ireland*, vol. VII, no. 3 (autumn 1972), p. 41.

36 Shovlin to author, 17 October 2007.

37 The most recent study of *Ireland To-Day* appears in *The Irish Literary Periodical 1923-1958*, by Frank Shovlin, pp. 67–95. Other less detailed references appear as follows: Brian P. Kennedy, '*Ireland To-Day*, A brave Irish periodical', in *Linen Hall Review*, Belfast, vol. 5, no. 4, winter 1988, pp. 18–19; Peter Denman, 'Ireland's Little Magazines', in *Three Hundred Years of Irish Periodicals* (Dublin 1987), pp. 130–32; and William Tierney, 'Irish Writers and the Spanish Civil War', in *Eire – Ireland*, vol. VII, no. 3 (autumn 1972), pp. 36–55.

6. A Call to Arms

1 Seán Russell (1893–1940), a 1916 Rising veteran, had just taken over as IRA chief of staff from Mick Fitzpatrick of Wexford. While Russell's name is inextricably linked to the 1939–40 bombing campaign, O'Donovan's is less well known and in most histories of the period he is recorded only as a footnote. Russell's file at the Military Archives in Dublin (G2/3010) contains no reference to O'Donovan, although both men were high-ranking IRA leaders in the 1938–40 period. By mid-1939, Russell was attracting major coverage in British newspapers. For example, a feature article entitled 'The Man Behind the Bombs' in the *Sunday Express* of 30 July 1939 includes photographs and a detailed profile of the IRA leader. By contrast, in August 1939, O'Donovan was able to pass through England and Wales undetected on his way back from a meeting with German military intelligence agents in Berlin; Russell continues to be a controversial figure and his statue in Dublin's Fairview Park (unveiled on 9 September 1951) was regularly daubed with anti-Nazi slogans. The 16-ft high stone statue, erected by Clann na Gael, was decapitated in 2005. In 2009, it was replaced with a bronze version to deter protestors, but the new statue has also been daubed with graffiti such as 'Hitler's friend' and 'Nazi scum' (see 'After four years, Seán Russell gets his head back', in *Evening Herald*, Dublin, 30 May 2009; and 'Vandals deface memorial statue of republican leader Seán Russell', in *The Irish Times*, 9 July 2009, p. 10).

2 Jim O'Donovan's handwritten memoir entitled 'How it came about', undated, *circa* 1962; It appears that even if O'Donovan had refused Russell's request, the bombing

campaign would have gone ahead. Russell had already dispatched his IRA colleague 'Peadar O'Flaherty to England to build up an organisation there' (Cronin, *Frank Ryan: The Search for the Republic*, p. 178); Jim O'Donovan's son Gerry notes that at the time of the treaty split, early in 1922, his father 'had proposed a plan to start bombing England. He proposed this plan to the [anti-treaty IRA] general staff and they decided against it. But Russell liked it and Russell came along to him then, in 1938, and asked him to flesh it out a bit and start planning, so he did' (author's interview with Gerry O'Donovan, 25 August 1999); Patrick McGrath was executed by firing squad in Mountjoy prison in September 1940, along with Thomas Harte from Lurgan. They had been tried by a military tribunal in the wake of a gun battle, during which two special branch detectives were fatally wounded.

3 Unpublished memoirs (undated) of IRA man Joseph Collins, alias Conor MacNessa. The author is grateful to Donal O'Donovan for supplying a copy of these memoirs. Joseph Collins died in 1974.

4 In fact, the bombing campaign began on Monday, 16 January 1939, four days after the 12 January letter to Lord Halifax. O'Donovan wanted copies of the Halifax letter sent simultaneously to the Vatican, the French and US presidents, and the German and Italian ambassadors, as well as the Scottish and Welsh nationalist parties, the British Labour Party and civil liberties groups in the UK and USA. It is not clear if such letters were ever sent, however (see Letitia Fairfield (ed.), *The Trial of Peter Barnes and Others: The IRA Coventry Explosion of 1939* (London 1953), p. 269). According to Donal O'Donovan, the 'ultimatum was sent to the British Prime Minister, Neville Chamberlin; his Foreign Secretary, Lord Halifax; the Northern Ireland Government; Adolf Hitler and Benito Mussolini' (Donal O'Donovan, *Little Old Man Cut Short* (Wicklow 1998), p. 24).

5 Jim O'Donovan erroneously refers to the *Morning Post*, which ceased publication in 1937. He confused it with the *Morning Advertiser*, which did carry extensive reports of the S-plan discovery in its issue of 7 February 1939, as did the *Daily Telegraph*, *News Chronicle* and *Daily Herald* of the same date. O'Donovan's S-plan blueprint was discovered when British police raided houses around London in early February. Twelve IRA men subsequently appeared at Bow Street magistrate's court on 6 February 1939, charged with conspiracy to cause explosions. The case provided many column inches in the national press, as prosecuting counsel read out lengthy extracts from the document O'Donovan had written six months earlier. The court also heard that police had seized gelignite, weapons and ammunition as a result of the raids and arrests.

6 O'Donovan memoir 'How it came about', p. 1.

7 Author's interview with Donal O'Donovan, 16 March 2005. Donal recalls that this car 'was an English-registered, two-tone Morris. I never knew who they actually were, but they were Irish living in England'. The chrome lettering on the car was inspired by James Clarence Mangan's poem 'My Dark Rosaleen' ('Róisín Dubh'); Donal O'Donovan also recalled his father's trips to Germany in 1939 'because we got nice presents. I got a lovely air-gun, a parachute knife and various things … like the first umbrellas known as Klebs, short six-inch folding umbrellas' (RTÉ broadcast, 25 July 2007).

8 Donal O'Donovan, RTÉ radio broadcast, 25 July 2007. Donal's wife, Jenny, notes that her father-in-law 'was soft inside with a hard exterior shell, rather like a crab. He

NOTES

was cold and would not show emotion. It may have been the Jesuit education'. Author's interview with Jenny O'Donovan (née McGrath), 2 June 2007.

[9] In his detailed memoirs, for example, O'Donovan refers only once to the major bomb explosion in Coventry on 25 August 1939, which cost five lives and injured seventy-two: 'It was so soon after the Coventry incident, the airports were being so well watched and all Irish more or less suspect, I had a queasy feeling' (undated memoir, *circa* 1962, entitled 'August 23rd 1939'). In fact, he got his dates mixed up. He had travelled back through England on 21 August, four days before the Coventry explosion. O'Donovan's 'queasy' feeling, therefore, arose not from the carnage in Coventry, but from the fear of arrest as he made his way through Croydon airport from a secret meeting with German military intelligence agents in Berlin (see chapter 8).

[10] From an unpublished work entitled 'The Irish Republican Army', signed 'by James L. O'Donovan', pp. 12–13 of chapter VIII. The author is grateful to Gerry O'Donovan for supplying a copy of this manuscript; James Hogan (1898–1963) was the Free State army's director of intelligence during the civil war, and professor of history at UCC from 1920 to 1963. For additional data see *James Hogan: Revolutionary, historian and political scientist* by Professor Donnchadh Ó Corráin (Dublin 2001); O'Donovan's daughter Sheila adds: 'I think it was crazy of him to go back into IRA work with Seán Russell. I thoroughly disapproved of it, but he said "Sheila, you don't know what it was like then", and of course I didn't. But I didn't approve of it at all. I think there were times when he regretted it himself. He said as much, later, when he was in the Manor.... By the time he got to Our Lady's Manor, he had regrets about the later years, the 1930s. I never talked to him about feelings of remorse over the deaths in Coventry and such places. Daddy had his own idea of what religion was about. He was excommunicated four times and totally ignored it. He was a practising Catholic' (author's interview with Mrs Sheila Hanna, 27 March 2000).

[11] J. Bowyer Bell, *The Secret Army: A History of the IRA 1916–1970* (London 1970), p. 147.

[12] Coogan, *Long Fellow, Long Shadow*, p. 159.

[13] Twomey (IRA chief of staff, 1926–36) had quit the army council, on 25 June 1938, in protest at the proposed bombing campaign in England. In a prophetic letter of resignation he said the IRA could not 'possibly develop or sustain a campaign of sufficient magnitude to compel the English to evacuate their forces from Ireland; after a limited number of operations ... the campaign would peter out in failure; a campaign in England ... would not result in favourable reactions to the Republican movement ... we would be assailed on every side; both "governments" in Ireland would respond to British demands to attack the Army [and] make the continuance of the Army impossible' (NLI file 22/307, Twomey memorandum to IRA army council, 21 May 1938); historian Cian Ó hÉigeartaigh notes that another army council member, Máirtín Ó Cadhain, also had misgivings about the S-plan: 'He was unhappy with the IRA's campaign manifesto, and argued that it should seek economic as well as political freedom. On the practical side, he argued, correctly as it transpired, that the IRA's English organisation was not ready to carry out the tasks assigned to it. In early December 1938 he proposed a postponement, and, on losing the vote, he resigned from the Army Council, though not from the Army' (Ó hÉigeartaigh,

'Máirtín Ó Cadhain: Politics and Literature' in the *Canadian Journal of Irish Studies*, volume 34, no. 1, Spring 2008, p. 29); At around the same time, Tom Barry resigned from the IRA, considering the S-plan to be 'impractical and immoral'. Seán MacBride resigned from the IRA in June 1938 (see Cronin, *Frank Ryan: The Search for the Republic*, pp. 178–79).

14 O'Donovan, *Little Old Man Cut Short*, pp. 21–22.

15 Dr Seán Cooney to Michael MacEvilly, 23 February 1986. The author acknowledges the help of Mr MacEvilly in supplying a copy of the cited letter.

16 Coogan, *The IRA*, pp. 158–99.

17 Bowyer Bell, p. 149; despite the supposed ban on IRA attacks in Scotland and Wales, an unexploded bomb was discovered under the main Glasgow–Edinburgh railway line at Shotts, Lanarkshire, on 3 September 1939 – ironically, the day Britain declared war on Germany (Fairfield, p. 262).

18 Owing to a typing error, the IRA awarded Lord Halifax (1881–1959) a non-existent title. Halifax had served as Viceroy of India from 1926 to 1931 on foot of which he was awarded the GCIE, or Knight Grand Commander of the Order of the Indian Empire. The mistake probably arose when a typist misread the handwritten version of the letter.

19 While Provisional IRA statements in the 1970–94 campaign were usually signed 'P. O'Neill' – a long deceased figure from the republican past – in this case the signatory was alive and kicking. The author is grateful to retired RTÉ journalist Colm Connolly for the following thumbnail sketch of his uncle, who was IRA chief of staff from 1945 to 1947: 'Paddy Fleming was born and raised in Tír na bPoll (the land of the holes), a townland outside Killarney in County Kerry. His rebel days began early when he led a strike of primary-school children in 1911. He was in 6th class. He was involved in the war of independence and carried a shrapnel scar on his upper lip for the rest of his life after a Mills grenade was thrown at him by a Black and Tan. As Secretary of the Army Council in 1939, he signed the IRA's declaration of war which was sent to Lord Halifax, the British Foreign Secretary. He was directly involved in the S-Plan operations in England and was subsequently arrested there. He gave his name as "Joseph Walker" but detectives suspected he was Paddy Fleming. Consequently, a Garda sergeant was sent from Killarney to confirm their suspicions but this man could not – or would not – identify Fleming. As a result, "Joseph Walker" received a relatively light sentence. If he had been properly identified as the signatory of the Declaration of War, he would have, at best, spent many years in jail. It is possible that he would have been hanged. "Joseph Walker" was held in various prisons – Winson Green, Brixton and Liverpool – before being interned along with some 30,000 other enemy aliens on the Isle of Man. Along with other Irishmen, he was held in Peel in a house requisitioned by the authorities. After some time there, this group devised a plan to escape back to Ireland. They first dug a tunnel out of the house and hid in the countryside while the army and police searched for them. Some local people befriended them and directed them to small fishing boats. Unfortunately, the boat chosen did not have an engine and the escape bid relied on the rowing power of the escapers at the oars. They covered some miles before a British navy gunboat intercepted them and returned them to internment. When World War II ended in 1945, the Irish internees were returned to Ireland. The

NOTES

Army Council of the IRA appointed Paddy Fleming as Chief of Staff. On 10th of March 1945, Fleming ordered a ceasefire with Britain to stop the S-Plan operations and conclude the Declaration of War on Britain. Thus, Fleming, who had officially started the S-Plan, also officially ended it. He became a psychiatric nurse, working in [St Ita's Hospital] Portrane [County Dublin]. Later, he became chief steward of Bord na gCon, the board of the Irish greyhound racing industry, with the responsibility of ensuring that race meetings at Shelbourne Park and Harold's Cross were run according to the board's rules and regulations. He married Eileen Tubbert, a member of a staunchly Republican family in Dublin. She was a member of Cumann na mBan [women's IRA] and along with her sister Alice, was held in Kilmainham Jail during the Civil War. Fearing that Cumann na mBan was moving too far to the left, Tubbert, along with other like-minded women, joined Mná na Poblachta [women of the republic], an organisation co-founded in 1933 by Mary MacSwiney, sister of Terence MacSwiney who had died on hunger strike in 1920. Frequent visitors to the Fleming home on Strand Road in Sandymount [Dublin] were Elizabeth O'Farrell, who accompanied Pádraig Pearse when he surrendered after the 1916 Rising, and Julia Grenan who had nursed the wounded James Connolly in the GPO during that week. Eileen predeceased Paddy who died in the Mater Hospital [Dublin] in 1983, following a stroke. He was 83.' (Connolly to author, 27 November 2007. The author is also grateful to Gerry O'Donovan for supplying a copy of the IRA's January 1939 ultimatum.)

[20] The photograph and O'Donovan's certificate for attending the course are contained in his NLI file 22/307.

[21] The Manchester gas mains explosion killed one person. In addition, electricity sub-stations and pylons were blown up in or around London. It can hardly have been coincidental that O'Donovan's expertise as a state electricity employee and explosives expert was resulting in so many attacks on the English power supply network. Bridges were also targeted, including Hammersmith Bridge, which was damaged by explosives on 29 March 1939. The latter bombing was carried out by two sisters from Belfast who were part of an IRA active service unit in London headed by a London-born IRA man 'with a Cockney accent' (anonymous source to author).

[22] As historian J. Bowyer Bell notes, such raw recruits were chosen because they would be 'unknown to the police' in England (Bowyer Bell, p. 150).

[23] MA file G2/3010 contains a document dated 20 March 1946 and signed 'N.L.'.

[24] Collins's unpublished memoir, which is in the author's possession. Historian Tim Pat Coogan notes that in addition to the Green Lounge on St Stephen's Green, Dublin, IRA training also took place in Killiney Castle, south County Dublin, then a derelict building but nowadays a large hotel (Coogan, *The IRA*, p. 158).

[25] Untitled IRA statement, 21 January 1939 – possibly for broadcast purposes – supplied by Gerry O'Donovan.

[26] The author is grateful to Diarmaid Fleming for permission to use these extracts from his 2006 interview with Dan Keating. The interview was broadcast on BBC Radio Ulster, on 9 April 2007, in a documentary entitled 'The Last Man Standing'. Diarmaid Fleming is a grand-nephew of Paddy Fleming, who signed the IRA's January 1939 ultimatum to Lord Halifax. In an earlier interview, Keating admitted his involvement in attacks on London's Grosvenor Hotel in Park Lane, a big

department store in Queen's Road, Bayswater, and an incendiary attack in King's Inn Road (MacEoin, *The IRA in the Twilight Years*, p. 624).

[27] IRA special order, 1939. The author is grateful to Gerry O'Donovan for supplying a copy of this document; The nation may have been 'on the march' and being guided 'to victory' in O'Donovan's rose-tinted view of things, but the reality (as he admitted over 20 years later) was that the S-plan was faltering because of widespread arrests and a lack of money, weapons and other equipment. On 29 October 1939 (nine and a half months after the bombing campaign was launched), O'Donovan used the secret radio hidden in his study to request 'arms and equipment' from Berlin. A month later, on 28 November, the Abwehr was in touch with the German naval high command seeking U-boats to bring 'agents to Eire' (Abwehr diary entries, translated in UKNA file KV 2/769, p. 4).

[28] The cited extracts are from Joseph Collins's unpublished memoirs, courtesy of Donal O'Donovan.

[29] Seosamh Ó Duibhginn, *Ag Scaoileadh Sceoil*, (Dublin 1962) pp.10–13. The author is grateful to Mr Seán Ó Briain for his help in translating the cited extracts from Deegan's book.

[30] Ó Duibhginn, p. 10.

[31] ibid, p. 11.

[32] ibid, p. 13. According to Fairfield, pp. 251–58, some eighty-seven people were imprisoned as a result of the S-plan campaign, with a further five sent to Borstal, including the young Brendan Behan, who based his celebrated *Borstal Boy* on that three-year sentence. In addition, Fairfield, pp. 259–63, puts the number of S-plan explosions at 226 (including incendiary bombs) plus an unspecified number of bombings of electricity pylons on 16 January 1939, the first day of the campaign. The S-plan attacks continued up to and including 18 March 1940, although the plan was not formally cancelled until 10 March 1945.

[33] Ó Duibhginn, p. 63. Ailtirí na hAiséirí (architects of the resurrection) was a pro-Nazi fascist group founded by Gearóid Ó Cuinneagáin, who resigned from a senior position in the department of defence when de Valera took power in 1932. Joe Deegan, a native of County Armagh, later became a member of Ailtirí na hAiséirí. He was Irish-language editor of de Valera's *Irish Press* newspaper from 1963 to 1979. The author Hugo Hamilton's father, John (who, like Jim O'Donovan, worked for the ESB) was also a senior member of Ó Cuinneagáin's party. O'Donovan himself did not join Ailtirí na hAiséirí but was associated with another right-wing party, Córas na Poblachta (company of the republic). A recent study of such fringe groups notes that when Córas na Poblachta began to hold its first public meetings, 'its members included such luminaries of the Irish ultra-right as Maurice O'Connor, Alec McCabe and Reginald Eager from the Irish Friends of Germany [and] Joseph Andrews of the minute pro-Nazi People's National Party'. The study also notes that 'James O'Donovan, the IRA's principal liaison with the Abwehr, was also associated with the movement [i.e. Córas na Poblachta]'. See R. M. Douglas, *Architects of the Resurrection: Ailtirí na hAiséirí and the fascist 'new order' in Ireland* (Manchester 2009), p. 79. John Hamilton appears in the book's index under his Irish-language name, Seán Gearóid Ó hUrmoltaigh.

NOTES

34 The cited recollections are based on the author's interview with Tom Byrne, 22 July 2001.

35 UKNA, file KV 4/232, 'IRA Outrages'.

36 The relevant reports were carried in *The Times* and *Daily Telegraph*, 20 July 1939.

37 This may have been the aim of the S-plan all along, given Russell's 1936 contacts with German diplomats in America and the unlikelihood of the bombing campaign forcing a British withdrawal from the Six Counties. In a 1965 memo, O'Donovan noted that 'Germany took cognisance of' the sabotage campaign in England, which was expected 'possibly even to interest Germany in making her decision, if it were at all her intention to engage England in a showdown'. There is a certain irony in the fact that, while his younger brother Jim was directing the bombing of England and engaging with German military intelligence, Irish diplomat Colman O'Donovan was meeting Monsignor Giovanni Montini (later Pope Paul VI, 1963–78) at the Vatican, on 3 October 1939, to discuss Irish efforts to help Poland, which had been invaded by Germany on 1 September 1939, thus sparking World War II. (See C. Crowe *et al.*, *Documents on Irish Foreign Policy, Volume VI* (Dublin 2008), pp. 62–63).

7. The German Connection

1 Mark M. Hull, *Irish Secrets: German Espionage in Ireland 1939–1945* (Dublin 2003), p. 92. Professor Hull claims that German intelligence 'should have realised that the IRA was unsuitable, hopelessly immature, badly disorganised and not a reliable partner for a protracted covert relationship'.

2 For details of Andy Cooney's visit to Germany, see chapter six. In 1940, Tom Barry told Irish military intelligence (G2) that Seán MacBride (IRA chief of staff, 1936) had paved the way for his 1937 visit to Germany (see Eunan O'Halpin, *Spying on Ireland: British Intelligence and Irish Neutrality during the Second World War* (Oxford 2008), p. 40); Hull charts the change in official German attitudes to the IRA, from negative to positive, which appears to have occurred following the Barry/Hoven initiative in 1937 (Hull, pp. 42–43, 47); Olier Mordrel (1901–85) was born Olivier Mordrelle in Paris. In May 1940, Nazi Germany recognised Mordrel as leader of the Breton government in exile in Berlin. Although sentenced to death in France in 1946, Mordrel eventually returned from exile in Spain in 1972. The Mordrel/Ryan meeting in Paris was either in March or June 1937, i.e. on his way to Ireland or back to the Spanish civil war (UKNA, KV 2/769, p. iii; Cronin, *Frank Ryan: The Search for the Republic*, pp. 102, 115); details of Le Helloco's 1938 visit to Ireland are contained in the report of MI5's interrogation of Abwehr officer Kurt Haller (UKNA, KV 2/769, report on Haller interrogation, 7 August 1946, p. v). Le Helloco was a founder of the Breton militant group Gwenn ha Du (meaning 'White and black'). As well as translating Dan Breen's memoirs, he was involved in anti-French explosions and gun-running in pre-war Brittany. He sided with the Germans and after the war was sentenced to death for high treason by the French authorities. He lived in exile in Britain for the rest of his life.

[3] Anonymous G2 memo, dated September 1945, in MA file G2/3783. The observation that Jim O'Donovan 'was not an actual member of the IRA' is misleading. As an IRA volunteer (and later a member of the GHQ staff), O'Donovan had sworn an oath of allegiance when joining the IRA as a UCD student in December 1917. His resumption of active service in 1938 did not require him to take another oath. As Ruairí Ó Brádaigh points out: 'There has been no "oath" since 1925. A simple promise or word of honour is all that is required' (Ó Brádaigh to author, 31 October 2007).

[4] Douglas Gageby, who was a student at Dublin's Trinity College in 1939, guessed that Hoven was a spy: 'In TCD we knew Jupp Hoven was a spy. He ran an Abwehr office in Brittany. Before he left TCD, Hoven organised a party in rooms there – John Smullen's room, No. 6. He came along with Martin Plass, an exchange student, both carrying a case of German wine. We said, "You see, he must be a spy. They get paid so well".' (author's interview with Douglas Gageby, 29 September 1999); Professor Eunan O'Halpin of TCD notes that 'Hoven's undercover work was inspired by geography rather than by politics: Ireland was of interest to the German navy because of her Atlantic location and her shipping links with Britain. Clissmann, on the other hand, had a brief to develop relations with the republican movement in anticipation of a future war…' (O'Halpin, *Spying on Ireland*, p. 33); in 1938, the director of the Aachen choir, Rev. Ernst Rehmann (an Abwehr agent), visited Helmut Clissmann and Jupp Hoven in Dublin 'to evaluate [their] operation' (UKNA file KV 6/79). The author is grateful to Professor Mark Hull for drawing his attention to this file on MI5's post-war interrogation of Hoven, dated 15 May 1945. In the mid-1930s, Hoven was best man at Helmut Clissmann's wedding to Elizabeth Mulcahy in Dublin.

[5] J. P. Duggan, *Neutral Ireland and the Third Reich* (Dublin 1985), p. 56; author's interview with Mrs Elizabeth Clissmann, 21 April 2005. In the same interview Mrs Clissmann confirmed that, in the 1930s, her husband had 'a certain amount of contact' with IRA members, including Tom Barry, although 'he had to mind his job'. Mrs Clissmann notes that the IRA-German links arose not because they had a common enemy in England (although they did from September 1939 onwards), but because the Germans 'were interested in revolutionary movements' in Ireland, Flanders, Brittany and elsewhere. Helmut Clissmann (1911–97) joined the Nazi party on 1 May 1934, but according to his wife, this did not involve a 'transition' from his previous membership of the left-wing Prussian Youth League. She adds: 'He had to be in the [Nazi] party, otherwise he couldn't have left the country. He could not have got the [student] exchange without being in the party'.

[6] Russell to Luther, 21 October 1936, in J. P. Duggan, *Herr Hempel at the German Legation in Dublin 1937–1945* (Dublin 2003), pp. 288–89. Historian Seán Cronin claims that Russell wrote to Dr Luther at the 'bidding' of Joseph McGarrity, head of Clan na Gael in America (see Cronin, *Frank Ryan: The Search for the Republic*, p. 177). In 1938 (after Russell became chief of staff) McGarrity had a secret conference with the new IRA leader in the Spa Hotel, Lucan, County Dublin. At that meeting, Russell unveiled his plans to bomb England, which were loosely based on 'Rory O'Connor's sabotage of British economic targets during the war of independence' (see National Graves' Association profile of Seán Russell at www.nga.ie/russell); in

NOTES

retrospect, Russell did not seem to care whom he did business with as long as it served the IRA's aims. In addition to working hand-in-glove with Nazi Germany, he was happy to accept funds raised in America by Clan na Gael. A recent study discloses that Russell was part of an IRA delegation which visited Moscow in mid-1925. He was accompanied by P. A. Murray of the GHQ staff, Mick Fitzpatrick and Sinn Féin TD Gerry Boland. Murray, who had been IRA O/C Britain in 1923, met privately with Stalin and an interpreter. (see Tom Mahon and James J. Gillogly, *Decoding the IRA* (Cork 2008), p. 249). The latter authors state that 'the IRA's clandestine relationship with the Soviet Union was utilitarian and not ideologically based'. It was, they contend, 'based on the financial and military needs of the IRA' (Mahon and Gillogly, p. 82). In fact, 15 years later in Berlin, money and weapons formed the bulk of Seán Russell's shopping list at his meeting with German foreign minister, Joachim von Ribbentrop, on 5 August 1940.

[7] Fred Taylor (ed.), *The Goebbels Diaries 1939–1941* (London 1983), p. 56. Amid references to U-boats, Finland's conflict with Moscow, and the German churches 'becoming insolent', Goebbels adds a single line on Ireland: 'The Irish are carrying out bomb attacks in London'; the Abwehr, for its part, seemed more thorough and continued to report IRA attacks in its war diary throughout 1930 and into 1940. For example, on 27 January 1940, it recorded the previous day's 'sabotage' by 'Irish activists' on a power station in Lancashire, which served a big steel plant nearby. Clearly, O'Donovan's ESB expertise was still being used by the IRA in England over a year after the S-plan began; German agent Kurt Haller told MI5 interrogators in 1946 that 'the IRA bomb outrages in England ... showed Abwehr that the IRA might be potentially valuable allies'. Haller added, however, that had the Abwehr been consulted by the IRA about the S-plan 'they would most certainly have deprecated the idea, since the military results were nil and it only served prematurely to weaken the IRA forces' (UKNA, file KV 2/769, p. vi). Haller's view of the negative effects of the S-plan echo what Moss Twomey said in mid-1938 when resigning from the IRA's army council in protest at the Russell/O'Donovan plan to bomb England (see chapter six). In 1939, the left-wing republican George Gilmore opposed Russell and O'Donovan's pro-German stance, noting that 'an alliance between the IRA and Hitler would be disastrous for Ireland' (Cronin, *Frank Ryan: The Search for the Republic*, p. 183).

[8] Although a former comrade of O'Donovan's on the IRA GHQ staff in 1921, some eighteen years later, Eoin O'Duffy was in political terms diametrically opposed to the 1939 IRA leadership. He was a former commissioner of the Garda Síochána (1922–33) and in the mid-1930s a pro-fascist Blueshirt leader who set sail to fight for Franco's forces in the Spanish civil war. But why was Pfaus sent to O'Duffy rather than to any member of the 1939 IRA leadership? Kurt Haller told post-war MI5 interrogators that 'Pfaus's Irish addresses, which he presumably obtained through his work with the Fichtebund [Nazi propaganda body], were mainly those of the Irish Blueshirts, Irish Fascists of the notorious General O'Duffy's organisation' (see MI5 file KV 2/769, p. vi; and Hull, p. 52 passim); O'Duffy's biographer, Dr Fearghal McGarry, suggests that O'Duffy facilitated the meeting between Pfaus and the IRA leadership because he believed that 'the IRA had been purged of socialism' and thus 'the prospect for co-operation between the far right and republican extremists had

improved' (McGarry, *Eoin O'Duffy*, pp. 325–26). McGarry contends that O'Donovan returned the favour the following year by facilitating a meeting in early November 1940 between O'Duffy and the German spy Hermann Görtz (McGarry, p. 335).

9 O'Donovan's undated memoir, p. B2.

10 O'Donovan misspelled the name of Dr Theodor Kessenmeier, then head of the Fichtebund. The Nazi propaganda body had been founded by his father, Heinrich Kessenmeier, in 1914 (see Hull, pp. 52–53). O'Donovan seems to have been unaware that Pfalzgraf was a cover name for Major-General Friedrich Carl Marwede, who had been establishing Abwehr-IRA links since 1937 (see also Enno Stephan, *Spies in Ireland* (London 1963), p. 27 passim). Marwede was head of Abwehr II's office 1 west in Berlin, working clandestinely with militant anti-government groups – in Ireland's case, the IRA; at their first meeting, Pfaus introduced Marwede to O'Donovan as Dr Pfalzgraf, 'a representative of the High Command'. Despite the rather important-sounding title, Marwede was a senior military intelligence officer and had nothing to do with the German armed forces' high command, the OKW (MI5 file KV 2/769, vii). In the latter file Kurt Haller discloses only two IRA-Abwehr meetings: May 1939 in Hamburg and August 1939 in Berlin. There were, however, three such meetings: February and April in Hamburg, and August in Berlin. Haller was co-operating fully with the British, so the discrepancy in dates may have been the result of a genuine lapse of memory, as well as the stress of continued interrogation sessions during 1945 and 1946.

11 Founded in 1934, the AO was an umbrella group for Nazi members living abroad. Siemens director, Oscar Müller-Dubrow, was AO chief in Ireland (and a neighbour of de Valera's on Cross Avenue, Blackrock, County Dublin).

12 O'Donovan is presumably referring to fake passports or other identity papers, which the Germans were willing to supply to him and his wife for their return journey through Britain – and to be used if they were arrested there. He is suggesting that the papers were designed to give him and his wife false identities aimed at perpetrating a 'political hoax' in the event of their arrest returning through Britain; O'Donovan refers to his wife's health as an excuse for visiting Brussels, but Kurt Haller told MI5 in 1946 that 'O'Donovan had certain business to transact with Siemens-Halske, and this would serve as adequate cover' (KV 2/769, p. vi).

13 UKNA file KV 4/232, 'Note on IRA cases', 6 January 1941.

14 Franz Fromme was the Abwehr agent who would collect Seán Russell in Genoa on his return from the USA in May 1940, and drive him to Berlin to meet Nazi foreign minister, Joachim von Ribbentrop.

15 Pfalzgraf (Marwede) was either trying to impress O'Donovan with his German thoroughness, or the Abwehr agents were genuinely afraid that the British might try to bug the hotel.

16 O'Donovan appears to have confused Fromme's two visits to Dublin. The first, in 1932, was to research a book which was published in Berlin in 1933 under the title *Irlands Kampf um die Freiheit*. Fromme revisited Ireland in April 1939 (two months after Oscar Pfaus) when he met Francis Stuart, among others.

17 O'Donovan memoirs, entitled 'Random Notes (1), (2) and (3)', undated. The author is grateful to Gerry O'Donovan for supplying copies of his father's notes. By

NOTES

O'Donovan's own admission, he over-egged the pudding in exaggerating the IRA's capabilities in 1939. In 1946, Kurt Haller (one of the key German agents dealing with Irish affairs during the war) told MI5 that the Germans 'took the fantastic daydreams of the IRA at face value and greatly overrated the strength and ability of this organisation' (UKNA file KV 2/769, p. i).

[18] MI5 file KV 2/769, p. vii; Haller quotes O'Donovan as saying that 'the IRA's one and only aim was the conquest of Northern Ireland; it had little interest in other military or political operations against the UK'. But this flies in the face of the S-plan, a military operation that was underway when the IRA-Abwehr meeting took place in Hamburg. The contradiction cannot have been lost on the senior Abwehr personnel, who had responded quickly to the S-plan by sending Oscar Pfaus to Dublin in February; Haller also told MI5 that 'at the end of the meeting O'Donovan was given a sum of money (not more than the equivalent of RM 30,000 in £5 notes) and another meeting was arranged for the near future'.

[19] O'Donovan memoir 'How it came about', p. B3.

[20] Fairfield, *The Trial of Peter Barnes*, p. 263.

[21] IRA army council's 'Message to America', bearing O'Donovan's handwritten alterations. The draft note was supplied to the author by Gerry O'Donovan.

[22] O'Donovan uses this jibe as a double-edged sword against de Valera, who for a time held the post of president of the Dáil before the treaty split. But it also underlines O'Donovan's view that the IRA leadership, of which he was a top figure, constituted the legitimate government of the Irish republic.

[23] 'German Gold and the IRA', broadcast on Easter Sunday, 9 April 1939. The five-page typescript includes a handwritten note by Jim O'Donovan.

[24] Bowyer Bell, *The Secret Army*, p. 158. See also Hull, p. 63.

[25] The author is grateful to Gerry O'Donovan for copies of his father's notes covering his four trips to the continent in 1939. According to the Danish archives in Esbjerg, Jacob Brink Nielsen of Strandbygade 45 worked as a wartime security guard at Esbjerg harbour (Denmark was occupied by Germany during World War II). The author is also grateful to Svenning Dalgaard of Danish television station TV2 for this information (Dalgaard to author, 29 January 2009).

[26] In August 1940, Paul Moyse was the Abwehr's first choice of agent to accompany Seán Russell by U-boat to Ireland, but he was dropped in favour of Frank Ryan (see Hull, pp. 135, 308).

[27] IRA letter to Cardinal Hinsley, 29 June 1939, in O'Donovan papers. The author is grateful to Gerry O'Donovan for a copy of this letter.

[28] Fairfield, pp. 260–61.

[29] UKNA, KV 2/769, p. 3. According to this file, based on MI5's 1946 interrogation of Lahousen, Dr Hempel 'advised Lahousen not to compromise Irish-German relations by any such action in the future'. Hempel's advice fell on deaf ears, however, since twelve more agents were sent to Ireland from August 1939 to December 1943 (see O'Halpin, p. 241).

[30] Bowyer Bell, p. 159.

[31] 'Did FBI foil an IRA plot to kill king?' in *Sunday Times*, London, 27 December 1998.

8. 'Our Friends' in Berlin

[1] This and subsequent recollections of his final visit to Nazi Germany are taken from Jim O'Donovan's unpublished 1960s' notes entitled 'August 23rd 1939'. O'Donovan's reluctance to be seen communicating with McGarrity in public is understandable. But both men presumably met aboard the vessel in one of their private cabins, although the notes do not mention any such contact.

[2] Seán Cronin, *The McGarrity Papers: Revelations of the Irish Revolutionary Movement in Ireland and America, 1900–1940* (Kerry 1972), p. 173.

[3] Hull, *Irish Secrets*, pp. 62, 308. McGarrity died in America in 1944.

[4] O'Halpin, *Spying on Ireland*, p. 41. Presumably, Professor O'Halpin is referring to the final meeting in Berlin in August, although he does not specify which one. O'Donovan's own memoirs do not refer to McGarrity attending any of the IRA-Abwehr meetings in Hamburg or Berlin.

[5] Donal O'Donovan, RTÉ interview, 25 July 2007.

[6] Hull, p. 62.

[7] The Abwehr war diary for 30 March 1940 reports that Abwehr agent Franz Fromme 'had conversation with brother of Jim O'Donovan [Colman O'Donovan, not named] in Rome who tells him that his brother in Ireland is at liberty, and with Bishop O'Rourke'. Assuming this was not a codename, Fromme's episcopal contact would have been Count Eduard O'Rourke (1876–1943), the Bishop of Danzig (the author is grateful to Mr Martin Fagan, archivist of the Irish College in Rome, for this information). This occurred a month before Seán Russell arrived in Genoa aboard a transatlantic liner, on 1 May. An earlier Abwehr diary entry on 19 March noted that Fromme was 'trying to contact members of IRA visiting Rome for Easter'. In 1946, however, Abwehr officers told MI5 interrogators that Fromme's attempt failed because 'there were no IRA sympathisers amongst the visiting Irish priests' (Abwehr diary translation and MI5 interrogation report in UKNA file KV 2/769, p. 6). The Abwehr's descriptions of Jim O'Donovan and Seán Russell appear in the diary entries for 20 and 26 April 1940 respectively (IMA, original German-language version, p. 5).

[8] Hull, pp. 131, 328. The Russell-Ribbentrop meeting was to finalise a plan to use the IRA in support of Germany's invasion of England, Operation Sea Lion, scheduled for that summer. Colman O'Donovan, like his brother Jim, had fought in the war of independence. Unlike Jim, however, he had long renounced the armed struggle, joining the department of external affairs in 1922 and Fianna Fáil in 1927 (author's interview with Donal O'Donovan, 16 March 2005). Official records from January 1941 show that, far from having extreme republican views, Colman O'Donovan was in fact trying to restrain the 'rabidly anti-British' views of the Irish College's rector, Monsignor Denis McDaid (see Crowe, *Documents on Irish Foreign Policy, Volume VI*, p. 433).

[9] Author's interview with Donal O'Donovan, 16 March 2005. Colman O'Donovan's transfer to neutral Portugal probably had less to do with his contact with Fromme than with the fact that he had acted without Dublin's permission on one occasion. Contemporary documents reveal that he lobbied the father general of the Jesuits for Monsignor Paschal Robinson (apostolic nuncio to Ireland 1929–48) to become a cardinal. This earned O'Donovan a rebuke from his boss, ambassador William

NOTES

Macaulay, who complained to Dublin in December 1939 that 'any canvassing on our part would do nothing but harm'; Joe Walshe may have been even less impressed the following year when Macaulay resigned and Colman O'Donovan dashed off a telegram to Dublin announcing that 'many people here ... have expressed the hope that I will be appointed to succeed'. In the event, O'Donovan remained in Rome for another eighteen months before being shunted off to Lisbon (Crowe, pp. 126, 367); having served as a diplomat in Brussels (1922–66), Washington (1930–33), Berlin (1933–35) and London (1935–38), Colman O'Donovan was appointed as a legation official to the Holy See on 1 July 1938. He was promoted as acting chargé d'affaires in 1940, remaining at the Vatican until February 1942. On 6 February 1942, he was appointed as Ireland's first ambassador to Portugal, where he remained until 13 May 1945. (The author is grateful to Ms Elaine Dalton, Department of Foreign Affairs, Dublin, for supplying Colman O'Donovan's service record.)

[10] Author's interview with Donal O'Donovan, 16 March 2005.

[11] Created as a result of the 16 June 1922 election, the Third Dáil did not meet until 9 September 1922. The last meeting of the Second Dáil was on 8 June 1922, although it was formally adjourned rather than dissolved. Strictly speaking, O'Donovan was correct in saying that the Second Dáil had never been formally dissolved but, in any case, the point is superfluous since the Second Dáil had ratified the Anglo-Irish treaty, thus accepting partition. Even if the Second Dáil had met, as originally intended, on 30 June, it had already been superseded by the Third Dáil, which was elected two weeks earlier.

[12] Kurt Haller quotation from MI5 file KV 2/769, p. i; Lahousen told MI5 interrogators in 1946 that he 'was unable to follow the proceedings at the Ribbentrop-Russell meeting because the "conversation was in English"' (Ribbentrop, a former ambassador to London, spoke fluent English). According to Lahousen: 'Canaris contemptuously referred to Russell as the "music professor".' (UKNA, KV 2/769, p. 8); Kurt Haller told MI5 that at the Berlin meetings Seán Russell had 'for the first time ... mentioned the potential strength of the IRA (including sympathisers), which he gave as 5,000–10,000 men. This figure was far below German expectations'. According to Haller, 'the German motive for sending Ryan [to Ireland] was that Russell, throughout his stay in Germany, had shown considerable reticence towards the Germans and plainly did not regard himself as a German agent'. Haller added: 'By sending [Frank] Ryan, Abw[her] II felt that their own interests would be better safeguarded, as Ryan accepted more easily his position as a German agent' (KV 2/769, p. xvii). Mrs Elizabeth Clissmann, a close friend of Ryan's, notes that his decision to work with the Germans was not 'difficult' because 'in 1940, Russia was an ally of Germany' (author's interview with Mrs Clissmann, 21 April 2005). But this does not explain why Ryan was still willing to work with Dr Veesenmayer (Ribbentrop's coup d'état specialist) and considered doing propaganda work at German Radio's Luxembourg studios long after Hitler's invasion of Russia in mid-1941. One obvious explanation, however, is that Ryan owed his life to Veesenmayer, who had saved him from death row in Burgos prison. Both men got on socially and, according to Mrs Clissmann, they used to play cards together with her husband Helmut.

13 O'Donovan's 1960s' memoir of that day is entitled 'August 23rd 1939', but he got his dates mixed up. By Wednesday 23 August, he was already back at his desk in Dublin.

14 Despite his mild protestations about using English in such circumstances, O'Donovan was not that averse to the language. Three years earlier, in one of his first editorials in *Ireland To-Day*, he wrote: 'greater than we have served Ireland nobly and farther afield through the tongue imposed on us' (Shovlin, *The Irish Literary Periodical*, p. 74). According to post-war MI5 files, Neumeister was a German foreign office counsellor 'who had served in Belgium in the 1914–18 war and had there become acquainted with the Flemish nationalists'. In late 1939, five months before Germany invaded Belgium, the Abwehr sent Neumeister back to Belgium to liaise with Flemish nationalists (UKNA, KV 2/769, p. v).

15 O'Donovan does not identify all five Abwehr agents by name but, according to a 1946 MI5 file, one of them was the top official Friedrich Carl Marwede, using the alias Dr Pfalzgraf, whom O'Donovan had already met in April in Hamburg (see UKNA, KV 2/769, Haller file, 7 August 1946, p. vii).

16 Ernst Röhm (1887–1934) was a co-founder of the Nazi Party and headed the Sturmabteilung, SA or stormtroopers. Seen as a rival to Hitler, Röhm and other SA leaders were rounded up in the so-called 'night of the long knives' on 30 June 1934. Röhm was shot, on Hitler's orders, on 2 July 1934.

17 Veesenmayer earned his reputation as a coup d'état expert by installing pro-Nazi puppet regimes in his native Austria, as well as in Croatia, Serbia, Slovakia and Hungary (UKNA, KV 2/769; Cronin, *Frank Ryan*, pp. 252–53). The only historian to track down Veesenmayer to his post-war residence in Darmstadt, Germany was Lt Col John P. Duggan, who recalled: 'He said repeatedly to me that the tactic [in dealing with the IRA] was "Give them all they needed but it was the Irish who were to do it. Arm them, give them plentiful supplies, maybe some leadership and guidance, but the Irish were to do the fighting."' Duggan describes Veesenmayer as 'very dangerous' and 'very powerful', adding, 'he was Ribbentrop's coup d'état specialist. You didn't get where he was [without the ability] to rise up in the Nazi meritocracy, and he got to the top.' (Author's interview with John P. Duggan, 15 October 2001.)

18 Hull, p. 63; Haller (KV 2/769, pp. viii–ix) has a different version of the radio codes story: when O'Donovan 'revealed the existence of an IRA short-wave WT station … it was agreed that on a date shortly after O'Donovan's return (late Aug 39) a trial transmission' would be sent from Ireland and answered by the Abwehr. On the day, the Abwehr 'slipped up' and 'failed to reply' to the IRA signal. But contact was re-established in October because Marwede had told O'Donovan at the Berlin meeting 'that complete codes and WT instructions would be sent over by courier in the near future'. The codes were brought from Brussels to London by Abwehr courier Paul Moyse, and thence to Dublin; in 1939, Moyse was using Leon Millarden as a courier to bring Abwehr messages and money from Paris and London to Jim O'Donovan in Dublin. Moyse met Millarden in London, but the Paris contact was a Breton nationalist named Marcel Guiyesse (UKNA file KV 6/80); Kurt Haller told MI5 that the radio link lasted for only two months (i.e. until the end of 1939), whereas O'Donovan's radio log shows he was in regular contact with Germany from

NOTES

28 November 1939 to 28 September 1940 (the author is grateful to Michael Hill for supplying a copy of O'Donovan's radio log). According to Haller (KV 2/769, p. x), the Abwehr was receiving 'a good deal' of what it considered to be 'frivolous messages' from the IRA. These included 'a telegram of congratulation to the Führer on the occasion of the sinking of the *Royal Oak*'. (This was the first British battleship hit during the war. It was sunk by a U-boat on 14 October 1939 at Scapa Flow, Orkney Islands, Scotland, with the loss of 833 crewmen).

[19] MI5 file KV 2/769, pp. vii–viii; the outbreak of war just over a week later put paid to the seven-point Berlin pact agreed between Jim O'Donovan and Major-General Marwede. The German arms, ammunition and explosives were never delivered, but money was sent via various agents. The radio link was up and running in October, and the courier service was also used. Meanwhile, the IRA ignored the Abwehr's plea to halt operations, pending 'receipt of express instructions from Germany', and continued its attacks in England for another six and a half months, until mid-March 1940; Haller also noted that 'O'Donovan was again given the equivalent of approx. RM 30,000 in £5 notes'. In his own unpublished memoirs, written in the early 1960s, O'Donovan never referred to either of the payments that Haller claimed he had received in Hamburg and Berlin; contrary to Berlin's 1939 plan to use the IRA to attack targets in Northern Ireland, the IRA ended up two years later advising the Luftwaffe on what parts of Belfast to bomb. On 20 October 1941, Dublin gardaí seized an IRA document entitled 'Comprehensive military report on Belfast' from the handbag of Miss Helena Kelly, 42 Frankfort Avenue, Rathmines. The 20-page report included a map showing areas 'as yet unblitzed by the Luftwaffe', including a power station, aircraft factory and Sydenham aerodrome. The IRA report added: '… if the objectives marked are bombed by the Luftwaffe as thoroughly as the other areas in recent raids [i.e. in April and May 1941, when 1,100 people died], Belfast will be rendered a negative quantity in Britain's war effort.' The report advised the Luftwaffe to avoid bombing the Falls Road – described as 'the chief site of Nationalism' – and Crumlin Road prison 'where some 300 to 400 Irish republican soldiers are imprisoned' (IMA file G2/1722).

[20] O'Donovan got his dates mixed up here. The IRA bomb, which killed five and injured seventy-two people in Coventry, happened four days later, on 25 August 1939.

9. Carnage in Coventry

[1] See *Midland Daily Telegraph*, 28 August 1939, p. 5.

[2] Jane C. Woods, 'To Blow and Burn England from her Moorings' (PhD thesis, University of Kentucky, 1995), p. 386.

[3] Author's interview with Ted Cross, 7 June 2007.

[4] Author's interview with Joan Cook, 6 June 2007.

[5] Fairfield, *The Trial of Peter Barnes and Others*, p. 277 (citing S-plan p. 10); former Sinn Féin president Ruairí Ó Brádaigh notes that: 'The explosion in the city centre was certainly not IRA policy and was unintentional and accidental with horrific results. People of that period told me that an electrical power plant was the target.'

Ó Brádaigh adds: 'I never met J. B. O'Sullivan.... The word was that he was a disturbed individual. He escaped from the Dental Hospital in Lincoln Place, Dublin, while there for treatment under escort in the 1940s.... He was sent to the awful conditions of Portlaoise Jail, following his recapture. That place would not have improved his condition.' (Ó Bradaigh to author, 17 November 2009).

[6] This and subsequent quotations are from the author's interview with Tony Rose, 6 June 2007.

[7] *Sunday Times*, 6 July 1969.

[8] *Irish Press*, 5 July 1969, p. 4; MacGiolla (born in Nenagh, County Tipperary, 25 January 1924) was an ESB employee. He held the presidency of Sinn Féin from 1962 to 1970, and was also chairman of the Official IRA's army council for a time. (MacGiolla interview in *Hot Press* magazine, July 2009. See also *The Irish Times*, 5 February 2010, p. 9, and 6 February 2010, p. 14.) Following the split with the provisionals, MacGiolla was president of Official Sinn Féin from 1970 to 1983. He was also a Workers' Party TD for Dublin West 1982–92. MacGiolla (who died on 4 February 2010) recalls that at the Sinn Féin ard comhairle meeting to discuss the repatriation and reinterment of Barnes and McCormick, the feeling was that 'whether they were innocent or guilty, they should be brought home anyway'. During his graveside oration, MacGiolla recalls: 'I was heckled by dissidents in Mullingar. The hecklers were the representatives of the provisional movement, but we didn't know that' (author's interview with MacGiolla, 11 August 2009); according to another account of the reinterment ceremony, Belfast republican Jimmy Steele attacked 'the movement's turn to the left', adding: 'One is now expected to be more conversant with the thoughts of Chairman Mao than those of our dead Patriots' (Brian Hanley and Scott Millar, *The Lost Revolution: The Story of the Official IRA and the Workers' Party* (Dublin 2009), p. 123).

[9] *Irish Press*, 7 July 1969, p. 4. Tomás MacGiolla thinks the 'unnamed high-ranking republican' quoted about Coventry in the *Irish Press* was Cathal Goulding (author's interview with MacGiolla, 11 August 2009). Goulding was official IRA chief of staff at the time; Seán MacStíofáin became the first provisional IRA chief of staff later that year.

[10] Ó Brádaigh to author, 31 October 2007. Ruairí Ó Brádaigh was IRA chief of staff from 1958 to 1959 and again from 1960 to 1962. He was president of Provisional Sinn Féin from 1970 to 1983, when Gerry Adams took over; on Sunday, 6 July 1969 (when Barnes and McCormick were being reburied in Mullingar) RTÉ Radio's 'This Week' programme broadcast an anonymous interview with the Coventry bomber. The interview was conducted by Mike Burns, who recalls tracing Joseph B. ('Joby') O'Sullivan through a file in the Scotland Yard archives, which had an address for him in Cork: 'When I went down to Cork, Joby was living over a greengrocer's shop in Werburgh Street, and working as a swimming instructor'. O'Sullivan was not at home, but some people arranged for Burns to meet the former IRA man that night in the countryside outside Cork city. The RTÉ man waited all night in his car, but O'Sullivan never showed up. Burns adds: 'When he [O'Sullivan] subsequently contacted us in Dublin he was fairly down-at-heel and staying in the Iveagh hostel. We met in the old Embassy Hotel (his choice) at the corner of Fitzwilliam Street and Baggot Street, and he then came out to RTÉ very late that Saturday night to record

NOTES

the interview.' Burns remembers that Joby O'Sullivan admitted to being the Coventry bomber: 'He said the bike got stuck in the tram tracks and, fearing it would explode prematurely, he decided to leave it.' Burns adds that O'Sullivan 'looked like a fellow who'd been drinking for years, but he was sober when I met him' (author's interview with Mike Burns, 21 October 2009). Mike Burns's RTÉ colleague Seán Duignan also recalls the meeting with Joby O'Sullivan: 'I accompanied Mike to a small hotel off Baggot Street (I think). I remember he [O'Sullivan] was a badly dressed, elderly, nervous man [and] that the interview was very long – we used quite a lot of it on 'This Week'. As I recall (very vaguely) he had the bomb on a bike, he panicked for some reason and abandoned it somewhere in the busy centre of Coventry ... we were strongly criticised, perhaps justifiably, for having broadcast the interview. Muiris McGonagle [a senior RTÉ producer] was particularly critical.' (Duignan to author, 10 November 2009). The interview was cleared for broadcast by the then head of news at RTÉ, Jim McGuinness, who had been a senior IRA figure in the 1940s and 1950s. Mike Burns remembers asking McGuinness to confirm that Joby O'Sullivan was the Coventry bomber, but McGuinness refused, claiming that he was still bound by the IRA oath. As a compromise, however, McGuinness agreed to nod his head when Burns mentioned O'Sullivan's name (author's interview with Mike Burns, 21 October 2009); Uinseann MacEoin's *The IRA in the Twilight Years 1923–1948* (Dublin 1997, p. 533) notes that Joby O'Sullivan was in Portlaoise prison 'for a period from 1942 before being transferred to Dundrum asylum'.

[11] Fairfield, p. 277.

[12] ibid, pp. 259–63 and 271.

[13] Bowyer Bell, *The Secret Army*, p. 149.

[14] When the author sought details of his late uncle's role in England, Mr Adams replied: 'Dr O'Donoghue, a chara, Thank you for your recent correspondence regarding James L. O'Donovan, 1896–1979. The era which you are researching is indeed an interesting time in Irish Republican history. Unfortunately my late uncle Dominic is no longer alive and I have no information which could be of help to your research. I regret that I am unable to be of more assistance to you. Good luck with your project. Is mise le meas, Gerry Adams, MP, MLA.' (Adams to author, 12 December 2007)

[15] McDade was the first member of the Provisional IRA to be killed in England since the start of the bombing campaign in Britain in March 1973 (McGladdery, *The Provisional IRA in England: The Bombing Campaign 1973–1997* (Dublin, 2006) pp. 89–90.

[16] *An Phoblacht*, 16 July 1974; and McGladdery, pp. 59, 239–40.

10. The Road to Internment

[1] UKNA, file KV4/9, p. 28.

[2] Author's interview with Elizabeth Clissmann (née Mulcahy), 21 April 2005. According to historian Seán Cronin, '[Helmut] Clissmann knew almost all the IRA leaders from his time as a student at Trinity College and then as Secretary of the

German Academic Exchange Board in Dublin' (Cronin, *Frank Ryan: The Search for the Republic*, p. 271).

³ David A. O'Donoghue, *Hitler's Irish Voices: The Story of German Radio's Wartime Irish Service* (Belfast 1998), pp. 41–42.

⁴ Extract from Professor Mark Hull's interview with Francis Stuart, 7 July 1999. The author is grateful to Professor Hull for supplying a transcript of this interview, which is thought to be the last Stuart gave before his death the following year. According to MI5's 1946 interrogation of Kurt Haller, before departing for Ireland Görtz 'brushed up his English by conversing with Rosaleen James, an Irish actress in Berlin, and Francis Stuart, lecturer in English at Berlin University' (KV 2/769, p. xii).

⁵ Hull, *Irish Secrets*, pp. 90–92; MI5 file KV 2/769, pp. xi–xii; some historians, though not Professor Hull, have confused Stephen Held (born in Ireland, but adopted by a German businessman, Michael Held) with Jim O'Donovan, and one even claimed they were the same person. The error probably arose because one of the Abwehr codenames for O'Donovan was V-Held; historian Seán Cronin notes that Held also handed the Germans 'a request to free Frank Ryan' from prison in Spain. The then IRA chief of staff, Stephen Hayes, recalled: 'We calculated that if the IRA could get him freed where the Irish government had failed, it would give us valuable publicity' (Cronin, *Frank Ryan*, p. 184).

⁶ de Valera to Eden, 29 January 1940, in UKNA file CJ 1/62. The department of external affairs' internal correspondence on the Coventry bombing, subsequent murder trial and death sentences is contained in *Documents on Irish Foreign Policy*, Volume VI, 1939–41, pp. 119–21 *passim*. These files contain a note 'Efforts to reprieve Barnes and Richards' by Joseph Walshe, head of external affairs, revealing that Tom Barry (1897–1980, leader of the IRA flying columns in Cork during the war of independence) had contacted de Valera at that time. Barry told the Taoiseach that 'if a delay of four days were granted, he would go to the Home Secretary in London and produce evidence to prove that the condemned men were not guilty of the Coventry outrage'. It is hard to fathom how Barry could prove that the two accused IRA men had nothing to do with the Coventry bomb, without revealing the identity of the culprit. It is understood that Barry was a personal friend of the bike-bomber, Joseph B. 'Joby' O'Sullivan, who hailed from Cork city. In any case, it appears that de Valera declined Barry's offer to go to London.

⁷ Taylor, *The Goebbels Diaries 1939–1941*, p. 117. Taylor notes that the incorrect total of eight hanged may be due to a transcription error, as the diary entries were dictated and typed up later by secretaries.

⁸ Taylor, p. 56.

⁹ Hull, *Irish Secrets*, pp. 71–75. Professor Hull, a US Army reserve major, has produced the most detailed account so far of German espionage in wartime Ireland, building on the initial spadework in Enno Stephan's 1963 publication *Spies in Ireland*.

¹⁰ Görtz was actually the fourth of thirteen German agents dispatched to neutral Ireland from 1939 to 1943. See Eunan O'Halpin, *Defending Ireland: The Irish State and its Enemies since 1922* (Oxford 1999), p. 241. While omitting Oscar Pfaus, Professor O'Halpin names other less active agents such as John Codd, James O'Neill and Jan van Loon, in addition to couriers Henry Lundborg and Christopher

NOTES

Eastwood. According to one MI5 file (UKNA, KV4/9, p. 53), another Irishman, Jack Vickers, was also trained by the Germans as an agent, but not deployed; Görtz narrowly missed meeting Seán Russell, who had only just arrived in Berlin. Abwehr liaison officer, Kurt Haller, told MI5 in 1946 that he had driven Russell to an aerodrome in Kassel, only to find that Görtz's plane had already taken off (UKNA, KV 2/769, p. xiii).

[11] While the authorities in wartime Britain did execute some spies who refused to work as double-cross agents against Germany, Ireland just interned them. See Nigel West, *MI5: British Security Service Operations 1909–45* (London 1983).

[12] In fact, Görtz was damaged goods in the espionage community, having done a three-year prison term in England for photographing British airfields in the 1930s. He was detained from November 1935 until his release in February 1939 (see Hull, pp. 79–83).

[13] Hull, p. 86. Professor Hull describes the IRA plan as 'amateurish'. In a 1962 article, Stephen Hayes (IRA chief of staff, 1939–41) described Plan Kathleen as 'ridiculous' (Cronin, *Frank Ryan*, p. 184).

[14] Kevin Kiely, *Francis Stuart: Artist and Outcast* (Dublin, 2007) pp. 133–34. Kiely notes that following her release, Iseult had an affair with the German spy.

[15] Hull notes that the surviving radio logs (discovered years later in the rafters by a subsequent owner of O'Donovan's house 'Florenceville') 'show an almost continuous period of monitoring from January through September 1940'. The dates covering Görtz's arrival remain blank on the log, however, presumably to avoid linking O'Donovan to the spy's arrival on Irish soil (see Hull, pp. 63–64); O'Donovan's radio set was variously operated and repaired by Pat Conway and Mattie O'Neill (see MacEoin, *The IRA in the Twilight Years*, p. 722).

[16] Donal O'Donovan, RTÉ radio interview, 25 July 2007.

[17] MA, Görtz diary, p. 13, pars. 56 and 57.

[18] MacEoin, *The IRA in the Twilight Years*, p. 432; Hull, pp. 148, 170; the author is grateful to Ms Ailbhe de Buitléar for permission to inspect her late father's papers; an entry in Görtz's Irish Military Intelligence file (G2/1722) suggests the spy may have been helped at Brittas Bay by a TCD lecturer named Einhart Kawerau. Describing Kawerau as a German refugee, the file adds: 'Görtz contact suggested, but no proof' (IMA, G2/1722, part VII). In the 1990s, Dr Einhart Kawerau worked as an assistant to the Professor of Biochemistry (William R. Fearon) at Trinity College, Dublin. (The author is grateful to Mr Thomas Turpin, formerly of TCD, for this information.)

[19] Hull, p. 133; Bowyer Bell, *The Secret Army*, p. 190.

[20] O'Donoghue, *Hitler's Irish Voices*, pp. 51–52, 56. Frank Ryan's prediction that he would be in the Irish government following a German victory could indicate that Veesenmayer planned to instal a puppet regime in Dublin, as he had done elsewhere. It is worth noting that when Ryan's U-boat docked at the Breton port of Lorient in mid-August 1940, Veesenmayer was there to meet him and escort him back to Berlin. According to MI5 files, Veesenmayer 'had already decided to use Ryan as Russell's successor in the IRA operation' – i.e. operation Taube (dove) 'an auxiliary offensive operation against Great Britain'. Under the German plan, Ryan was 'to approach the

Irish govt. and suggest that the German invasion of Britain would be an opportune moment for the seizure of Northern Ireland.... German support [would be] assured, but the Germans would act only after de Valera had committed himself. Ryan had told Veesenmayer that de Valera would support such a plan as this, provided he considered it a legitimate risk to take'. (UKNA, KV 2/769, pp. iii–iv; see also Cronin, *Frank Ryan*, pp. 252–3). A mid-1945 MI5 file records that 'In August of that year [1942] he [Frank Ryan] is said to have been received by Hitler' (UKNA file KV2/1292, 'Note on Frank Ryan', 6 July 1945, p. 1).

[21] Press Association report on release of MI5 files to UK national archives, Kew, 20 April 2000; UKNA, Lahousen file KV2/173; and UKNA, Lahousen interrogation file WO 208/4347; Canaris was executed by the SS (on suspicion of working for the British) just two weeks before the war ended; as regards the Russell/Ryan relationship, a 1946 G2 assessment noted that: 'As over 50 per cent of the IRA leaders on Seán Russell's staff were anti-socialist and most of them held communist views, Seán Russell kept any arrangement he had with the Germans to himself as he knew he could not trust any of the information to his staff' (MA, G2/3010). If this G2 assessment is correct, it might explain why, following Russell's death in August 1940, Ryan chose to return to Berlin: he was not privy to Russell's plans and probably felt he would be safer back with his Foreign Office mentor, Edmund Veesenmayer, awaiting further orders on foot of expected German military advances, including a planned invasion of England (codenamed Operation Sea Lion).

[22] A comprehensive list of those who aided Görtz in Ireland is contained in Hull, pp. 141–47, 170–71.

[23] NLI file 21/155, Görtz to O'Donovan, 29 August 1940. Some Görtz letters in this file are written in code; see also Hull, p. 170 *passim*; the discovery by the Garda special branch of the Görtz letters among O'Donovan's papers in September 1941 certainly did not help the IRA man, but internment was inevitable once he was named in the Stephen Hayes confession. In addition, while in custody in Mountjoy prison in June 1941, Hayes told gardaí about O'Donovan's IRA role in Germany two years earlier. Just a month before, on 2 May 1941, Hayes had written to O'Donovan about plans to get Görtz back to Germany. He also told O'Donovan about the involvement of a senior Irish army officer (Major General Hugo McNeill) who is understood to have had at least one meeting with Görtz (see Hull, pp. 170–71).

[24] Stephen Hayes's confession (long version) pp. 45–46. Dr Ryan, as reported by Hayes, was right about O'Donovan's links to Germany but wrong in thinking that he was 'too well placed' to be arrested; the author is grateful to Michael MacEvilly for a copy of the confession's long version, which supports his contention that it 'was a strange mixture of fact and fiction' (MacEvilly, Unpublished biography of Dr Andy Cooney, p. 297).

[25] NLI file 22/309, O'Donovan's handwritten note dated 22 September 1969; according to Professor Eunan O'Halpin of Trinity College, Dublin, the Hayes confession 'would not have disgraced a Stalinist show trial' and while many of Hayes's accusers felt 'he must have been a traitor, so far as can be judged he was not. But in becoming the focal point of his comrades' paranoia, he unintentionally did the state an enormous favour. The Hayes affair diverted the IRA's energies for months, it

further discredited the movement in the eyes of the public, and it left a legacy of confusion and bitterness in republican circles ... the IRA was reduced to a minor irritant after 1941.' (O'Halpin, *Spying on Ireland*, p. 249); republican opinion was certainly divided over the former chief of staff. Jim O'Donovan told a fellow internee (Jim Savage from Cork) in the Curragh camp that the Hayes confession was 'rubbish'. Conversely, another internee (Eddie Keenan from Belfast) thought Hayes was guilty: 'I knew Seán McCaughey and Charlie McGlade and others associated with the arrest and detention of Hayes. I knew them to be sincere, honourable soldiers of the Republic. None of them were pro-Nazi ... they had the same attitude as Tone had in '98 and the men of 1916 when they accepted help from the French or Germans – England's difficulty, Ireland's opportunity. I would accept their conclusions as to the guilt of Hayes...' (Keenan to Brendan Ó Cathaoir, 25 November 1994. The author is grateful to Mr Ó Cathaoir, a retired *Irish Times* journalist, for supplying a copy of Keenan's letter).

[26] NA, Department of External Affairs file A34 re Hermann Görtz.

[27] Coogan, 'Today with Pat Kenny', RTÉ Radio One, 30 September 2008; historian Cian Ó hÉigeartaigh notes that, for some years after taking power in 1932: 'Fianna Fáil had an uneasy relationship with the IRA, with qualified support on one side and qualified tolerance on the other' (see Ó hÉigeartaigh, 'Máirtín Ó Cadhain: Politics and Literature' in the *Canadian Journal of Irish Studies*, volume 34, no. 1, Spring 2008, p. 28).

11. A Guest of the Nation

[1] Author's interview with Donal O'Donovan, 16 March 2005. Professor Tierney was a neighbour of O'Donovan's in Shankill. The UCD professor's wife was a daughter of Eoin MacNeill, with whom O'Donovan had studied Irish in Omagh on holidays years before; Gerry O'Donovan recalls the raid as follows: 'I remember the morning of his arrest and the special branch bringing each of the children, separating them and quizzing them about visitors. I remember being asked if my father had any hiding places that he used to use ... all that kind of thing, very underhand. I didn't tell them anything. I didn't know anything.... The maid we had at the time, Katie Clarke, was quizzed in the same way. She was asked about the guests, who were Todd Andrews, Dermot Lawlor and his wife. They were all above-board names. There were a few, I suppose, that were a bit iffy. She forgot that every Saturday night a man came to transmit on the radio [*laughs*]. It went out of her head.' Gerry O'Donovan also recalls: We used to be in and out of Michael Tierney's house ... there we would meet Eoin MacNeill and Major-General Hugo MacNeill, who was in the army then, James McNeill, the ex-governor general, and [Séamus] Delargy [of the Folklore Commission]. They were all friends of Tierney's. My father would be there sometimes. After mass he might drop in and there'd be a discussion, so there was some communication between the two sides. I was at school with the Tierney children, both in Presentation College, Bray, and at Glenstal. I was at Blackrock College and they went there as well. Michael Tierney was a great Blueshirt man' (author's interview with Gerry O'Donovan, 25 August 1999).

² MA file G2/3783. Davis recoilless guns were patented in America in 1910. In World War I, they were mounted on British warplanes and used to attack airships and ground targets (see Ian V. Hogg, *The Guns 1939–45* (London 1977), pp. 140–41). It is not clear why O'Donovan had instructions for such a weapon which, by 1941, was no longer in general use; Donal O'Donovan recalled that 'the aerial ran from the chimney of our house across a valley to a big tree. It was a huge aerial' (RTÉ radio documentary, *Codename Paddy O'Brien*, 25 July 2007). The author is grateful to RTÉ producer Ciarán Cassidy for permission to cite extracts from his documentary.

³ MacEvilly, Unpublished biography of Dr Andy Cooney, p. 313; Hull, *Irish Secrets*, p. 146; MA file IC/P/743.

⁴ MA files G2/3783 and IC/P/743; given the line of questioning, it is clear that the special branch detectives had no idea that O'Donovan had sheltered Görtz. O'Donovan's daughter Sheila remembers that the German spy 'lived in Donal's tree-house in the old eucalyptus at the bottom of the orchard. At night, apparently, he came in and lived in the bedroom of the coachman's house' (author's interview with Mrs Sheila Hanna, 27 March 2000).

⁵ O'Donovan to Guiney, 14 October 1941, MA file IC/P/743.

⁶ MA, IC/P/743. Michael O'Rahilly had been Pádraig Pearse's aide-de-camp in the GPO. He died leading twelve men in a charge against a British barricade in Moore Street, Dublin, during the 1916 Rising. Richard was married to Monty's elder sister Elgin. Elgin visited the camp on at least one occasion, according to O'Donovan's internment file.

⁷ O'Donovan to Boland, 6 November 1941, MA file IC/P/743; NLI file 22/307 reveals that O'Donovan's decision to write personally to Boland was prompted by the latter's 'statement to Seán Ó hUadhaigh [O'Donovan's solicitor] that parole for me was out of the question'.

⁸ Mackey to G2, 19 February 1942, MA file G2/3783.

⁹ MA file G2/3783. According to Donal O'Donovan, Toner was a native of Strabane who worked for Healy's outfitters in Dame Street before qualifying as a solicitor in middle age. In addition to founding the Irish Film Society in 1936, Toner was also business manager of O'Donovan's literary magazine *Ireland To-Day* (1936–38). This was the same man who accompanied Monty O'Donovan on her monthly visits to her husband in the Curragh internment camp (1941–43). The Strabane man was married to Molly MacDonagh, a niece of 1916 Proclamation signatory Tomás MacDonagh. See also O'Donovan, *Little Old Man Cut Short*, pp. 12–16, 34 and 38.

¹⁰ Mackey to G2, 4 May 1943, MA file G2/3783, S/463/P-secret. While the ESB struck O'Donovan off its payroll for the duration of his internment (twenty-three months), his army pension and disability payments continued to be paid.

¹¹ O'Donovan essay 'Germany and Small Racial Groups', June-July 1942, Curragh camp. The author is grateful to Gerry O'Donovan for supplying a copy of this essay; when this author asked Gerry O'Donovan if he thought his father admired the Nazis, he replied: 'Well, they had done an unheard of job on Germany. Germany had worthless money and huge unemployment of 20 million or more. And in five years it was gone. They had 280 different values of the Mark … but they had done wonderful things in Germany and I suppose he would have had some admiration. If

you say you admired anything about Germany, people say it means that you were for the Holocaust. That didn't come into it at all. There was no abject or unquestioning admiration. Anyone who knew him would realise that, because he never wholly admired anything; he always had something to criticise in it. Certainly, in 1936, he was anti-German, but whether he changed a bit – as I say, Ireland's opportunity was the most important thing in his life' (author's interview with Gerry O'Donovan, 25 August 1999).

[12] The author is grateful to Professor Colum Kenny (Dublin City University), who brought the book to his attention, having found it in a second-hand bookshop.

[13] Callaghan to Guiney, 23 June 1942, MA file IC/P/743; the author is grateful to Martin Ferris TD for additional details on O'Donovan's three 'students'; O'Donovan would have been fascinated to learn that in mid-1942 Kurt Haller was seeking plans of the Fort William electricity plant in Scotland with a view to blowing it up. The Abwehr diary of 16 May noted that 'agents have been earmarked for this purpose'. O'Donovan would have been even more interested to discover that the agents were in fact two British army POWs from Ireland: Private James Brady from Strokestown, County Roscommon, and Private Andrew Walsh from Fethard, County Tipperary. Walsh was to be parachuted into Glasgow, while Brady would attempt a similar operation near Ballycastle, County Antrim. In the event, neither mission went ahead (see Hull, p. 222; and MI5 file KV 2/769, pp. 11–12).

[14] The author provided a copy of O'Donovan's notebook to two professors of chemistry at Trinity College, Dublin – Professor Seán Corish and Professor David Grayson – who confirmed that it contained preliminary notes for a lecture on explosive techniques. Professor Corish notes that one part of the book relates to 'what you need to do to blow up a bridge', as well as checking detonators to 'make sure they would not blow up in your face'. Professor Corish adds: 'There is no doubt he had a great deal of knowledge about how to make explosives ... he's clearly passing on instructions on how best to cause explosions.' Professor Grayson adds that the lecture notes contain references to relevant quantities of explosive material, including ammonium nitrate, TNT and aluminium powder. He noted that one page of O'Donovan's copy-book 'looks like an instruction manual for detonator circuits'. In addition, Professor Grayson notes that O'Donovan 'refers to the use of a P[ost] O[ffice] Box for testing purposes' and also 'sets out some "examination questions"' for his students. Both TCD academics confirm that the copy-book contains references to electrical detonation, size of charges, quantity of gelignite and drilling holes in which to place explosives; the aforementioned material is based on the author's interview with both professors at the department of chemistry, Trinity College, Dublin, on 24 November 2008. The author is grateful to Professor Seán Corish (Fellow Emeritus and former Professor of Physical Chemistry, TCD) and Professor David Grayson (Head, School of Chemistry, TCD) for their help in deciphering Jim O'Donovan's bomb-making lecture notes.

[15] Henry to Guiney, 6 July 1942, MS file IC/P/743.

[16] Author's interview with Donal O'Donovan. Jim O'Donovan's children were unaware that their father had also been granted parole ten days earlier owing to his sister's serious illness. Despite being out of the camp on that occasion for four days,

he did not visit his children in their respective boarding schools. Donal discovered the first parole period only when examining his father's internment file in August 2008.

[17] Donal O'Donovan, RTÉ radio documentary, 25 July 2007.

[18] G2/3783, Bryan to G2 Curragh Command, 19 May 1943.

[19] Guiney to G2, 27 May 1943, MA file IC/P/743; a copy of the same text was sent to Colonel Dan Bryan of G2 the following day by the G2 representative at Curragh command, Commandant D. Mackey.

[20] MA file IC/P/743, Mackey to Guiney, 7 July 1943.

[21] O'Donovan called the clippings his 'box of "census" papers'. They were confiscated when he left the camp on 8 September 1943. Nine days later he wrote to the camp governor asking for the papers to be returned. They were sent to O'Donovan on 28 September 1943. The relevant correspondence is in his internment file, MA IC/P/743.

[22] See, for example, 'The Spy who loved Daddy', in *The Guardian*, 4 February 1999, pp. 10–11.

[23] O'Donoghue, *Hitler's Irish Voices*, p. 94; Professor Eunan O'Halpin of TCD plays down Bowen and Betjeman's intelligence roles (see O'Halpin, *Spying on Ireland*, pp. 138–39, 210–12).

[24] O'Donovan papers, NLI; the broadcaster and playwright Ulick O'Connor recalls that during the war Gogan took him 'and some friends to 58 Northumberland Road [the German Legation] to see films about Hitler. Someone there asked me: "You will visit Germany after the war, yes?"' (author's interview with Ulick O'Connor, 20 August 2001); William Joseph Gogan (born 1891) joined the National Museum's staff in 1914 as assistant keeper of antiquities, but was suspended in 1916 for his pro-republican activities. He was reinstated following independence in 1922 and promoted to the post of keeper of the museum's art and monuments archive in 1936. He wrote a book on the Ardagh chalice. (The author is grateful to the current director of the National Museum, Dr Patrick Wallace, for the aforementioned information on Liam Gogan.) The National Museum's Austrian director, Dr Adolf Mahr, was on leave of absence in Berlin during the war where he worked for the German foreign office and the Reich radio service. Mahr was a member of the Nazi party. (For further details on Mahr's multi-faceted career, see O'Donoghue, *Hitler's Irish Voices*, and Mullins, *Dublin Nazi No. 1*).

[25] Gerry O'Donovan remembers that his father 'inflicted an awful lot of worry and pain on my mother … she never had any money. She used to get some sort of an allowance from him for the housekeeping, but if she wanted to go anywhere, do anything, buy anything – even a present for him – she would have to either work it out of the housekeeping or ask him for the money. In her lifetime she never knew what he earned. The only money that she ever had that she could call her own, he spent it on this City Chemical and Colour Company. He blew it. I don't know to what extent he regretted that, if at all … he was of a particular upbringing where it was none of the woman's business what you earned and therefore she never knew. It was a very old world attitude, but particularly hard on her because she was expected to keep this big house and garden with no income from him except the IRA disability pension' (author's interview with Gerry O'Donovan, 25 August 1999).

NOTES

[26] Author's interview with Donal O'Donovan. Donal was a regular contributor to the Blackrock College annual. In his final year, 1946, he penned an essay in Irish entitled 'An tSaoirse' (Freedom). Although it deals with the 1918–21 period, the essay makes no reference to his father's or other relatives' roles in the war of independence; Gerry O'Donovan recalls that 'Donal and I both entered Blackrock College in January 1942 and he stayed until he finished secondary school. I left in summer 1947' (G. O'Donovan to author, 14 April 2009). Mrs Aedine Sànta (née O'Donovan) recalls that her mother 'went to Belvedere [College] and tried to get them [Donal and Gerry] in there, but that didn't work out' (author's interview with Mrs Sànta, 31 May 1999); see also John Cooney, *John Charles McQuaid: Ruler of Catholic Ireland* (Dublin 1999), p. 142; a year earlier, in September 1940, Jim O'Donovan's other brother Colman (then posted to the Vatican as a diplomat) was busy trying to find out who the Pope would appoint as the new archbishop of Dublin. See Crowe, Kennedy *et al. Documents on Irish Foreign Policy, Vol. VI*, p. 364.

[27] Author's interview with Tom Byrne, 22 July 2001.

[28] Jim O'Donovan also taught German in the Curragh, according to one source. (See John McGuffin, *Internment* (Dublin, 1973), chapter 4, p. 8.)

[29] The words mean 'Give me your hand, your white hand; live well my dear, live well. Then we march, then we march against England'. This popular song of the Nazi era was banned by the British in occupied post-war Germany. But the locals got round the ban by singing 'Denn wir fahren mit der Eisenbahn' (Then we march with the railroad). The author is grateful to historian Enno Stephan and Professor Mark Hull for details of the song and its history.

[30] Author's interview with Eddie Keenan, 24 August 2000.

[31] In addition to giving Russian language classes – he had learned the language while living in Moscow in the 1930s – Neil Goold Verschoyle also taught Marxist theory and tried to pass on his communist beliefs to others. In July 1942, he signed the camp's autograph book while adding a quotation from Lenin: 'The proletariat has no other weapon in the struggle for power except organisation' (Curragh internment camp autograph book 1941–4, p. 54). The author is grateful to Martin Ferris TD for providing a copy of this book; Neil Goold Verschoyle's younger brother Brian, who was also a communist party member, died on 5 January 1942 in the Sol'Iletsk gulag (a town in Orenburg Province, near the border with Kazakhstan; he was earlier held in the Solovetsky gulag). He had been imprisoned on suspicion of 'spying for a foreign power'. The two brothers were born to an Anglo-Irish family at the Manor House, Dunkineely, County Donegal. Their father was a barrister and their mother the daughter of a British army colonel (see Barry McLoughlin, *Left to the Wolves: Irish Victims of Stalinist Terror* (Dublin 2007), pp. 191, 195 *passim*). Neil Goold Verschoyle married a Russian woman, Olga Dobrova, while living in Moscow in the 1930s. He lived in Dublin and London in the 1940s and 1950s, but returned to Russia in the 1960s. He died in Moscow in 1985, aged 88. His son still lives there. The author is grateful to Professor David Simms of TCD's mathematics department for details of his two uncles.

[32] Author's interview with Billy Joe McCorry, 24 August 2000.

[33] Author's interview with Jim Savage, 18 August 2000. Before interviewing Mr Savage in Cork, the author received a letter from him about Jim O'Donovan stating:

'He was a friend of Seán Russell but unlike Russell he was a full-blown Nazi and didn't deny it. Before the war he spent time in Germany ... I slept next to him in the Curragh internment camp but had nothing in common with his views, no way.... His stay in the camp was brief as he had great pull.... He wasn't a popular fellow as I'm sure he felt he was above the rest. I only spoke to him a half a dozen times.' Savage adds, 'O'Donovan could have risen to the top had he joined Fianna Fáil. It is to his credit that he did not.' (Savage to author, 20 July 2000); O'Donovan's former IRA comrades differ on his approach to Nazi Germany, depending on their own left- or right-wing perspectives. However, the historian Seán Cronin notes that O'Donovan's 'politics were pro-German' (Cronin, *Frank Ryan*, p. 182). Whether or not O'Donovan was also anti-Semitic is less clear. According to Cronin, IRA chief of staff Stephen Hayes blamed the 'anti-Jewish flavour' of some scripts O'Donovan had allegedly written (for broadcast on a secret IRA radio transmitter, which was seized by police in December 1939) not only for the loss of the transmitter, but also for making the government aware of 'German influence in our ranks' (Cronin, p. 183). Hayes's views appeared twenty-three years later in a series of ghost-written articles for *The People* newspaper (London, November 1962). But Cronin adds the following caveat: '*The People* was a sensational Sunday paper and not to be trusted in the handling of such material' (Cronin, p. 271). In the course of researching this biography, the author did not find any specifically anti-Semitic material written by James L. O'Donovan.

[34] Author's interview with Mick O'Riordan, 27 April 2001.

[35] Better known as Seán Óg Ó Tuama, this Corkman was a teacher in Dublin and well known as a traditional sean-nós singer. He was a second cousin of Professor Seán Ó Tuama of University College Cork. The author is grateful to Finín Ó Tuama of Raidió na Gaeltachta for this information.

[36] Author's interview with John Murphy, 10 April 2000.

[37] Author's interview with Ruairí Brugha, 9 March 2001.

[38] MA file IC/P/743, Mackey to G2, 4 May 1943.

[39] Author's interview with Donal O'Donovan; Donal's brother Gerry has similar feelings about the medal incident: 'Sent to an internment camp. I mean, Jesus. I always think it's much harder if you haven't got a little bit of fame out of it – at least having a bit of fame or notoriety – but to be one of hundreds, I mean all the people who died. You know the four who died, McKelvey, Rory O'Connor and those [Dick Barrett and Liam Mellows]. There were another four the next night, but nobody ever heard of them. It's very sad that they really got nothing. But I've always held myself that it was a very middle-class revolution, and that really the ordinary man in the street was dragged in by the toes or the short hairs. But he got no thanks at all for it.... When you think of all the people who sided with de Valera all got marvellous jobs, and the people who sided with Collins all got great jobs' (author's interview with Gerry O'Donovan, 25 August 1999). O'Donovan's sons were, however, mistaken in thinking that their father's medal was sent to the Curragh camp. MA file IC/P/743 makes it clear that the medal was, in fact, mailed to the O'Donovan household in Shankill, County Dublin.

[40] Over sixty years later, no member of O'Donovan's family could recall where the medal was or what had become of it. Given the long-standing enmity between de Valera and O'Donovan – they died within a few years of each other, Dev on

NOTES

29 August 1975 and O'Donovan on 4 June 1979, never having been reconciled – the medal seemed to be more a source of embarrassment than anything else within the O'Donovan family. Nonetheless, some 30 years later, in mid-1971, Jim O'Donovan was awarded the Truce (1921) Commemoration Medal. This award, marking the 50th anniversary of the truce on 11 July 1921, was given to a, by then, dwindling number of old soldiers, including O'Donovan, who was aged 74 and Richard Mulcahy, then aged 84.

[41] O'Neill to Guiney, 19 May 1943, MA file IC/P/743.
[42] O'Neill to Guiney, 14 August 1943, MA file IC/P/743.
[43] Fleming to Guiney, 8 September 1943, MA file IC/P/743.
[44] Author's interview with Donal O'Donovan, 28 August 2008.
[45] Byrne to Guiney, 9 September 1943, G2/3783.
[46] Guiney to G2, 22 October 1943, MA file G2/3783.
[47] Bryan to G2 Curragh command, 6 November 1943, MA file G2/3783.
[48] Mackey to Bryan, 9 November 1943, MA file G2/3783; Donal O'Donovan maintains that his father was never suicidal. He recalls that, in the 1970s, his father once told him in Our Lady's Manor nursing home, 'You can be assured I would never kill myself' (author's interview with Donal O'Donovan, 28 August 2008).

12. A Time for Reflection

[1] O'Donovan, RTÉ radio documentary, 25 July 2007.
[2] ibid.
[3] MacEvilly's unpublished biography of Andy Cooney, p. 318. MacEvilly uses the Irish word *meitheal* (working party).
[4] Deputy Garda Commissioner to department of justice, October 1941, MA file G2/3783.
[5] Author's interview with John O'Brien, 2 April 2001; O'Donovan's daughter Aedine recalls: 'After the war, my father got his ESB job back. I don't know if there was a problem internally, but he got it back and that was, to him, all that mattered. He told me that he expected to get his job back. There must have been enough sympathy somewhere in the ranks for him to have expected that. I don't think Dick Browne, the then [ESB] director, was particularly interested one way or the other, but there were quite a few staunch IRA people on the staff ... Paddy Corr was one' (author's interview with Mrs Aedine Sànta, 31 May 1999).
[6] Author's interview with Tomás MacGiolla, 19 November 2001. MacGiolla believes that the ESB's blacklist system had been abolished by the late 1970s; in a subsequent interview with the author, MacGiolla said that O'Donovan 'was involved in some bombing. He wasn't acceptable to the ESB [in 1943], but the government made a signed order saying he was acceptable.... People would point him out in the canteen' (author's interview with MacGiolla, 11 August 2009). This version of events suggests that O'Donovan had friends in high places at the time – perhaps de Valera himself, who was Taoiseach in 1943, or Seán T. O'Kelly, who was a close friend of Jim O'Donovan's brother Dan.
[7] Author's interview with Jack Wyley, 2 September 1999.
[8] Author's interview with Pádraig Ó Conaill, 2 April 2001.

[9] Author's interview with Jan van Loon, 28 August 2001.

[10] Hull, *Irish Secrets*, p. 258.

[11] Author's interview with Douglas Gageby, 29 September 1999. In the 1950s, Gageby became editor of de Valera's *Evening Press* and later, editor of *The Irish Times*, 1963–74 and 1977–86 (Fergus Pyle was editor 1974–77). For details of Gageby's career, including his time in Irish military intelligence, see obituary in *The Irish Times*, 28 June 2004, p. 4.

[12] Author's interview with Donal O'Donovan, 16 March 2005.

[13] Author's interview with Donal O'Donovan, 12 February 1999.

[14] Colman O'Donovan may have fallen foul of Walshe when he lobbied the Father General of the Jesuits in Rome to have Monsignor Paschal Robinson (apostolic nuncio to Ireland 1929–48) made a cardinal. The move earned a rebuke from O'Donovan's boss, ambassador William Macaulay, on 28 December 1939. The irony was that Joe Walshe had studied to be a Jesuit priest before joining the diplomatic corps. In September 1940, O'Donovan sought Macauley's job when the latter resigned and left for America. But Walshe kept O'Donovan on only as acting chargé d'affaires before posting him to Lisbon. See Crowe, *Documents on Irish Foreign Policy, Vol. VI*, pp. 126, 367; the author is grateful to Ms Elaine Dalton, Department of Foreign Affairs, Dublin, for details of Colman O'Donovan's diplomatic career.

[15] Author's interview with Donal O'Donovan, 16 March 2005.

[16] Author's interview with Mrs Sheila Hanna (née O'Donovan), 27 March 2000. Margaret O'Donovan (née Brennan) died in 1930; her husband, Daniel O'Donovan, died in 1931.

[17] Francis Stuart broadcast on German Radio, 6 February 1943. See O'Donoghue, *Hitler's Irish Voices*, p. 107. This book details the story of German Radio's Irish service or *Irland Redaktion*, which was on air from December 1939 to May 1945.

[18] NLI file 21/987, O'Donovan to Boland, CTS, London, 13 February 1945. O'Donovan's 'prisoner's companion' idea may have originated in 1930 when he sent a prayer book to Seán Russell, who was at that time imprisoned in Mountjoy. Russell wrote: 'I was delighted at the thought that you considered my friendship of any consequence.' See NLI file 21/155, Russell to O'Donovan, 27 March 1930. (This was eight months before O'Donovan joined the ESB.) According to O'Donovan's daughter Aedine, prayer was important to her father: 'My father was a church-goer and a great favourite of prayer. He would go to church every Sunday. Prayer was very important to him, his direct line. He prayed at home quietly. At one stage, at confession, he was given the rosary to say. He said "Whoever created the rosary should have been shot. It is the most mechanical thing that ever existed". He said that to the priest – that it was no real penance because you just said it. It didn't mean anything' (author's interview with Mrs Aedine Sànta, 31 May 1999).

[19] Harry White escaped the gallows, serving two years for manslaughter instead, thanks to the efforts of his lawyer, Seán MacBride, who had briefly been IRA chief of staff a decade earlier. According to O'Donovan's son Gerry, it is not clear if the article was ever published. White's memoirs were published in 1985 under the title *Harry*. It was the first publication to name Archie Doyle as the man who shot Kevin O'Higgins in 1927; the British government also wanted White's execution stopped, but for different reasons. See O'Halpin, *Defending Ireland*, p. 250.

[20] Jim O'Donovan's daughter Mrs Aedine Sànta recalls: 'The boy's name was Ernst Dirksen. Of our family I was the nearest in age to him, so had the most contact. We shared an interest in philately and exchanged stamps.... As Ernst's mother was still alive (his father died early in the war, I believe) Peter and Ethel [O'Donovan] weren't allowed to adopt him officially' (Sànta to author, 24 September 2009).
[21] *The Irish Times*, 24 May 1947.
[22] Cronin, *Frank Ryan: The Search for the Republic*, pp. 205–14.
[23] For the background to Görtz's mission to Ireland, see Hull, p. 75 *passim*. Mahr joined the Nazi party in April 1933 while he was on the Irish state payroll. He spent the war years in Berlin working for the German foreign office and German Radio's overseas services (including the nightly broadcasts to neutral Ireland).
[24] Duggan, *Herr Hempel*, p. 223.
[25] MacWhite to Boland, 2 June 1947, NAI, DFA file A/34.
[26] Boland to MacWhite, 2 July 1947, NAI, DFA file A/34.
[27] Hull, p. 312.
[28] Author's interviews with O'Brien and Ó Conaill, 2 April 2001; in fact, O'Donovan's chances of promotion were also hampered by illness. His daughter Sheila recalls that 'he had multiple sclerosis from the age of 50. Donal always says that was brought on by the hosing down and things like that that he used to get [in the Curragh camp]. Apparently, whenever they were hosed, they used to dance around and pretend they were enjoying themselves, even though they were bloody freezing, just to annoy the guards' (author's interview with Mrs Sheila Hanna, 27 March 2000); O'Donovan's younger daughter Aedine adds: 'In 1947, he contracted multiple sclerosis and was very near kicking the bucket. He lost his sight and hearing. It was very bad for a few weeks. Then it began to get a bit better. It took him nearly a year to learn how to walk again ... he got a remission until 1957.... He went into the home in 1969, and died in 1979. He had been in a wheelchair for fourteen years before he died' (author's interview with Mrs Aedine Sànta, 31 May 1999).
[29] The author is grateful to Brendan Delaney, ESB archives manager, for this information.
[30] The author is grateful to the current state chemist, Dr Dermot Hayes, for clarifying this matter. Hayes to O'Donoghue, 8 June 2007.
[31] Author's interview with Donal O'Donovan, 28 August 2008; the old republicans' antipathy to what they termed the 'Free State army' seemed to be pretty universal. Colm Connolly told the author that his uncle Paddy Fleming (IRA chief of staff 1945–47) disapproved of his decision to join the FCA in the 1960s (Connolly to author, 27 November 2007).
[32] Despite their detailed correspondence, Florence O'Donoghue's book *No Other Law* makes only two brief references to Séamus O'Donovan (pp. 208–9 and 290). However, as O'Donoghue was a member of the advisory council of the Bureau of Military History at the time, he may have been encouraging O'Donovan to make a personal deposition to the bureau (which the latter did, although only covering the early stages of the war of independence).
[33] Birkenhead to O'Donovan, 20 March 1962, NLI file 21/987.
[34] *Studies*, September 1950, pp. 307–15.
[35] Donal O'Donovan confirmed to this author that his father had not supported the Provisional IRA's campaign. Gerry O'Donovan recalls that his father 'always professed

to scoff at it [the Provisional IRA campaign] a bit – not that he wouldn't have done the same. And it wasn't really that their planning or anything was wrong, it was just that his efforts didn't bear fruit and he felt nobody else's could either' (author's interview with Gerry O'Donovan, 25 August 1999).

13. Belated Thanks from the Third Reich

[1] Published in 1958 by Odhams, the authors were Charles Wighton and Günther Peis. Enno Stephan's 1961 work, *Geheimauftrag Irland* (published by Gerhard Stalling Verlag, Hamburg, and which appeared in English in 1963 as *Spies in Ireland*, published by Macdonald, London), was largely based on Abwehr II's war diaries, as was *They Spied on England*. Stephan told this author that Kurt Haller (who was a liaison officer between the Foreign Office and the Abwehr) had approved the manuscript of *Geheimauftrag Irland* on his deathbed. Enno Stephan had fought in the German army and ended the war as a prisoner of the French, thus learning to speak their language fluently. Putting his newly found linguistic abilities to good use after the war, Stephan rose through the ranks of German Radio's foreign service to become head of its French language department.

[2] Clissmann letter, *The Irish Times*, 9 June 1958.

[3] In fact, Jim O'Donovan was linked by name to the Abwehr war diary in a 1953 book by Dutch historian Louis de Jong (director of the Netherlands state institute for war documentation). The book appeared in English in 1956 entitled *German Fifth Column in the Second World War*. But no British or Irish papers appear to have spotted the reference. O'Donovan refers to the book in his own notes of the early 1960s.

[4] MI5 file on Kurt Haller, 1 November 1945, UKNA, KV 2/769.

[5] Stuart in conversation with Professor Mark Hull, 7 July 1999. The author is grateful to Professor Hull for supplying a transcript of his interview with Francis Stuart (who died the following year).

[6] O'Donovan's unpublished notes, *circa* 1962. It is noteworthy that O'Donovan refers to the senior Abwehr officer, Friedrich Carl Marwede, in this recollection. But Marwede is not named in O'Donovan's notes of his three 1939 trips to Hamburg and Berlin. Marwede used the cover name Pfalzgraz when he met O'Donovan with other military intelligence officers. O'Donovan mentions the cover name, but it is not clear when the IRA man first became aware that Pfalzgraz and Marwede were the same person.

[7] O'Donovan's unpublished notes.

[8] Author's interview with Mick O'Riordan, 27 April 2001.

[9] Author's interview with Jim Savage, Cork, 18 August 2000.

[10] Donal O'Donovan's book appeared in 1989 under the title *Kevin Barry and his Time* (Glendale Press, Dublin).

[11] Enno Stephan's message to O'Donovan, when translated, reads: 'For Jim O'Donovan with cordial thanks for the helpful support during my stay in Dublin and for the hospitable welcome.' The photograph was signed and dated 30 January 1960. The Drohl mentioned in O'Donovan's notes is Ernst Weber-Drohl, another German spy, who was landed from a U-boat off Sligo in February 1940. Hermann Görtz arrived three months later. O'Donovan misspelled the name, but Margarete was the

NOTES

codename for Mary Mains, a 45-year-old Irish woman living in Spain, who acted as an Abwehr courier and met O'Donovan in Dublin in November 1940. She gave him $10,000 for Görtz, as well as invisible ink and a new radio code. Her trip from Spain to Ireland aboard a Japanese liner was facilitated by Leopold Kerney, the Irish ambassador in Madrid. On her return to Spain, Mains carried a situation report from Görtz for the Abwehr (see Hull, *Irish Secrets*, pp. 142–44). Mary Mains's codename appears in the Abwehr II war diary, and resurfaces in UKNA file KV 2/769, MI5's 1946 'Special Interrogation Report' on Kurt Haller (Foreign Office liaison officer with Abwehr II). According to this report, Mains also 'notified' the IRA that Seán Russell had died three months earlier. On 14 November 1940, the Abwehr diary recorded that Mains had arrived safely in Ireland and that 'she will return to Spain shortly'. Haller told MI5 that Mains 'met O'Donovan several times and through him Görtz'. Haller said Mains inquired 'whether Frank Ryan, who was now in Germany, would be welcomed by the IRA', but O'Donovan replied 'that it was a matter of indifference to the IRA whether Ryan was in Germany, Spain or Ireland' (KV 2/769, p. xix). O'Donovan's caustic comment suggests that there would have been no senior IRA role for Ryan if he returned home.

[12] RTÉ radio documentary, 'Codename Pat O'Brien', 25 July 2007.

[13] O'Donovan's contemporaneous notes (unpublished).

[14] Author's interview with Mrs Elizabeth Clissmann, 23 June 2008.

[15] *The Irish Times*, 'Spies from Germany: a chapter of history completed', 19 October 1963, p. 12.

[16] O'Donovan's notes, *circa* 1962.

[17] Jim O'Donovan to Patrick O'Donovan, 6 June 1966, NLI file 22/336.

[18] *The Irish Times*, 24 April 1969, p. 12. Polling day for the Third Dáil was on 16 June 1922, and it first met on 9 September 1922. See also Hickey and Doherty, *A New Dictionary of Irish History*, pp. 197–98.

[19] O'Shannon to author, 22 June 2000.

[20] RTÉ documentary, *Kevin Barry*, October 1970. The author is grateful to Cathal O'Shannon for his insights and to Ciarán Cassidy for a copy of the documentary. Béaslaí's book is entitled *Michael Collins and the Making of a New Ireland* (two-volumes, London, 1926).

[21] O'Shannon to author, 13 January 2005. O'Shannon found Mrs Monty Barry to be 'a delightful woman' but did not interview her for the Kevin Barry programme because 'she had never talked about her brother for any public purpose and she was not going to do so now.'

[22] Author's interview with John P. Duggan, 15 October 2001; Gerry O'Donovan also recalls his father's disillusionment in old age: 'He looked around him and was very disappointed with the deterioration in the state – after all the trouble that his generation went to, that they end up with such a materialistic, dull and dreary country. I think that disappointed him.... Censorship was another thing that he didn't have time for' (author's interview with Gerry O'Donovan, 25 August 1999).

[23] Author's interview with Donal O'Donovan, 16 March 2005. Donal O'Donovan adds that his father 'never had a drink problem. At weddings he'd drink four whiskeys and would slump down in his chair'.

[24] Briscoe to author, 9 May 2007. According to Donal O'Donovan, his father voted twice for Fianna Fáil in the 1932 Dáil and Seanad elections, but was dismayed 'when he saw de Valera wearing a top hat [the symbol of the English ruling class] to go to [the League of Nations in] Geneva. And then of course the IRA campaign began, the military courts were reinstated and the whole thing fell apart. I suppose that is when he began to think that maybe somebody like Seán Russell should come along' (author's interview with Donal O'Donovan, 16 March 2005). Dr Briscoe's and Donal O'Donovan's recollections are not necessarily contradictory. While unhappy with de Valera's decision to enter the Dáil in 1927, five years later Jim O'Donovan presumably felt obliged to vote Fianna Fáil to put an end to ten years of Cumann na nGaedheal rule. Donal O'Donovan confirms Dr Briscoe's view that Jim O'Donovan was opposed to the bombing in the North in the 1970s, adding that his father 'was so disgusted at what he had done that he did not support the Provisional IRA's campaign, although he had supported the previous Border campaign of 1956–62' (author's interview with Donal O'Donovan, 2 October 2008); O'Donovan's daughter Aedine recalls that her father used to joke about de Valera in later years: '[He said that] the best thing de Valera could do was be a dead de Valera [*laughs*]. Then when he [de Valera] did finally die [in 1975], he said, "It's a pity I can't complain about him any more". He also said that if he reached 100 he didn't want "the bloody five pound note from de Valera" [*laughs*]' (author's interview with Mrs Aedine Sànta, 31 May 1999).

[25] Author's interview with Professor Risteárd Mulcahy, 2 April 2007. Jim O'Donovan once told his son Donal that 'if the circumstances were right, I'd rather meet Dick Mulcahy than Frank Aiken' (author's interview with Donal O'Donovan, 26 January 2007).

[26] Jim O'Donovan died in Dublin's Meath Hospital on 4 June 1979, aged 82. His wife died on 25 January 1985, aged 78. The author is grateful to Sister M. B. Murphy, administrator of Our Lady's Manor, for details of Jim O'Donovan's final years at the nursing home (Sister Murphy to author, 28 September 1999). See also 'Sister of Kevin Barry is buried', *Irish Press*, 28 January 1985; Mrs Aedine Sànta also recalled her father's talks with Fr Jordan: 'He had quite a good relationship with the priest who was attached to the place. They used to have long chats and discussions. Confession had gone by that time but he remained hopeful in his faith so I imagine that he had at some stage come to terms. At the time he died I think he probably had made a personal confession without actually going to the confessional ... he said on a few occasions that they had very good heart-to-heart talks. Also, he never seemed afraid to die. He just kept thinking, why doesn't He take me now? At some stage I said to him, "That's probably your punishment" ... He said, "You're probably right". He just laughed it off' (author's interview with Mrs Aedine Sànta, 31 May 1999).

[27] RTÉ radio documentary, 25 July 2007.

Postscript

[1] *The Irish Times*, 20 June 1979, p. 9.
[2] *The Irish Times*, 27 June 1979, p. 11.
[3] Fisk, p. 380.

SELECT BIBLIOGRAPHY

Béaslaí, Piaras. *Michael Collins and the Making of a New Ireland* (2 vols., London, 1926)
Bowyer Bell, J. *The Secret Army: A History of the IRA 1916–1970* (London, 1970)

Connolly, S.J. (ed.). *The Oxford Companion to Irish History* (Oxford, 1999)
Coogan, Tim Pat. *The IRA* (London, 1970)
   De Valera: Long Fellow, Long Shadow (Dublin, 1993)
Cooney, John. *John Charles McQuaid: Ruler of Catholic Ireland* (Dublin, 1999)
Cronin, Seán. *The McGarrity Papers: Revelations of the Irish Revolutionary Movement in Ireland and America, 1900–1940* (Kerry, 1972)
   — *Frank Ryan: The Search for the Republic* (Dublin, 1980)

Crowe, C., Kennedy *et al. Documents on Irish Foreign Policy, Volume VI, 1939–1941* (Dublin, 2008)

Douglas, Ray M. *Architects of the Resurrection: Ailtirí na hAiséirí and the fascist 'new order' in Ireland* (Manchester, 2009)
Duggan, John P. *Neutral Ireland and the Third Reich* (Dublin, 1985)
— *A History of the Irish Army* (Dublin, 1989)
— *Herr Hempel at the German Legation in Dublin 1937–1945* (Dublin, 2003)

Fairfield, Letitia (ed.). *The Trial of Peter Barnes and Others: The IRA Coventry Explosion of 1939* (London, 1953)
Fisk, Robert. *In Time of War: Ireland, Ulster and the Price of Neutrality 1939–45* (London, 1983)
FitzGerald, Garret, *All In A Life: Garret FitzGerald, an Autobiography* (Dublin, 1992)
Foley, Conor. *Legion of the Rearguard: The IRA and the Modern Irish State* (London, 1992)

Garvin, Tom. *1922: The Birth of Irish Democracy* (Dublin, 1996)
Judging Lemass: The Measure of the Man (Dublin, 2009)

Hanley, Brian and Scott Millar. *The Lost Revolution: The Story of the Official IRA and the Workers' Party* (Dublin, 2009)
Hickey, D.J. and J.E Doherty *A New Dictionary of Irish History from 1800* (Dublin, 2003)
Hogan, James J. *Badges, Medals and Insignia of Óglaigh na hÉireann (Irish Defence Forces)* (Dublin, 1987)
Hogg, Ian V. *The Guns 1914–18* (London, 1973)
— *The Guns 1939–45* (London, 1977)
Hull, Mark M. *Irish Secrets: German Espionage in Ireland 1939–1945* (Dublin, 2003)

SELECT BIBLIOGRAPHY

Kautt, W. H. *Ambushes and Armour: The Irish Rebellion 1919–1921* (Dublin, 2010)

Keogh, Dermot. *The Vatican, the Bishops and Irish Politics 1919–39* (Cambridge, 1986)

Kiely, Kevin. *Francis Stuart: Artist and Outcast* (Dublin, 2007)

Larkin, F.M. (ed.). *Librarians, Poets and Scholars* (Dublin, 2007)

MacEoin, Uinseann. *Harry* (Dublin, 1985)
— *The IRA in the Twilight Years 1923–1948* (Dublin 1997)

MacEvilly, Michael. Unpublished biography of Dr Andy Cooney.

McGarry, Fearghal. *Eoin O'Duffy: A Self-Made Hero* (Oxford, 2005)

McGladdery, Gary. *The Provisional IRA in England: The Bombing Campaign 1973–1997* (Dublin, 2006)

McGuffin, John. *Internment* (Dublin, 1973)

McGuire, James and Quinn, James. *Dictionary of Irish Biography from the earliest times to the year 2002.* Nine volumes (Cambridge, 2009)

McLoughlin, Barry. *Left to the Wolves: Irish Victims of Stalinist Terror* (Dublin, 2007)

Mahon, Tom and James J. Gillogly. *Decoding the IRA* (Cork, 2008)

Molloy, Geraldine. *Michael Leo Whelan RHA (1892–1956)* (MA thesis, UCD, 2008)

Mulcahy, Risteárd, *Richard Mulcahy (1886–1971): A Family Memoir* (Dublin, 1999)
— *My Father, The General: Richard Mulcahy and the Military History of the Revolution* (Dublin, 2009)

Mullins, Gerry. *Dublin Nazi No. 1: The Life of Adolf Mahr* (Dublin, 2007)

Neeson, Eoin. *The Civil War in Ireland 1922–1923* (Cork, 1966)

Ó Corráin, Donnchadh. *James Hogan: Revolutionary, historian and political scientist* (Dublin, 2001)

O'Donoghue, David A. *Hitler's Irish Voices: The Story of German Radio's Wartime Irish Service* (Belfast, 1998)

O'Donoghue, Florence. *No Other Law* (Dublin, 1954)

O'Donovan, Donal. *Kevin Barry and his Time* (Dublin, 1989)
— *Little Old Man Cut Short* (Wicklow, 1998)

Ó Duibhginn, Seosamh. *Ag Scaoileadh Sceoil* (Dublin, 1962)

O'Halpin, Eunan. *Defending Ireland: The Irish State and its Enemies since 1922* (Oxford, 1999)
— *Spying on Ireland: British Intelligence and Irish Neutrality during the Second World War* (Oxford, 2008)

O'Malley, Cormac and Anne Dolan. *'No Surrender Here!': The Civil War Papers of Ernie O'Malley 1922–24* (Dublin, 2007)

O'Malley, Ernie. *The Singing Flame: A Memoir of the Civil War, 1922–24* (Dublin, 1978)

Regan, John M. *The Irish Counter-Revolution 1922–1936: Treatyite Politics and Settlement in Independent Ireland* (Dublin, 2001)

Shovlin, Frank. *The Irish Literary Periodical 1923–1958* (Oxford, 2003)

Stephan, Enno. *Spies in Ireland* (London, 1963)

Taylor, Fred (ed.). *The Goebbels Diaries 1939–1941* (London, 1983)

West, Nigel. *MI5: British Security Service Operations 1909–45* (London, 1983)

INDEX

1916 Rising *see* Easter Rising

A

Abwehr 112–13, 115, 122–3, 128, 131, 134–43, 168–9
Adams, Dominic 165
Aiken, Frank 56, 60
An t-Óglach 25, 36
Andrews, David 51–2
Andrews, Todd 51–2, 78–9, 232
Anglo-Irish treaty 12, 38–48, 226
Ansell, Laura 155
Arbour Hill prison 57–9, 193
Ardmore film studios 14
army *see* Irish army
army pensions 23–37
Arnott, John 154–5

B

Ballyseedy massacre 16
Barnes, Peter 156, 161, 169
Barrett, Richard 16, 55
Barry, Kevin 63, 233, 240–41
Barry, Mary Christina 'Monty' *see* O'Donovan, Mary Christina 'Monty'
Barry, Tom 16, 112–14
Barton, Robert 39, 73
Béal na mBláth 14, 15, 52
Béaslaí, Piaras 15, 240
Behan, Brendan 194
Bender, Albert 80–81
Berlin 133–46
Betjeman, John 189
Birkenhead, Lord 226

Birmingham 91, 129, 165
Black and Tans 21–2
Blackrock College 187, 191–2
Bliss, Fr Geoffrey 4
blitz 153, 158–9
Bloody Sunday 27
Blueshirt movement 15, 16
Blythe, Ernest 72
Boland, Freddy 222–3
Boland, Gerald 58, 180, 181–2
Boland, John 219–20
Boucher-Hayes, Ethel 218
Bowen, Elizabeth 189
Bowyer Bell, J. 89, 127–8, 165, 226
Bray Heritage Centre 53
Breiz Atao 129
Brennan, James 62
Brennan, Moll 218
Breton military intelligence 113
Breton nationalists 112, 129
Briscoe, Joe 242–3
Briscoe, Robert 48
British military intelligence 113, 119–20, 168, 174, 189
Brown, Paddy 29
Browne, Dorothy 217
Broy, John 224
Brugha, Cathal 34, 40
Brugha, Ruairí 42–3, 205
Brussels 117, 128–9
Bryan, Dan 188–9, 208, 209, 216
Byrne, Thomas 208–9
Byrne, Tom 105–10, 192–4

C

Callaghan, William 184–5
Canaris, Wilhelm 138, 174
Catholic church 50–51, 129–31, 219–20
Catholic Truth Society 219–20
Cavalcade 124
Charleton, Joe 223
chemical warfare 9–10
Childers, Erskine 65
Christle, Colm 214
Christle, Joe 214
City Chemical and Colour Company 31, 60–62
civil war 12, 38–48, 50–59
Clan na Gael 125, 126, 132, 135
Clancy, Peadar 27, 28, 34, 36
Clancy, Seán 21–2
Clay, James 155, 156
Cleary, James 189
Clissmann, Helmut 113–14, 167–8, 173, 221, 229, 231, 233, 235
Collins, Joe 84–5, 93–6, 99–102
Collins, Michael 7, 13, 15, 26, 39, 41, 43, 47, 52, 240–41
Collins, Timothy 185
Collins barracks 14
Cologne 117–18
conscription 4–5, 6, 22
Conroy, Mick 201, 202
Coogan, Tim Pat 41–2, 176, 225–6
Cook, Joan 157–9
Cooney, Andy 58, 90, 112, 175, 179, 212
Cooney, Seán 90
Córas na Poblachta 10
Corr, Paddy 230–31
Cosgrave, W.T. 39, 57, 60, 68–9, 70–71, 72–3, 77, 145
Costello, John A. 217
Costello, Michael J. 236
Costello, Thomas 185
Cotter, Jim 62
Coughlan, Patrick 58
Coughlan, Timothy 66
Coventry bombing 96, 131, 153–66
Coventry cathedral 153, 158–9
Coventry police museum 153–4
Cronin, Seán 135, 239
Cross, Ted 156–7
Cumman na mBan 63

INDEX

Cumman na nGaedheal 65, 69, 71–3, 77
Curragh camp, internment at
  arrest and interrogation 178–80
  correspondence 181–3
  health 207–8
  impact on family 180–81, 187, 191–2
  lectures and studies 187, 190–91
  memories of internees 105, 192–205
  passes on explosives knowledge 185–9
  request for parole 180–82
  writings and press clippings 184–6, 189, 190–91
Curragh military hospital 26, 49
Curragh mutiny 16, 17

D

Daily Telegraph 124
Dalton, Emmet 14, 39
Daly, Una 75
Dartmoor prison 155
de Barra, Leslie 16
de Buitléar, Éamon 172
de Valera, Éamon
  and Catholic church 51
  Dan O'Donovan as secretary 217
  as GHQ President 39–40
  imprisonment 57
  O'Donovan's dislike of 73–4, 79, 126, 145, 176–7, 211, 220
  possibility of coup d'etat 144
  rumoured to offer state chemist position to O'Donovan 225
  as Taoiseach 23, 126, 169, 206–7
Dean's Grange cemetery 64, 222
Deasy, Liam 55
Deegan, Joe 102–5, 107–9, 190, 225
Derrig, Tom 58
Dillon, Thomas 5, 7, 24
Dowling, John 90
Doyle, Archie 66, 67–8
Drumcondra 3
Duffy, Gavan 19
Duggan, Denny 102
Duggan, John 241–2

E

Easter Rising 5, 7
Eden, Anthony 169
Electricity Supply Board 17, 68–70, 212–15, 219, 223–5
emergency powers, introduction of 50
Erne hydro-electric scheme 226–7
ESB *see* Electricity Supply Board
Evening Press 229
executions 14–15, 16, 27, 54–5, 65
explosives 19–22, 24–9, 84–5

F

Farrell, James T. 90
FCA 225
Fianna Fáil 52, 72, 74–5, 211–12, 217
Fine Gael 15, 16
FitzGerald, Francis 29
Fitzpatrick, Diarmuid 189, 195–6
Fitzpatrick, Michael 94
Four Courts 26, 48
Franco, Francisco 16
Fromme, Franz 120–21, 136, 168, 173

G

G2 94, 113, 172, 182–3, 188–9, 208, 209, 216
Gageby, Douglas 216, 229, 234–5

Gallagher, Frank 58
Gannon, Bill 66
Garda Síochána 16, 66–7, 212–13
Garvin, Tom 41, 52, 56
gas, poisonous 7–9, 22
Gentle, Reginald 155
Germany 16–17, 81–2
   contact with Irish government 137–8
   contacts with IRA 90, 112–17, 167–70
   O'Donovan's visits 117–24, 127–9, 133–52
   military intelligence 112–13, 115, 122–3, 128, 131, 134–43, 168–9
   Nazi leadership 115, 136, 137–8, 143, 146, 151, 230
   propaganda 138, 219
   spies in Ireland 170–73, 174, 215–16, 220–23
   books and articles on 228–38
   suggested links to S-plan 89, 123–4, 126–7
Glasgow 2, 91
Goebbels, Joseph 115, 138, 169–70, 219
Goold, Neil 195, 198, 199
Görtz, Hermann 169, 170–73, 174, 176, 179, 194, 215–16, 220–23
Goss, Ritchie 102
Greenwich, explosives shop 29
grenades 20–22, 24–7
Griffith, Arthur 47–8
Griffiths, Jackie 102
Guilfoyle, Joe 224
Guiney, James 181, 186, 188–9, 207, 209

H

Hales, Seán 15, 54
Halifax, Lord 89, 91–3, 109, 226
Haller, Kurt 122–3, 138, 148–50, 169, 173, 229–31
Hamburg 118–23, 127–8, 135–6
Hanson, Fr Eric 3
Harris, Tom 49
Haughey, John Joe 200
Hayes, Richard 172, 216
Hayes, Stephen 95, 125, 168, 174–6, 180, 201, 233
Healy, Joe 172
Healy, John 234, 235–6
Held, Stephen Carroll 169, 171
Hempel, Eduard 131, 168, 174, 207, 222
Henderson, Frank 59
Henry, F.J. 186–7
Hinsley, Cardinal Arthur 129–31
Hitler, Adolf 143, 146, 151, 207
Hoare, Samuel 110
Hobson, Bulmer 78
Hogan, James 78, 88
Holy Ghost Fathers 191–2
Hoven, Jupp 113–14, 168
Hull, Mark 135
hunger strikes 60, 194

I

incendiary devices 27–8, 84–5
independence 12
invalidity pension 23–6
IRA *see* Irish Republican Army
IRB *see* Irish Republican Brotherhood
Ireland Today 58, 77–82, 201
Irish army
   dispute over control of 40–42, 43–8
   military intelligence 94, 113, 172, 182–3, 188–9, 208, 209, 216
Irish Book Lover magazine 64–5
Irish Builder and Engineer magazine 61–2
Irish Press 58, 162
Irish Republican Army
   army council 43–5, 48, 90

INDEX

contacts with Nazi Germany 90, 112–17, 167–70
O'Donovan's visits 117–24, 127–9, 133–52
fundraising, USA 125, 131–2
GHQ members 12–18
   meetings of 34–5, 38–40
   portrait of 11–14, 35
members blacklisted 213–15
O'Donovan's service 1920s 19–37
pro-treaty/anti-treaty split 38–48
propaganda and statements 54, 96–7, 125–6
S-plan bombings *see* S-plan bombings
Irish Republican Brotherhood 16, 17, 72, 94
Irish Times 49, 221, 222–3, 228–9, 231–2, 237, 239, 246

J

Joyce, John 30

K

Kavanagh, Patrick 78
Kearney, Pete 175
Keating, Dan 97–8
Keenan, Eddie 194–8
Kell, Vernon 110
Kennedy, Brian 78
Kennedy, Raymond 183
Kennedy, Sam 95
Kerney, Leopold 221
Kessenmeier, Theodor 118–19
Ketterick, Tom 58
Kevin Barry (RTÉ documentary) 240–41
Kilmainham jail 59

L

Lahousen, Erwin von 131, 136, 137, 138, 174, 230
Le Helloco, Henri 113, 131
Leicester 129
Lemass, Seán 30
Lincoln 129
Liverpool 91, 102–10
Lloyd George, David 12
London 91, 97–8, 129, 131
Loon, Jan van 215–16
Luther, Hans 114–15
Luzio, Monsignor 51
Lynch, Liam 42, 50, 55–7
Lynch, Michael 24, 32
Lynch, Tommy 190

M

MacBride, Seán 10, 114, 214–15, 236
McCabe, John 2–3
McCarvill, Patrick 59
McCaughey, Seán 174
McCormick, Frank 156, 161, 169
McCorry, Billy Joe 198–9
McDade, James 165–6
McDonnell, Andrew 59
MacEntee, Seán 74–5
MacEvilly, Michael 212
McGarrity, Joe 125, 132, 135
McGarry, Seán 68
MacGiolla, Tomás 162, 214–15
McGrath, Joe 68, 70, 80
McGrath, Paddy 84, 95
McGuinness, Bernard 99–101
McKee, Dick 27, 28, 32, 34
McKelvey, Joe 16, 55
McKenna, Dan 180
Mackey, D. 183, 188, 209
McLaughlin, Raymond 165–6
MacMahon, Seán 17, 34, 39
MacNeill, Eoin 19
MacNeill, Turlough 5
McQuaid, John Charles 191–2
McSweeney, Dinny 200
McSweeney, Tommy 200
MacWhite, Michael 222
Magan, Tony 193–4

Mahr, Adolf 81, 221
Manchester 91, 99–101, 129
Mangan, Séamus 108
Martin, Tom 104–5
Marwede, Friedrich Carl 113, 118, 120–21, 122–3, 148–9, 169
Mellows, Barney 59
Mellows, Liam 14–15, 34, 39, 42, 43, 46, 50, 55, 75
MI5 113, 119–20, 168, 174, 189
Midland Daily Telegraph 155
military service pension 23, 24, 27–37
Millarden, Leon 113
Mitchell, Gearóid 185, 190, 198
Moloney, Jim 236–7
Moloney, Kathleen 69
Monasterevin 25, 48
Mordrel, Olier 112
Morning Post 124
Mountjoy prison 56, 60, 176, 194
Moyse, Paul 128, 129, 148
Mulcahy, Richard
  as army commander in chief 52
  as Cumann na nGaedheal minister 72, 77
  as GHQ chief of staff 13, 15, 24, 27–9, 30, 34–5, 39–40
  pro-treaty position 41, 43–8
  receives war of independence service medal 206
  at UCD 10
  visits O'Donovan in nursing home 244
Mulcahy, Risteárd 41, 47–8, 244, 246
Murphy, John 203–5

N

Naas military barracks 26, 49
National Museum, Dublin 81
Nazi leadership 115, 136, 137–8, 143, 146, 151, 230
Nazi Germany *see* Germany
Neumeister (Abwehr agent) 136, 139–42, 144, 148
neutrality 176, 206–7
SS New York 127
Newbridge jail 49, 52
News Review 124, 126–7
Norton, William 217

O

Ó Brádaigh, Ruairí 163–4, 165
O'Brien, John 213–14, 224
Observer, The 238–9
Ó Cadhain, Máirtín 190, 202
Ó Conaill, Pádraig 215, 224
O'Connell, J.J. 'Ginger' 14, 39–40
O'Connor, Frank 78
O'Connor, Joe 203
O'Connor, Rory 13, 16, 34, 39, 42, 43, 48, 54–5, 65
O'Donnell, Bernard 173
O'Donnell, Peadar 48, 58, 78, 79, 121, 229
O'Donoghue, Donal 114
O'Donoghue, Florence 39–41, 225
O'Donovan, Aedine 3, 63, 191
O'Donovan, Colman 2, 136–7, 168, 217–18
O'Donovan, Dan 2, 52, 74, 191–2, 208, 217
O'Donovan, Daniel 2
O'Donovan, Donal
  biography of Kevin Barry 233
  birth 61
  on Colman O'Donovan 137, 217
  on Dan O'Donovan 208
  during O'Donovan's internment 187, 191–2
  on Eileen O'Donovan 218
  on *Ireland Today* 79

INDEX

on Jim O'Donovan
  arrest and internment
    178–9, 206, 208
  ESB employment 69–70
  disapproval of Rising 7
  dislike of de Valera 73
  family conference 216–17
  German contacts 137,
    171–2
  illness and death 242,
    244–5
  injury to hand 25, 26–7
  and religion 51
  S-plan 86–7
  joins FCA 225
  joins Fianna Fáil 52, 211–12
  on Monty O'Donovan 63, 234
  reviews *Spies in Ireland* 237
O'Donovan, Eileen 218
O'Donovan, Gerry 3, 62, 63, 187, 191
O'Donovan, Jim
  anti-treaty position 38–48
  appointment to GHQ 27
  army pension applications 23–37
  arrests and imprisonment 25–6, 29–30, 48–50, 56–9; *see also* internment at Curragh
  article on Erne hydro-electric scheme 226–7
  attends Görtz's funeral 222–3
  bankruptcy 17, 62
  Bureau of Military History statement 20–21, 22–3
  City Chemical and Colour Company 31, 60–62
  civil war 52–9
  correspondence 226
  on Cumman na nGaedheal government 71–3
  on death of Kevin O'Higgins 65–9, 76–7
  death threats while under arrest 71, 89
  as director of chemicals 27–37
  dislike of de Valera 73–4, 79, 126, 145, 176–7, 211, 220
  early life 1–4
  ESB employment 17, 69–70, 212–15, 219, 223–5
  explosives development 19–22, 24–8
  family 62–3, 180–81, 187, 191–2, 211, 216–18
  German contacts, books and press coverage 228–38
  German spies, contact with 170–73, 174, 176
  Germany, visits to 117–24, 127–9, 133–52
  health 207–8
  hunger strike 60
  illness and death 241–6
  'In Memoriam' (poem) 56–7
  injury to hand 25–7, 29–30
  internment at Curragh
    arrest and interrogation 178–80
    correspondence 181–3
    health 207–8
    impact on family 180–81, 187, 191–2
    lectures and studies 187, 190–91
    memories of internees 105, 192–205
    passes on explosives knowledge 185–9
    request for parole 180–82
    writings and press clippings 184–6, 189, 190–91
  invalidity pension 23–6
  IRA activity 1920s 19–37
  Ireland Today journal 77–82
  Irish Book Lover column 64–5
  Irish–English dictionary project 190–91
  military service pension 23, 24, 27–37

named in Hayes confession 175–6, 180
poems 56–7
poison gas accident 7–9, 22
The Prisoner's Companion 219–20
propaganda and IRA statements 54, 96–7, 125–6
proposed prayer book 219–20
'Quid Retribuam?' (poem) 57
radio broadcast on Kevin Barry 233
raids on home and office 53–4
receives thanks from Third Reich 230
recruitment as volunteer 5
and religion 51–2
S-plan *see* S-plan bombings
at UCD 4–10
war of independence service medal 206
on World War II 144–6, 238
O'Donovan, Marguerite 187, 218
O'Donovan, Mary 'Minnie' 2, 218
O'Donovan, Mary Christina 'Monty'
during O'Donovan's internment 181, 182–3, 191, 206
illness 241, 243, 244
marriage and family 62–3
visits to Germany 117, 134–6, 139, 141, 150, 234
O'Donovan, Patrick 238–9
O'Donovan, Peter 2, 218, 220
O'Donovan, Sheila 5, 62, 63, 188, 191, 218
O'Duffy, Eoin 39–40, 64, 66, 79, 116
Ó Faoláin, Seán 78
Offences Against the State Act 179
O'Halpin, Eunan 135
O'Hegarty, Diarmuid 31, 36–7, 72–3
O'Higgins, Kevin 65–9, 76–7

O'Kelly, Seán T. 208, 217
O'Kelly, W.D. 8
O'Mahony, Maisie 179
O'Mahony, Seán 127
O'Malley, Ernie 33, 42, 47, 48–50, 52, 56, 78
O'Neill, C.A. 207
O Néill, Seósamh 191
O'Rahilly, Richard 181, 246
O'Reilly, Joseph 70–71
O'Reilly, Michael 179–80
O'Riordan, Mick 200, 201, 232
O'Shannon, Cathal 240–41
O'Sullivan, Gearóid 15, 39–40, 67
O'Sullivan, Joby 156
Ó Tuama, Seán Óg 190, 202
Our Lady's Manor nursing home 241, 244

P

papal envoy 51
Parkhurst prison 102
partition 12, 226–7
pension applications 23–37
Pfaus, Oscar 113, 115–18, 120, 127, 131, 135–6, 169
Plant, George 203
Plunkett, George 58, 202
Plunkett, Jack 202
Poland, invasion of 152
Portobello barracks 71, 89
Power, Johnny 195, 201
Prevention of Violence Bill 104, 110–11
Price, Eamonn 'Bob' 16, 39
propaganda
German 138, 219
IRA 54, 96–7, 125–6

Q

Queen Mary 109
Quinn, Frank 185

INDEX

R

Regan, John M. 57
Rehmann, Theodor 168
Ribbentrop, Joachim von 136, 138, 173, 174, 221, 229–30
Ribbentrop-Molotov non-aggression pact 152
Richards, James *see* McCormick, Frank
Robinson, Archbishop Paschal 71
Roscommon 2
Rose, Tony 153–4, 159–61, 165–6
Rotterdam 147–8
Rowlands, Gwylim 155
Royal Hibernian Academy 12
Russell, Patrick 226
Russell, Seán
  anti-treaty position 42, 43, 63–4
  contacts with Germany 114–17, 136–7, 138, 144, 173–4, 221
  explosives work with O'Donovan 20, 25, 27, 32, 48
  fundraising trip to USA 125, 131–2
  as GHQ director of munitions 16–17, 34, 39, 75
  S-plan 83, 86, 88, 90, 94–5, 103–4, 165
  U-boat plan 144, 173–4
Russia, invasion of 152
Ryan, Frank 17, 112, 138, 144, 173–4, 221, 230
Ryan, Hugh 5, 7, 8, 33, 225
Ryan, James 175
Ryan, Seán 224

S

S-Plan bombings
  accounts of 93–6, 97–110
  Birmingham 91, 129
  condemned by Cardinal Hinsley 129–31
  Coventry 96, 131, 153–66
  issuing of ultimatum 91–3
  Leicester 129
  Lincoln 129
  Liverpool 91, 102–10
  London 91, 97–8, 129, 131
  Manchester 91, 99–101, 129
  methodology 85–8, 94–5
  planning of 83–91
  propaganda 96–7
  suggested German links 89, 123–4, 126–7
St Aloysius' College 2–4
Savage, Jim 199–203, 232–3
Save the German Children 220
Schwendy (Abwehr agent) 136, 139–40, 142
service medals (war of independence) 206
Sheehy Skeffington, Owen 78, 79–80, 81
Shovlin, Frank 77–8, 80, 81–2
Smith, Paddy 201
Spanish civil war 16, 78, 79–80, 81–2
Spies in Ireland (Stephan) 234–8
Stack, Austin 25, 59
Staunton, Martin 107–9
Stephan, Enno 230–31, 233–8
Stuart, Francis 167–70, 173–4, 219, 230
Stuart, Iseult 167, 171–2
Studies magazine 226–7
Sunday Review 234–6
Sunday Times 161–4
Sweetman, Malachy 58–9

T

Tallon, Joe 62
They Spied on England 228–9
Third Reich *see* Nazi leadership
Tierney, Michael 5, 78
Timms, Muriel 155

Toner, Edward 26, 181, 183
Toner, James 26
Twomey, Moss 90, 94, 114, 116, 175

U

University College Dublin 4–10

V

Veesenmayer, Edmund 138, 144, 173, 221, 230
Vize, Joe 39

W

Walshe, Joe 137, 217
Walshe, Maurice 218
Washington 128, 134–5
Weber-Drohl, Ernst 170, 171
Weckler, Friedrich 224
Whelan, Leo 11–14, 35
White, Harry 66, 220
World War I 3–6, 22
World War II 12, 22, 152, 153, 158–9, 176, 215, 219, 238
Wyley, Jack 215